Christian Theology and African Traditions

Christian Theology and African Traditions

MATTHEW MICHAEL

RESOURCE *Publications* · Eugene, Oregon

CHRISTIAN THEOLOGY AND AFRICAN TRADITIONS

Resource Publications
An imprint of Wipf and Stock Publishers
199 W. 8th Ave., Suite 3
Eugene, OR 97401

www.wipfandstock.com

ISBN 13: 978-1-61097-812-5

Manufactured in the U.S.A.

To the members and elders
of Evangelische Freie Gemeinde
at Reutlingen in Germany

"There will always be differences of opinion in a finite world."

—G. R. Osborne

Contents

Foreword

I FIRST MET DR. Matthew Michael at the Jos ECWA Theological Seminary (JETS) in 2006 as a doctoral student. I was amazed at his brilliance as a young scholar whom I immediately considered to be my colleague rather than as my student. Dr. Michael is well endowed and gifted theologically and has the potentials of soon becoming a foremost and a distinguished evangelical theologian in Africa. As I read his new book, *Christian Theology and African Traditions*, I observed that Dr. Michael is seeking to "reveal the defining nature of African Christianity and the attending importance of its theological thinking." Furthermore, he is seeking "to understand Christian theology particularly in the context of the African worldviews and religious traditions since these categories gave African Christianity its unique regional stamp." Based upon the foregoing, Dr. Michael is emphasizing "the onus of Christian theology to engage as well as interact with the formidable cultural determinants that appear to make Christian theology at home with the African people."

This book is his emerging and maturing theological reflections on a crucial subject, *the interactions, the engagement, and the dialogue between Christian Theology and African Traditions*. The primary goal of his theological project is the transformation of the African mind and its worldviews and traditions. Christian theology must engage, or be in dialogue with the African traditions as a prerequisite to transforming Africa. The major flaw of Western Missionary Christianization of Africa was its serious failure to engage or dialogue with the African traditions. The book in its entirety is a systematic examination of how Christianization, engagement, or dialogue can take place within Africa. In his methodology, Dr. Michael took the familiar classical Christian doctrines by re-interpreting their Western Christian experience and doctrinal interpretations in the light of the Holy Scripture for modern African understanding. With this new understanding and approach to Christian theology as drawn from the

Western Christian experience and its interpretations, and also from the Holy Scripture, Dr. Michael uses that as a means of engaging or dialoguing with the African traditions. His interpretations and explanations of the important Western classical Christian doctrines in the light of the Holy Scripture become the means by which he engages or dialogues with similar African traditions. The whole theological schema uses both the Christian evangelical presuppositions and the Holy Scripture as the foundations of engaging the Western classical Christian doctrines and their interpretations, on the one hand, and the African traditions, on the other. With this theological methodology, Dr. Michael brings freshness, innovation and creativity to the current theological discourse in Africa. His method proposes that we go beyond the Western classical Christian experience and interpretations of Christian dogma as found in the likes of Augustine or Thomas Aquinas, the Western missionary Christianization of Africa, and the pioneering African theologians in the likes of John S. Mbiti or E. Bolaji Idowu. The religious and cultural dimensions of Africa's traditions affect all aspects of African life, Christian presence and witness in Africa. A meaningful and effective Christianity cannot flourish well within the African context without a serious theological and practical engagement with the African traditions.

No doubt this new book by Dr. Michael is a concrete response to the growing need for a serious Christian engagement with the African traditions which had been neglected by the missionary Christianity. Prof. Paul Bowers posed a very serious challenge to African theologians in this regard in his series of Lectures at the Jos ECWA Theological Seminary (JETS), 2008, "Christian Intellectual Responsibilities in Modern Africa." In these lectures, Prof. Bowers posed the challenge of engaging the African mind as the most needed theological task for modern Africa. In a similar vein, Prof. Yusufu Turaki has developed a 2 volume Manuscript on "A Systematic Examination of the Interactions between Christianity and African Traditional Religion" (2008). It proposes an "appropriate way for African Christianity to understand and address Africa's traditional religious heritage." In methodology, Dr. Michael took after that of Professor Samuel W. Kunhiyop's in his book, *African Christian Ethics* (2009). In this book, Prof. Kunhiyop re–interpreted Western traditions of morality and ethics in the light of the Holy Scripture and then used that understanding to engage the African moral and ethical traditions. Certainly, Dr. Michael's *Christian Theology and African Traditions* is within the sphere of these new approaches to the study of Christianity in Africa. This new book will definitely arouse great interest in Christian Systematic Theology and Christian Studies which needs to be studied side by side with African Traditions.

Yusufu Turaki, PhD
Professor of Theology and Social Ethics
Director, Centre for the Study of Religion,
Church and Society Jos ECWA Theological Seminary
Jos, Nigeria
March 2011

Acknowledgments

T HE PRESENT WORK BECAME a reality through the love and support of several individuals and organizations. In particular, I want to recognize the immense contribution of the members and elders of *Evangelische Freie Gemeinde* at Reutlingen in Germany for their love and friendship during my doctoral research visit to *Eberhard Karls Universität Tübingen*. Looking back now, it is the friendship of this loving congregation that started a chain of events which now culminate in the publication of this work. Specifically, the love and encouragement of the families of Elder Reinhard Schultze, Martin Schill, Stefan, Anna and Leonie Epp cannot be overemphasized.

In the same way, I also appreciate the ministry of *Hilfe für Brüder* which provided the needed funds toward the publication of this book. In this regard, I want to recognize the kindness of Eva-Maria, of *Hilfe für Brüder*, who has truly made the difficult task of converting lecture notes into book truly pleasurable.

In addition, I am also grateful to the friendship and encouragement of Prof. Yusufu Turaki, Prof. Chris Wright, Prof. Paul Bowers, Prof. Scott Cunningham, Prof. Dogara J. Gwamna, Prof. Zamani B. Kafang, Prof. and Dr. Mrs. Bulus Galadima, Prof. Wolfgang Bluedorn, and Prof. Waje Kunhiyop who in variously ways had contributed to my spiritual and academic developments.

However, my greatest recognition goes to my wife and the many students who were the first to listen to the concerns and issues raised in this book, first at home, and subsequently in the different lectures on theology at the classroom. To my wife and these students, I say thank you for listening and making helpful suggestions which now translate to this present work.

Preface

CHRISTIAN THEOLOGY COULD BE readily defined as "theology that has Christian presuppositions." To put this definition simply, one could also say that "Christian theology consists of Christian teachings about God or other concerns related to this central subject." In this understanding, Christian theology has its source in the Bible and thus the Bible becomes the "textbook" of "Christian theology" since it is the "only" authoritative document accepted by Christians for faith and practice. Despite the use of "only" in the preceding definition to describe the Bible as the source of Christian theology, in the course of its history various external categories such as scientific traditions, philosophical traditions, ecclesiastical traditions, and Western academic traditions played a defining role in our conception and description of the nature, task, and goal of Christian theology. These traditions often provided the worldview or mental lenses from which the study of the Bible had taken place. Consequently, Christian theology is not naively the study of the Bible "only" or alone but the interactions and engagement of the Bible with these human traditions. To this end, the present work is also the study of the Bible in close dialogue with African traditions. In this sense, Christian theology is primarily tailored to speak or engage the different traditions that have now become synonymous with the African people. In fact, for Christian theology to remain relevant to a given people, such dialogue or interaction becomes inevitable because as a human enterprise it must by its nature engage the human context of its reflection in order to remain relevant. In this perspective, Christian theology cannot afford to isolate itself from daily human existential challenges. Any theology that ignores the human context and its myriad problems has isolated God from the human context, and thus it is a theology only fit for "angels" and not human beings. Consequently, theology of necessity must be theocentric as well as anthropocentric. In its anthropocentric dimension, it must seek to engage the different facets of human life. In Africa, Christian theology must engage the worldviews of the African people especially in terms of the beliefs, values and traditional orientations of the African people. On the theocentric dimension, Christian theology must also seek to be faithful to the Scriptures in its postulations, and not be merely an echo of contemporary ideological ramblings. In this particular understanding, first and foremost, Christian theology must seek to understand the defining issues on the pages of the Bible and the attending conflicts and tensions in the practice and description of these issues. Secondly, it must also relate these theological issues to contemporary life, hence it must never remain as a mere theological reflection on the pages of the Bible, but it must be able to transport itself to contemporary life. Unfortunately Christian theology becomes "incompetent" or "ill-equipped" to carry out such a contemporary function within the African context because in the history of its transmission it has been fashioned and shaped to address the needs and aspirations of the Western church and the imposing heritage of the enlightenment period. The African context must "reprocess" or reconstruct "Christian theology" in order to engage African questions which often are ignored by "standard" works on Christian theology.

From these highlighted concerns, this book discusses "standard" topics in "Christian theology" in light of African similar or dissimilar forms. It begins by underscoring the place of Christian theology on the African continent, the nature of African traditions, and Christian faith. Similarly, it discusses the place of the written word in the African context, particularly in the oral inclination of African society. In addition, it stresses the nature of divine revelation in Christian theology. This preliminary reflection on divine revelation entails the discussion on what I termed "kindergarten issues" in theology, which pertains to the definition, problem, and limitation of theology. It also discusses general and special revelation, the limitations of general, special revelation, the "Scandal of Particularity," the problem of religious experiences in the mediation of divine revelation, the consistency of the Judeo-Christian revelation, divine ontology, divine attributes in the context of suffering and theological issues surrounding divine revelation and eschatology. It also highlights biblical teachings on angels, the human person, Christ, the church, and the future life. As much as possible, these theological-biblical categories are highlighted in view of the biblical revelation, but also in sensitivity to the religious, social-cultural, and political concerns of the African context. Significantly, it is anticipated that this theological work will be a contribution to the on-going quest for an African systematic Christian theology.

1

Introduction

The Paradigm Shift

CHRISTIAN THEOLOGY IS GRADUALLY becoming a non-Western theological exercise. This shift has also become paradigmatic and defining for the future of Christianity since numerical and qualitative growth of Christianity is taking place away from areas which are traditionally labeled as the "hinterland" of Christianity. Underscoring this new situation, Philip Jenkins, in his thought-provoking studies of global Christianity, has described Christianity in the non-Western regions of Asia, Latin America, and Africa as the "Next Christendom."[1] This description envisaged that the next major theological discussions and decisions are going to take place within these regions. Concerning the defining role of African Christianity in this "Next Christendom," Andrew F. Walls described African Christianity as "*the* representative Christianity of the twenty-first century"[2] because "what happens within the African churches in the next generation will determine the whole shape of church history for centuries to come . . ." and "what sort of theology is more characteristic of Christianity in the twenty-first century may well depend on what has happened in the minds of African Christians."[3] Walls further observed, "A high proportion of the world's serious theological thinking and writing will

---

1. Jenkins, *The Next Christendom*, 3.
2. Walls, "Africa in Christian History," 2.
3. Walls, "Towards an Understanding of Africa's Place," 183.

have to be done in Africa if it is to be done at all."[4] Similarly, T. C. Tennent has also noted that "At the dawn of the twenty-first century, the typical 'face' of Christianity may more likely be encountered in Lagos than in London."[5] These different observations reveal the defining nature of African Christianity and the attending importance of its theological thinking. Consequently, it is needful to understand Christian theology particularly in the context of the African worldviews and religious traditions since these categories gave African Christianity its unique regional stamp. This consideration places the onus of Christian theology to engage as well as interact with the formidable cultural determinants that appear to make Christian theology at home with the African people. The great reception accorded to Christianity by traditional African society implies that Christianity and traditional African religious categories already shares a defining continuity rather than superficial discontinuity, thus Christian theology must seek to understand the various cultural and religious forms that make such continuity possible. In addition, Christian theology must also seek to understand the force of the so-called superficial discontinuities in order to create a lasting home for Christianity on the African continent. Such concern of Christian theology is predicated on the urgent need to do a "self-theologizing" or re-evaluation of classical Christian theology in light of the dominant African religious worldviews and traditions in order to create a self-defining theology that is grounded in the Scriptures but which also has the unique engraving of the African people. Interestingly, it was such "self-theologizing" that was deemed absent at the beginning of African reflection on Christian theology. Thus for example, in the early seventies John Mbiti categorically observed that the African church is "without a theology, without theologians, and without theological concerns."[6] Idowu Bolaji described the same situation when he also said that African Christianity has "a prefabricated theology, a book theology . . . what she reads in books written by European theologians. . ." and "what she is told by Europeans is accepted uncritically and given out undigested in preaching or teaching."[7] Similarly, the theological discourse of those times is characterized by unhealthy reactionary to Western misrepresentations of African cultures and traditions, which

---

4. Ibid., 182.

5. Tennent, *Theology in the Context*, 105.

6. Mbiti, "Some African Concepts of Christology," 51.

7. Idowu, *Towards an Indigenous Church*, 22.

normally failed to engage positively the African traditions in creative theological reconstructions to the biblical or classical Christian teachings. Signaling the era of new creative engagement of the African traditions and Christian theology, Kwame Bediako rightly noted,

> The era of African theological literature as reaction to Western misrepresentation is past. What lies ahead is a critical theological construction which will relate more fully the widespread African confidence in the Christian faith to the actual and ongoing Christian responses to the life-experiences of Africans.[8]

After these initial setbacks, the dialogue between Christian theology and the African people has generally continued and hence given rise to the present record of Christian growth on the continent. We must underscore the merits and demerits of this encounter between Christianity and the African traditions for the benefit of the universal church. It appears that now we have gone beyond the past stage of mere criticism towards the actual engagement of the traditions of the African people in tandem with Christian theology. In particular, this chapter looks at the relationship between Christian theology and the African continent. It also highlights the close connection between the African continent and Christian theology, the basic constitutions of the Christian faith and the nature of African traditions.

Christian Theology and the African Continent

Christian theology has a long history of association with the African continent. This association goes back to the second century in the planting of the church at Egypt, and subsequently in the founding of churches at Numidia, Nubia, and Abyssinia in third to fourth centuries respectively. The names Numidia, Nubia and Abyssinia may be unknown to some readers because these great African kingdoms, apart from Ethiopia, have now disappeared from the pages of world history and have been replaced by the Arab nations of Morocco, Tunisia, Libya, and Sudan. However, despite the obscurity of this heritage, these great Christian kingdoms practiced Christianity and provided theology for the universal church when Europe was still roaming in barbarism and the Western church was merely a footnote in theological debates of those times. Underscoring the significant

---

8. Bediako, "Understanding African Theology," 17.

role played by the African continent in the shaping of Christianity, B. B. Warfield rightly noted,

> It is from African soil, enriched by African intellect, watered by African blood, that the tree of Western Christianity has grown up until it has become a resting-place for the nations of the earth. If we abjure speculation upon what might have been on this or that supposition, and give attention purely to what actually has been and is, we must need confess that there is a true sense in which North Africa is the mother of us all. Christianity is what it is today, in all its fruitful branches at least, because of what North Africa was a millennium and a half ago, and because of what was done and thought and felt there. The very language in which it still defines its doctrines and gives expression to its devotion is of African origin; and the doctrines and aspirations themselves bear ineffaceably impressed upon their very substance the African stamp.[9]

It is from this close connection between Christianity and the African continent that Mbiti significantly observed, "Christianity in Africa is so old that it can rightly be described as an indigenous, traditional and African religion."[10] However, despite this defining relationship between the continent of Africa and Christianity often Christianity is viewed as a newcomer to the African continent. We often hear the quick association of Christianity as a "Western religion" and thus unfit for the African people. This description of Christianity as a "Western religion" usually comes from the oversight in seeing Christianity as just coming to Africa during the eighteenth- and nineteenth-century missionary enterprise to Africa from the West. For many Africans, this is the only history of African Christianity known. Unfortunately, such treatment of Christianity as a "newcomer" on the African continent often distorted the theological strides registered by the African continent in defining and shaping Christian thought in earlier times. Describing his indebtedness to Christian theology of this earlier time, Thomas Oden has brilliantly asserted,

> The same point applies to the inestimable African tradition of Christian theology. Anyone who reads these pages will quickly see how deeply indebted I am to the early tradition of African Christianity—few authors will be referred to more often than Athanasius, Augustine, Origen, Clement of Alexandria,

---

9. Warfield, "Africa and Christian Latin Literature," 518.

10. Mbiti, *African Religions and Philosophy*, 229.

Tertullian, and Cyprian. I am especially troubled when Christianity is portrayed as an essentially European religion, since it has its roots in cultures that are far distant from Europe and preceded the development of modern European identity, and some of its greatest minds have been African.[11]

Unfortunately, Athanasius, Augustine, Origen, Clement of Alexandria, Tertullian, and Cyprian have been de-Africanized and now Westernized, thus their contributions in the field of Christian theology are presumed to be the initiatives of Western Christianity. To counteract this Westernizing agenda of Western theological academia, Oden has even went further to describe the contribution of African Christianity in the shaping of Western civilization in a thought-provoking piece of work, *How Africa Shaped the Christian Mind*. This work generally aims at a "rediscovery of how the African continent provided the 'seedbed' for Western Christianity."[12] The preceding historical references to the greatness of African Christianity and its defining part in the shaping of Christian theology in the past naturally creates the need for Christian theology to become at home in a continent that has continually wrestled, debated, and formed theological opinions on the essence of the Christian religion. Describing the exploits of this African Christianity, Mbiti also observed,

> African Christianity made a great contribution to Christendom through scholarship, participation in church councils, defence of the faith, movements like monasticism, theology, translation and preservation of the Scriptures, martyrdom, the famous catechetical school of Alexandria, liturgy, and even heresies and controversies.[13]

From this rich historical heritage, it is expected that Christian theology would be a familiar subject on the minds of many African people, however, on the contrary, African people as well as African Christians are still groping in the dark to understand the true essence of the Christian faith. Consequently, the concern of the present work is to describe the engagement of some basic teachings of the Christian faith and the African traditions. It underscores the problems of such engagement or encounter. Similarly, it provides light and clarification between these two systems.

11. Oden, *The Living God*, 9.

12. Oden, *How Africa Shaped the Christian Mind*, 42–61.

13. Mbiti, *African Religions and Philosophy*, 229.

The Christian Faith

The use of this label is to describe the basic teachings of the Christian church particularly as reflected in the pages of the Bible. These teachings form the core of the Christian religion. It is the essence of Christian thought. The church had at various times conceived its faith in the form of creeds,[14] thus we have the Apostles' creed, the Nicene creed, the Chalcedonian creed, the Athanasian creed, and other variants of these creedal affirmations.[15] In these creeds, there is a consistent emphasis on the oneness of God, the Trinitarian character of the divine being, the virgin birth, the death and suffering of Jesus Christ, his resurrection and exaltation, his second coming, the judgment of the world, the resurrection of the saints, salvation, the founding of the church, the communion of the saints, and the expectation of a future life in the world to come. Historically, it is these basic teachings which have defined the Christian faith and give the Christian religion its unique character. Unfortunately, these distinctive Christian emphases are often missing in modern church worship. To this end, Gerald Bray has rightly observed,

> The confusion and uncertainty surrounding our public worship has its roots in a widespread failure to appreciate the importance of Christian doctrine. The modern church has been so concerned to extol the virtue of love that it has ignored the claims of truth, and conservatives too have fallen into this trap. Our churches can proclaim a gospel which often is grounded in personal experience and is only vaguely related to theological principle. . . . Conservative Christians cannot escape from the charge that they have replaced instruction in the things of God with religious entertainment, and that the doctrinal backbone to their preaching is decidedly weak. Many have no idea that creeds and confessions are an essential aid to Christian growth, and that the quality of our spiritual life is directly dependent on our understanding of spiritual truth. They do not know that the great centuries of the Church have been marked not by an aversion to doctrine and theological controversy, but by a passion for these things. Of course, controversy can be unpleasant and divisive, but the New Testament is full of it, and the great arguments of the past have seldom diminished our respect for the truths for which men fought and died.[16]

14. Demarest, "Creeds," 179.

15. Grudem, *Systematic Theology*, 1168–1207.

16. Bray, *Creeds, Councils and Christ*, 9.

Thus in talking about the Christian faith in this book we are engaging these basic teachings in dialogue with African traditions. Generally speaking, the engagement of biblical teaching with the traditions of a given human context is not a new practice since there is precedence of this endeavor in the history of the Christian faith. In its quest to find a home among different people groups, the Christian faith has on many occasions engaged, challenged, and corrected the various traditions along its path.[17] For example, the Christian faith first sought a home within the cultural and religious matrix of the Jewish community of the first century. During this period, the apostles and the writer of the book of Hebrews sought to make Jesus Christ the fulfillment of the hopes and longings of the Jewish nation and people, thus Jesus Christ was defined in terms of Messiah, the expected Davidic King, and the high Priest which annulled the Aaronic priesthood. Later, through the itinerary preaching and missionary journeys of Paul, the Christian faith also sought a home within the context of the Greco-Roman world. This new context generally necessitated the need to explicate an originally Jewish teaching of Jesus into the world and thought of the Greco-Roman world, thus epistolary letters became generally the mode by which Paul sought to translate the significance of the Jewish gospel of Jesus Christ to the gentile world. Interestingly, even though the epistolary form of mediation for the inspired writing was something strange in the Hebrew canon of the Old Testament, Paul employed this mode to speak to the Greco-Roman world. In this temporal domain, the Christian faith engaged with the issues and concerns of the Greco-Roman world. After the hellenization of the Christian faith in these Greek-styled epistles, the Christian faith moved into the Western world, and has generally stayed there until recent times. During its sojourning in the Western world, the Christian faith has engaged the issues and concerns of the Western world. These concerns basically range from philosophical to scientific issues which the Christian faith addresses in order to remain relevant to the Western world. In all these encounters of the Christian faith with the new contexts, its creedal elements of faith have remarkably provided Christianity with its continuous unique identity despite the precarious task of adjusting or translating its message to a new setting as it seeks eternally to find a new home in different cultures.

In the same quest to engage the African continent, since the coming of Christianity to Africa, the Christian faith has continually sought to engage the worldviews and traditions of the African people. In

17. Walls, *The Missionary Movement*, 1.

contemporary times, the greatest challenge faced by the Christian faith is the challenge of transforming African worldviews and traditions as it has greatly influenced and transformed in the past the course of human civilization and history especially within the Western world. Unfortunately, the Christian faith in Africa has refused to seriously engage African traditions at a deeper level of engagement, but has merely scratched the surface of the African cultural consciousness, which has led to the enigmatic character of the Christian faith as the religion of many African people, but with little or no impact seen in the social, political or economic sectors of African society. Regretfully, after almost two centuries of the presence of the Christian faith on the African continent,[18] the Christian faith appears incapable or powerless to transform African society especially in creating new values that would replace the pre-Christian values of African traditional society.[19] It is not an exaggeration to note that the Christian faith without a true engagement of the African traditions at a deeper level of dialogue becomes not only incapable of transforming Africa, but also incompetent to address the problems of African society.

The African Traditions

There is a common saying in Africa that "traditions are hard to die." The reason is because by their nature traditions are highly esteemed beliefs, customs, or way of doing something that have been handed down from one generation to the other. This particular way of viewing traditions, presupposes that traditions are "unchangeable" and "rigid" since every generation merely serves as "conduit" for them. This understanding holds a stereotyped view of tradition since every generation only becomes a mere vehicle to transfer the cherished beliefs and values of a preceding time. However, tradition is also conceived as dynamic since no traditions could be transferred in its exact form to the world of another generation without

18. The presence of Christianity in Africa is often dated at the beginning of the eighteenth century when Western missionaries began extensive mission work on the African continent.

19. Describing the same situation in the late sixties, Mbiti observing the strides recorded by Islam and Christianity, noted that, "Although Islam has generally accommodated itself culturally more readily than Western Christianity, it also is professed only superficially in areas where it has recently won converts. Neither faith has yet penetrated deeply into the religious world of traditional African life; and while this is so, 'conversion' to Christianity or Islam must be taken only in a relative sense." See Mbiti, *African Religions and Philosophy*, 15.

certain modification and adjustments to the realities of this new context. Consequently, while traditions generally claimed certain rigidity yet in actual practice they are flexible since every generation must adapt or bend the received traditions in order to engage with the realities of their times. The adjustment or modification of such traditional may be done on the periphery of such tradition or even the redefinition of the core elements of these traditions. In Africa, African traditions have similarly undergone such modification and adjustment in the light of colonization, intrusion of Western civilization and the presence of Christianity on the continent. This modification could be readily seen as bad and unhealthy for the African people by some individuals because some salient positive aspects of such traditions are lost in the course of such adjustment, however, others, in the light of negative traditions, welcomed the modification or even disappearance of bad traditions. Thus for example, in some African societies, there was the tradition of human sacrifice before the advent of Christianity and colonization; however, such practices have largely become extinct because of the emphasis in Christianity on the sacredness of human life and the emphasis of the same by the colonial administration. On the other hand, many Africans in the urban areas had lamented the disappearance of traditional values such as respect of the elderly and one's responsibility towards the extended family and the clan. For such people, the coming of modern civilization has caused the extinction of these cherished cultural practices, and hence they saw civilization, modernity and even Christianity as agents which sabotage the African traditions. Often the laments of these people come from their observation that traditions of a given people is closely tied to their identity, hence a disappearance of a key aspect of people's traditions is a direct assault on their identity as a people group. This connection of identity naturally makes tradition an interesting subject since it presupposes that traditions' change is directly an alteration of one's identity. Significantly, since we have seen that tradition, despite its claims to "unchangeability," is no doubt foible or flexible in the real life, hence this understanding has bearing in our conception of the relationship between African traditions and the quest for identity.

In the history of the African people, the quest for identity has been closely tied to the observance of cultural or religious traditions, which were practiced in the past, thus after independence most African countries, in their quest to assert an African identity, went back to revive traditional cultural practices which were condemned by the early missionaries. In fact, a celebration of the cultural practices and traditions become a hallmark of one's Africanness. This African renaissance is clearly ideological since it presupposes that African identity is to be found in the cultural past, and thus the revival of the cultural practices and traditions of the African past. A classic illustration of this tradition-identity syndrome is the FESTAC festival in 1977 whereby Nigeria and surrounding African countries came together in order to assert culturally the worth, dignity and beauty of the black culture. The overwhelming conviction behind such an elaborate festival was that African identity cannot be divorced from African traditions, thus traditions of the past were conceived as intricately connected to the identity of the African people of modern times. Despite the good of such African renaissance, however, the African people are clearly faced with issues of identity crisis particularly as seen in the daily bombardment of its cultural practices and traditions by Western cultures which has attained certain dignified status among the different cultures of the world.[20] This bombardment of African culture can be seen in the Hollywood cultures of the entertainment industry, the Westernized media, the internet, satellite channels and airwaves, thus changing the language, clothing, housing, lifestyle, and education of the African people. For example, in the past, a Yoruba man could be easily pointed out among group of people by his traditional tribal marks, his accented speech and clothing; however, with modern socialization such criteria become inadequate in order to identify a Yoruba person. The same is true of many African people whose traditional tribal marks, tribal fashion, and language could not be used as a means of identifying them. If we can no longer be identified by means of traditional tribal marks, clothing or language, we must ask ourselves what constitutes the African traditions, or to put it simply, since the traditional mode of identifying a particular African tribe has now changed, on what basis should the African person now be identified? As one could easily see, this identity has nothing to do with clothing, traditional tribal marks, language, housing, or even music since these categories have readily changed with the intrusion of Western culture. Today, we see African people clothed in Western clothing, speaking Western language, living in a Western style houses, working in a Western conditioned job, listening to Western music, and driving a Western car. In all fairness, could we call such a person African? If yes, is it all about his skin color? Is the black skin color enough criteria, reason or basis for African identity? These questions are valid since Black Americans have black skin color, but their worldview

---

20. On African identity crisis see Oduyoye, *Hearing and Knowing*, 54; Ujomu, "The Crisis of African Identity," 14–17; Magesa, "Africa's Struggle," 235–39.

or way of life is practically Western. Are they less African because of the absence of an African way of thinking or worldview? Is there anything like an "African way of thinking" or "worldview"?

The answer to the last question is yes, there is a particular way the African people look at the world. This often is the force behind their existence. It is the architect of their identity and way of life. Thus despite modernization of the African people in terms of modern and Western advancement such as planes, internet, satellites, and other modern inventions, yet in their thinking or worldview Africans have always remained African. Thus African identity is not about the externalities of its traditions such as traditional tribal marks, language, unique tribal clothing, festivity or location, but it is a worldview. It is such worldview that gives the tradition its force or vitality. Without such an African worldview underpinning and enforcing the traditions, African traditions in the midst of expedient modification and adjustment would have become extinct by now. But on the contrary, African traditions have remained strong on the continent despite the onslaught of colonization, civilization, and even Christianity because these antecedents have merely scratched the surface or externality of the African way of life. They have not readily engaged the African people at the level of their worldview. An African on the plane with his laptop on his lap, and his handset by his sides, still thinks, believes, and lives in deep recognition of the world of spirits as passed down to him by generations of traditions. In many cases, such a worldview appears to be something that is inherited rather than the art of environmental conditioning. It seems Africans are born with certain intuition and premonitions of these spiritual realities.

Unfortunately, it is at this level that Christianity has failed to change the African people. The early missionaries have stopped them from singing, drumming, and dancing, but most Africans after the missionaries went away reintroduced these banned practices. In South America, the African slaves in Brazil in particular reintroduced their own form of Christianity based on their worldview, which they carried with them across the Atlantic Ocean. Roman Catholic Christianity was reconstructed in order to accommodate the spiritual worldviews of the traditional African society, even if some of this contextualization was possibly suspect from an orthodox perspective.

The power of traditions as the origin of worldview cannot be underestimated, thus we must take seriously the challenge that the African worldview poses to biblical Christianity in Africa. The Christian faith must engage the African people at the level of their worldview. It is the worldview that now defines the African people. Since it is the worldview that provides the African people with a continuous identity from one generation to the other, it is fitting to engage this seat of African identity. For the African Christian is also faced with certain dilemmas because he or she is called to observe certain apostolic traditions, which have their origin in the Bible. Even though Jesus frowned against traditions, as readily seen in his indictment of the Pharisees (Matt 15:1–6; Mark 7:1–13; cf. Col 2:8), yet the teaching of Jesus was handed down in what is known as the apostolic traditions (1 Cor 11:23; 15:1–10). The apostles were the direct successors of Jesus Christ who were commissioned personally by him to teach or carry on his teachings (Acts 1:20–22; Matt 28:19–20; 10:1–23).[21] In the same sense, African Christians must prioritize between whose traditions should he or she venerate whether the traditions of his dead ancestors or of the living Christ? Interestingly, the apostolic traditions are enforced by a biblical worldview. Such biblical worldview is expected to engage the African worldview, thus leading to a transformation of the African worldview by a biblical one. The African Christian can no longer put his allegiance wholly on the African worldview, but on a transformed African worldview. Interestingly, the African and the biblical worldviews share certain relationships and common interest. For example, both worldviews acknowledge the existence of God, angels, demons or evil spirits respectively. From these shared categories or forms, the African worldview can be easily engaged and transformed. The transformation of the African worldview has serious implication for African culture or traditions. Everywhere, the Christian faith aims at such transformation because without such transformation of the indigenous worldview the true meaning of the Christian faith is neither fully known nor experienced.

Conclusion

The Christian faith has a long interaction with the African continent. The failure of Christianity to have a formidable impact on the continent is because of the failure of Christianity to engage the worldview of the African people. These African worldviews are daily encouraged and practiced on the continent despite the increasing Westernization of the Africa in terms of clothing, housing, language, occupation, and lifestyles. It is at

---

21. On the history of the Christian traditions, especially the Reformation, see Pelikan, *The Christian Tradition*.

this basic level that Christianity must engage, thus aiming at the ultimate transformation of African worldviews.

The formidable task before the African church is the task to Christianize the African people. This Christianizing agenda has unfortunately taken place without adequate understanding of the African worldview. The church has merely taken interest in the external issues surrounding the African people, however, it has not adequately engaged the African worldview in terms of close dialogue. Admittedly, the African continent has witnessed great conversions of people from the traditional religions to the Christian faith, and Christian theologians have sought to underscore the significance of this encounter between Christianity and traditional African society, however, these people thronging to the church are often left without a biblical blueprint that should provide them with direction in dealing with the inherited African worldview. The struggle often is the parallel observance of the things from the Bible and the African worldviews, thus leading to dual allegiance of these Christians. The thought of reaching Christian maturity becomes nearly impossible in the context of this divided loyalty. Christian theology must seek to help these Christians to better engage the traditional African worldview by advocating a transformation of the African worldview in the light of biblical revelation.

2

Kindergarten Issues

Introduction

THERE IS A COMMON oversight among different fields of learning. This oversight often reveals itself in their preoccupation with the sophisticated and complicated forms in their fields of learning, assuming that there is no need to be preoccupied with the preliminaries of these fields. The problem with such an approach is that some of the preliminary discussions in a given field of study are often indispensable towards a meaningful understanding of the nature, trends and developments of these fields. Most importantly, however, is that this preoccupation with the complexities of such fields often wrongly assumes that these preliminaries are free from theological complication too. In reference to theology, most preliminary discussions are often left to the new students who are taught the "basic" or primary forms in their new "theological kindergarten."[1] However, those often tagged "kindergarten issues" in theology, such as definitions, goals, and nature of theology and theological enquiry are usually depicted in simplistic fashion, which assumes that such forms have no serious complications or difficulties.[2] It is against such mindset that this present work seeks to reveal the complexity in such often assumed simple theological subjects in prolegomena to theology. Thus,

---

1. For helpful spiritual principles to aid the beginning student in his or her study of theology, see Thielicke, *A Little Exercise for Young Theologians.*

2. On the general problem of theology particularly dogmatic theology, see Harnack, *History of Dogma*, 76–128.

this section reveals the problem of theology, the understanding of theology in both the classical and modern theological traditions and lastly it underscores the general limitation of theology and hence, the contemporary quest for multiplicity of theologies.[3]

The Problem of Theology

Theology is ordinarily defined as "the human study of God." However, this definition though simple is yet profound and indeed introduces serious theological complications.[4] The complication inherent in this definition is the presence of two participants in the definition, namely humans and God respectively. In this deduction, the human is the subject, which by implication is the active participant, and God, the object and hence, a passive category in theological discussion. This understanding of theology raises serious problems because it envisages a hypothetical situation whereby humankind with all their obvious limitations in time and space become the interpreters or investigators of a profound being that is infinite in nature. The dominant human role in theological investigation is both intriguing and also problematic in this last sense, since the whole enterprise began on a hypothesis that the finite human being could indeed reflect on the infinite divine. However, even beyond this stated problem of epistemology (or whether the divine being could be known), is also the concern whether humans could actually capture or interpret the divine infinite being in the category of creeds, beliefs and religious systems as easily seen in contemporary religious professions.[5]

3. Paul Tillich introduced some helpful discussion on the preliminaries to theology; see Tillich, *Systematic Theology*, Vol. 1.

4. The usage of "The Problem of Theology" is similar but different from the usage by Karl Barth. It is similar because, like Barth, my major concern is with the "Subject–matter" of theology, while it is different because Barth's treatment and reflection is strictly narrowed to the eighteenth century. Also, Barth did not concern himself with "the general consciousness and life" of the eighteenth century. For Barth's investigation of the problem of theology in the eighteenth century see Barth, *Protestant Theology*, 80–135.

5. One significant weakness of modern theology is its growing complication and abstraction. This trend often separates theology from the life of the church. In his work, "Rescuing Theology from the Theologians," Gerald Bray presupposes that such a trend is unhealthy for theology in its basic conception and the light of the church. Thus he noted, "Few disciplines have suffered more from the follies of its practitioners than this one has, and yet none is more important for the eternal destiny of the human race. We can get to heaven without knowing anything about computer science,

Interestingly, the classical answer to such a theological question in the Christian tradition is a categorical "yes."[6] The Christian tradition believes that the divine is revealed in the New Testament and thus, a tacit justification for human reflection on the divine. In this sense, humans, particularly the Christians, can reflect on the divine despite the recognition that no religious confession can in the long run capture the entire divine essence as often depicted in stereotyped traditional theological reflections.[7]

The Understanding of Christian Theology

The understanding of theology must be configured in the classical and modern perspectives. However, the usual problem associated with this kind of enquiry is the problem of gross generalization in underscoring one's thesis particularly in assuming that theological trends in the classical and modern periods are harmoniously the same or to configure the investigation in the citation of dominant trends and denying the variation or dissident understanding of theology within these periods. Some attempt at overcoming these general difficulties would seem appropriate; however, the confining nature of this work made such desirable end unreachable. Thus, a sample of classical and modern theologians is undertaken in order to merely capture the classical and modern trends in the definition of theology.

At the beginning of the medieval period, Augustine critiques the threefold divisions of theology by one of his contemporaries Varro.[8] This Greek thinker conceived his contemporary theology to be of three dimensions namely, *fabular* or fabulous theology, natural theology, and civil theology. The first or fabulous theology is actually understood by Varro

molecular biology or geophysics, but to be deprived of the knowledge of God is to be deprived of eternal life, and theology is nothing if it is not about knowing God." In this understanding, Bray observed that the first prerequisite "for any theologian is a personal encounter with the living God." See Bray, "Rescuing Theology," 48, 49.

6. Grudem, *Systematic Theology*, 73–135.

7. Unfortunately, many systematic works on theology, which it is assumed should introduce the beginning student to some of these issues in the study of theology, often do not reflect on these issues all and instead dive headlong into issues of bibliology and theology proper without emphasizing the problems inherent in theological discourse. For an example of such treatment of theology see Erickson, *Christian Theology*; Berkhof, *Systematic Theology*.

8. On his critique of Varro's tripartite understanding of theology see Augustine, "St. Augustine City of God and the Christian Doctrine," *A Select Library of the Nicene and Post-Nicene Fathers*, 112–15.

to be a mythical theology that contains "many fictions, which are contrary to the dignity and nature of the immortals."[9] Consequently, he observed,

> For we find in it that one god has been born from the head, another from the thigh, another from drops of blood; also, in this we find that gods have stolen, committed adultery, served men; in a word, in this all manner of things are attributed to the gods, such as may befall, not merely any man, but even the most contemptible man.[10]

For Varro, the second theology, namely "natural theology" or entertainment theology, is found in Greek theatre and revealed in Greeks poetry and plays and thus such theology has the clearly defined purpose of amusement and entertainment. Lastly, Varro described the third theology as civil theology because it is closely associated with the Greek state and politics. While reviewing the nature of these theologies, Augustine rejected the contextual concurrence of these theologies and emphasized that theology must be based on the authoritative canon of the Christian Scriptures and not on the conflicting contextual realities of his Greek context. Thus, he accorded status to the Hebrew prophets and the apostles that outweighed the many brands of Greek philosophies who no doubt are behind contemporary understanding of theology as explicated by Varro. Even though Augustine's understanding of theology is well intentioned, the problem of such theology lies in unfounded assumptions that theology should be neutral to the contextual realities of his Greek context. The point worth stressing is that theology cannot lose its immanent contextual character even when claiming to address the transcendent dimension of its task. Whether this contextual understanding is based on "cultural accepted myth," entertainment or political ideology of the state, as Augustine's Greek immediate context, is beside the point. This is because whatever might be the challenge of our context each theology must seek to come to terms with these contemporary trends or challenges as expressed and experienced in the popular myths, religious conception, and political ideology of the time.

Writing from the medieval context, Thomas Aquinas defined theology variously as the "first philosophy," "metaphysics," or "divine science."[11] According to Aquinas, it is "first philosophy" in the sense "that all the other

---

9. Ibid., 113.

10. Ibid.

11. Aquinas, *Selections*, 37, 147, 150–51.

sciences follow after it in receiving their principles from it."[12] Similarly, it is "Metaphysics" (or "beyond physics") "because it comes after physics in the things that we learn; for we must proceed from sensible objects to the non-sensible ones."[13] In this medieval understanding, physics is understood to be the label for natural science. Lastly, Aquinas conceived of theology as a "divine science." Aquinas understood theology as a "divine science" because it seeks to give an organized understanding of God that is separated from the world of matter. For Aquinas, this divine science or theology is further divided into two spheres. Hence, he noted,

> And so, theology or divine science is of two kinds. One in which divine things are considered not as the subject of the science but as the principles of the subject, is the kind of theology that the philosophers seek. The other, which considers these divine things themselves in their own right as the subject of a science, is the kind of theology that is handed down in sacred scripture.[14]

For Aquinas, "both deal with things that are separate from matter and motion as far as their act of being is concerned." The understanding of Aquinas seemed to be that theology should be devoted to abstract philosophical enquiries about God and other related metaphysical entities. The problem with this understanding of theology as conceived in classical theological reflection is that it neglects the existential context of the church and unfortunately assumes an ivory tower disposition and mentality. This understanding of theology often prided itself in its philosophical and academic assumptions and enquiry that often have little or no serious warrant from the context of reality.

Turning from such classical understanding of theology in the modern times an alternative understanding of theology has sought to question the validity of the traditional conception of theology. Among the various modern understandings of theology, Rudolf Bultmann had been rated as "one of the greatest theologians of the last century." He simply defined theology as "the conceptual account of man's existence as being determined by God."[15] In this definition, human existence is placed in the same conceptual framework as God. Although this definition assumed the supremacy of God in such understanding of theology, yet in theological emphasis such preoccupation with the Christian deity is virtually absent,

12. Ibid., 37.

13. Ibid.

14. Ibid., 150.

15. See Schmithals, *An Introduction to the Theology of Rudolf Bultmann.*

and as such theology invariably becomes anthropology because of its preoccupation and obsession with existential human categories. Equally problematic in Bultmann's understanding of theology, despite his lofty conception of the enterprise, is the problem of Bultmann's Christology. For Bultmann, "Jesus' expectation of the near end of the world turned out to be an illusion. . . ."[16] Following from such skepticism on New Testament Christology and hence theology, Bultmann claimed that neither in the Synoptic Gospels nor in the Pauline Epistles is Christ entirely regarded as God. Consequently, Bultmann concluded that the portrayal of Christ as God is found "Only in the 'deutero-pauline' literature . . . and moreover the interpretation of them is disputed."[17] It is not farfetched to say that it is from such problematic christological commitment in his theology that led to Bultmann's theological methodology of demythologization of the Scriptures. In particular, the difficulty of Bultmann's understanding of theology is that it becomes anthropocentric in nature and does not bridge theology in its basic understanding with Christology.[18] Similarly, even when Christology is discussed in this theological scheme or reflection, Christ is not treated in the category of God or divine as conceived in classical Christian theological reflections.[19] It seems that Bultmann by definition has a lofty understanding of theology; however, his understanding of theology harbours a poor Christology. Is it possible to have a proper view of God and still lack a biblically based christological commitment?

Following these theological trends as engendered by Western liberal tradition and their revolt against traditional or classical theology, the theological enterprise began to involve the context of theological enquiry into the understanding and construction of theology, not only about God but about any other category of human and ecclesiastical forms. This is not to suggest that prior theological postulations did not carry the elements of their context into their theological reflection, however modern understanding made the human context a viable and indispensable partner of theological reformulations. Significantly, it is this revolt against the traditional understanding of theology that gave birth to contemporary Third

16. Bultmann, *Theology of The New Testament*, 22.

17. Bultmann, *Essays Philosophical and Theological*, 275.

18. For an evangelical criticism of Bultmann see Pinnock, "Theology and Myth," 215–26.

19. While classical theology in definition has understood theology and Christology as two different spheres, yet such a dichotomy often is problematic because it seems to emphasize discontinuity between the two persons of the godhead rather than the harmony that exist in such a trinitarian unity.

World theologies such as Indian theologies, African theologies, Asian theologies, Dalit theologies, Minjung theologies, Liberation theologies, Feminist theologies, theologies of African Independent Churches, and other forms of theologies within the Third World context. Defining theology, Gustavo Gutiérrez observed,

> The classic meaning of theology is an intellectual understanding of the faith—that is, the effort of human intelligence to comprehend revelation and the vision of faith. But faith means not only truths to be affirmed, but also an existential stance, an attitude, a commitment to God and to human beings.[20]

For Gutiérrez, theology "is a progressive and continuous understanding, which is variable to a certain extent."[21] It is not "merely the understanding of abstract truth." In addition, Gutiérrez observed that since theology is a "reflection" it presupposes that "it is a second act, a turning back, a reflecting, that comes after action."[22] To this end, Gutiérrez noted, "Theology is not first; the commitment is first."[23] Commitment here means action on behalf of the poor, which is readily captured by the all-embracing term "praxis." All liberationists conceived theology to be primarily defined around the praxis instead of the "pure theology" which dominates traditional Christian theological reflection. Gutierrez agreed with other liberationists that theology comes short of its name if it is divorced from the praxis or the suffering context of theological reflection. As such, theology must not begin with a lofty commitment towards explication of the mysteries of creation or the transcendence of the Creator, but rather the fulcrum on which its pendulum must forever swing is the existential context of the people.[24] Consequently, for Gutierrez the existential context, what is termed *praxis*, must come first in theological investigation or inquiries. The pragmatic involvement in the church's context to fight the injustice and political ills of Latin America and other fronts of oppression in the Majority world becomes the goal of liberation theology. It is not that Gutierrez rejected theological reflection about God or other preoccupations of classical theological reflections, however, his commitment with the praxis of oppression made him postpone mere talk of theologizing.

20. Gutiérrez, *Essential Writings*, 24.

21. Ibid.

22. Ibid.

23. Ibid.

24. Gutiérrez, *The Power of the Poor in History*.

Hence, theology is understood to encompass not merely the investigation of transcendence as often envisaged in classical theological discussion, but rather the reflection of the contemporary contexts in terms of political and economic variables. Such "afterward" postponement of divine enquiry has warranted serious criticisms of liberation methodology, however, the thrust of liberation commitment towards freedom and liberation of oppression particularly in the serious contextual realities of the church's context of reflection has inevitably sought to remedy the one-sided nature of classical theological enquiry with its often disjointed Christology and eschatology that seems to condition many Christians into passive thinking. Such passivity unfolds before ungrounded "spiritual conviction" or "religious devotion" that suggests the attitude of "This World is not my home" or "There is pie waiting for me in the sky by and by." This attitude has generally robbed Christians in the Majority world context of serious engagement with the negative political and economical trends that have become the "normal" ideological face of Majority world countries.[25]

The Limitations of Theology

Nonetheless, with all its many problems as seen in the classical writing of Augustine and Aquinas and the modern writing of Bultmann and Gutierrez, the human dimension reminiscent in theology is both liberating and not always problematic as already shown, since it provides a crude justification for differing ways of understanding the transcendent in view of the diverse theological understanding of such a being within, even the Christian theological traditions and among Third World theologies. If we recognize the human dimension inherent in theologizing, it goes along to show that theological differences are actually a healthy necessity in light of diverse human understanding and the Christian theological understanding of God and his activities in time and space. The thrust of this last assertion also reveals the limitation of every theology, since every theology, Christian theology in particular, seeks in the long run to capture the eternal claims of the divine in the light of the present spiritual, economic, and political context, as well as the background of class, gender, and other human determinants. In this understanding, every theology develops not in isolation or a vacuum but rather it reflects the cultural, spiritual, and political trends of its contemporary context. This suggests that every theology must be ready to accept its temporary and human dimension

25. See Gutiérrez, *A Theology of Liberation*; Brown, *Theology in a New Key*.

even when it claims to speak for the infinite divine being. Every theology is limited and thus must be subjected to critical evaluation and review in order to engender healthy theological discussion. It is assumed that such fresh and critical reflection of theologies will engender newer and more biblically honest theological understanding in the long run. It was from this perspective that Hans Küng had observed:

> serious theology does not claim any complete, total possession of the truth, any monopoly of truth. It claims to be no more that scholarly reflection on its object from one particular standpoint, which is anyway one legitimate standpoint among others. Theology can never be a comprehensive, systematic world view, worked out down to the smallest details and rendering ultimately superfluous any further reflections . . .[26]

Thus, theology or theologies as any human endeavor to understand or interpret the divine is inherently saddled with diverse forms of limitations. These limitations had been expressed in many ways and many forms, however three salient limitation of theology are forever certain and thus the necessity to tolerate, appreciate, and also be sympathetic to the weaknesses revealed by many theologies in their quest to capture the infinite transcendent being for their time, generation, and human context. Firstly, all theologies are limited in scope. No single theology has ever captured all dimensions of the human existential experience; instead every theology in every sense is narrow, limited, and preoccupied with a particular time, context, and agenda. It is thus unhealthy and absurd to develop a theology that will truly cut across all races, gender, class and other different categories of human society. Even though many theologies claim this impossibility, a closer look at these theologies reveals that often those claims are bogus generalizations and not founded on reality. It is true that most theologies seek to be universal in their relevance to the entire globe, but it is also true that such desire is just wishful thinking since theology itself from its simple definition encompasses ultimately the reflection of humans in their various contexts about the divine being who no single person, group, or time could ever capture for every people and time.

Secondly, theology is also limited in methodology. The revolt of existential theology and philosophy against traditional theology and philosophy is in this sense justifiable since no human methodology or system could in every sense captured the full dimension of the human existential experience. Thus, in this particular sense every theological

26. Küng, *On Being a Christian,* 87.

methodology whether expressed or unexpressed has a salient limitation and hence reveals that no one single method of theology could in every sense translate the divine or interpret the full scale of human socio-economic experiences. Consequently, Majority world theologies with their liberation or differing contextual methodologies are still limited despite their innate quest to speak in holistic terms to the entirety of the human experience in the Majority world environment. Lastly, theology is limited in its theological agenda. It is now known that no single theological agenda whether of traditional theology, or feminism or Black theology, or any other theology in that sense could be sufficient and transcends all cultural boundaries, age group, gender distinction, racial categories, and economical and social status. Thus, every theology is limited in its choice and identification with a theological agenda whether this agenda is expressed or unexpressed.

Conclusion

Following the preceding discourse, it seems that the tasks of theology whether as seen in classical or modern understanding could be reduced into two categories, which have been and ought to be the task of every theology. These two categories that explicate the task of theology are namely the theological commitment to transcendence and secondly its commitment to immanent or contextual realities.[27] Concerning the former, theology must seek a conscious commitment to the transcendent. By its name, it is rightly assumed that theology should have the divine being at its core or focus. Unfortunately, this defining task of theology has often eluded many Christian theologies. These types of Christian theologies have sound humanitarian or contextual concerns but a faulty transcendent concern and thus, inevitably such Christian theologies become shallow and inadequate to address the humanitarian or contextual concerns of the human community. Similarly, the flaw of many Christian theologies with a strong transcendent commitment is their inability to articulate a coherent commitment to the context of human experience.

In relation to the second, every theology must have an immanent commitment. Most theology is wrapped in philosophical categories around transcendence so that no room is left to address the human situation in which theological reflection takes place. Traditional theology as revealed in Western theology often is abstract, impersonal, reflective, and

27. Grenz and Olson, *20th Century Theology*.

unable to address the human socio-political, racial, gender, and other cogent and volatile components of human society. With such disposition in academic shibboleths and devoid of the existential factors in the human context, theological preoccupation becomes a reflection of mirage and not really the felt needs of human society. Unfortunately, it is such lack of praxis—the insensitivity of classical theology, that caused the rise of multiple theologies to address the many human concerns that have generally been ignored in the theological agenda of classical theology reflection. Theology must have both a transcendent focus and an immanent locus; without these two horizons kept in balance theology becomes irrelevant and obsolete. It is true that these Christian theologies, without these concerns are inadequate to deal with the human existential crisis of modern times and also the postmodern crises of future times. Thus for me, theology should be defined as "a study of God and other spiritual forms or realities in the framework of the existential human context." In this definition, we must capture for theology, the two differing theological emphases of classical and modern theology and sought to redefine theology based upon the conceived task of theology as expressed in these two concerns.

3

General and Special Revelation

Introduction

AFRICAN TRADITIONAL RELIGION IS often placed within the scope of general revelation, and Christianity, on the other hand, is placed within the sphere of special revelation. The placement of these two revelations does not come from an arbitrary scheme, but from a proper understanding of the concept of revelation. Before engaging with these concerns, we must first begin by the definition of revelation and other related issues. Simply stated, divine revelation could be defined as the voluntary "self-disclosure" of God to humanity.[1] Defining "revelation" in traditional African religion, J. O. Kayode noted,

> Revelation is an act of God and to the understanding of African peoples, divine messages can be obtained through the situation of things in their environment. Man has consciousness or self-awareness of the Divine Order. Without any hesitation, the African affirms that God has point this awareness in man and for this reason his traditional religion is found everywhere.[2]

For the African people, everywhere and everything can be a channel and mean of revelation from God, hence nature is replicate with messages from God. It is from this context that Africans have generally held a reverential

---

1. For the historical study on theological discussion pertaining to general revelation see Demarest, *General Revelation*.

2. Kayode, *Understanding African Traditional Religion*, 2.

attitude towards nature. In fact, without understanding this self-disclosure of the divine being in nature, there is the impossibility in understanding or knowing the divine being by most Africans. Since God is a being beyond the comprehension and articulation of man, in biblical thought as well as the African religious traditions, the onus for his disclosure to human society must rest securely on himself and none other.[3] To this end, the initiative and prerogative of divine revelation has its ultimate source in God himself without any reference or bearing on the human capacity to comprehend or know the divine being.[4] This chapter investigates the nature of general and special revelation, the limitations, and related issues such as the scandal of particularity, the place of experiences in the mediation of revelation, the consistency of the Judeo-Christian claims to divine revelation, and the relationship between divine revelation and eschatology.

The Nature of General and Special Revelation

General revelation underscores the universality of such disclosure of the divine being within the purview of nature, history, morals, and other human customs or cultures that serves as a pointer to the existence of God and that also indicates his benevolence and compassion.[5] Stressing the universality of such divine revelation of himself, Paul noted, "For the invisible things of him from the creation of the world are clearly seen, being understood by the things that are made, *even* his eternal power and Godhead; so that they are without excuse" (Rom 1:20). Similarly, the Psalmist revealed that "The heavens declare the glory of God; and the firmament reveals the work of his hands" (19:1). The writer of Ecclesiastes made reference to "eternity in their heart," in his universal appraisal of life under the sun (Eccl 3:11). Jeremiah made reference to the consistent flights of birds to illustrate Israel's disobedience and the faithfulness of birds through their strict obedience to divine given instincts (Jer 8:7). The writer of Proverbs points to the ants to illustrate to his contemporary the necessity of diligence and hard work in line with divine covenantal stipulations. Thus he said, "Go to the ant, you sluggard; consider its ways and be wise! It has no commander, no overseer or ruler, yet it stores its provisions

---

3. On Karl Barth's rejection of general revelation see Barth, *Church Dogmatics*, 86–128. For response to Barth see Brunner, *Man in Revolt*, 527–48.

4. See Walvoord, "The Person of the Holy Spirit," 55–168.

5. On the relationship of general revelation to civil government see Chafer, *Systematic Theology*, 4:234–43, 1:4–5.

in summer and gathers its food at harvest" (Prov 6:6–8). Also, Proverbs observed, "Ants are creatures of little strength, yet they store up their food in the summer" (Prov 30:25). Similarly, Isaiah speaks of the faithfulness of the cow and donkey in obeying their master in comparison to the inability of Israel in obeying Yahweh (Isa 1:3). Isaiah also made reference to the stars to illustrate Yahweh's care and faithfulness (Isa 40:26). Similarly, Jesus used illustrations from the flowers and birds to underscore divine love and care (Matt 6:28, 30).

This general revelation of God is also known as natural revelation and has the distinctive characteristics of universality, rationality, and simplicity. The sufficiency of general revelation to engender an adequate conception of God has often been denied because of the biblical understanding that such general revelation is insufficient to warrant salvation. It is this insufficiency of general revelation that occasioned the necessity of a special revelation (Job 42:5; Matt 11:25, 27; 16:17, Rom 1–3; Heb 1:1–3). Complementing general revelation, special revelation seeks to explicitly reveal the saving knowledge of God thus, while general revelation has its sphere within the first person of the Godhead, the concern of special revelation is within the purview of the second and third persons of the Trinity.[6] Even though such a narrow designation is problematic since there is possibility of partial proto-christological forms within general revelation. Thus, it seems general revelation may have some proto-christological expectations or expressions and hence, the invalidity of such divisions of the persons of the Godhead along the sphere of revelations whether general or special revelation. However, in its classic expression special revelation is often depicted as the revelation of the redemptive acts of God through the mediation of Jesus Christ. Special revelation is not universal as is general revelation. It is also not simply apprehended by observation or logical inferences drawn from nature. The centrality of special revelation lies in its salvific nature and the particularity of such divine expression within the Christian religious faith.[7] While general revelation is conceivable by the medium of observation or logical inferences, in special revelation the emphasis is on personal faith in Jesus Christ. In the Bible several channels of revelation were used by God. Such revelatory modes include theophanies, dreams, visions, miracles, supernatural occurrences, the written scriptural words, and then ultimately the self-disclosure of himself in Jesus Christ.[8]

6. On the necessity of divine revelation see Gerstner, "An Outline of the Apologetics of Jonathan Edwards," 195–201.

7. See Helm, *The Divine Revelation.*

8. See biblical theophanies Gen 16:7; 18; 22:11–12; 32: 29–30; Exod 3:2–6; Josh

The Limitations of General and Special Revelation

In discussing God and revelation as found in the Bible, it merits special attention to engage preliminarily the subject of the two natures of revelation and the inherent limitations of both. General revelation as already highlighted is the kind of revelation that comes from reflection, observation, and considerations of external factors such as nature in formulating theological conclusions about the existence of the divine being and his loving relationship with his creation. This understanding of revelation conceived of God in general terms with deep consideration of his general attributes of benevolence, compassion, and love as understood from the comprehensive interaction with external factors or forms of creation.[9] In general revelation, such conclusions about God could be reached from theoretical assumptions formulated or gathered from personal experiences, legends, and myths of the processes or dimensions of divine activity in reference to an individual or a specific community. In this last understanding, every human community or person has some limited comprehension of the divine being and in a loose sense, the human desire for virtues and morals are fundamentally informed by such a partial comprehension of revelation in the theological category of general revelation.[10] Within this persuasion, internal considerations such as values, moral consciousness, or the inner working of human conscience are all categories within the domain of divine revelation in general terms. The obvious limitation of general revelation is that it places on humans the onus of understanding, interpreting and concluding the invisible presence of the divine being as expressed in nature, human consciousness, and moral inclinations, thus the inevitable propensity towards misinterpretation. Similarly, diverse subjective readings from nature often account for the diversity of religious beliefs thereby muddling even further general revelation as the fountain of religious ideas. In putting all the preceding categories within the grasp of human comprehension, general revelation becomes a diverse, subjec-

---

5:14–15; Judg 6:11–14; 1 Chr 21:16, 18, 27. For biblical dreams see Matt 1:20; 2:12–13; 27:19; Gen 20:3; 28:12; 31:24; 37:5, 7; 41:1; Judg 7:13–15; 1 Kgs 3:5; Dan 7:1; See also Rom 3:2; Matt 22:43; Acts 1:25, 30; and 2 Pet 1:21.

9. See Berkouwer, *General Revelation*.

10. Unfortunately pioneering theological works in Africa have often stressed or built their theological edifice on general revelation or natural theology without adequately underscoring the limitation of such an avenue in the African religious quest to know God. See Idowu, *Olòdúmare* and the already cited works of Mbiti particularly *Concepts of God in Africa* and *African Religions and Philosophy*.

tive, and even contradictory source of obtaining divine revelation since man ultimately becomes the arbiter who can readily interpret or judge for himself the degree of divine presence in the stated category of divine revelation. Fundamentally, such diversity or subjectivity comes from the diversity already inherent in human society thus negating the possibility of arriving at a coherent theological understanding of the divine being from such diverse interpretations and reflections. Since man is conceived to be incompetent to tap fully into this divine revelation as seen in natural events, forms, and moral persuasions, it already sets a limit on how much human beings can actually conceive or understand God through these general means.

On the other hand, special revelation presupposes that the divine being took the initiative in revealing himself in the specific person of Jesus Christ. Building on Jewish traditional religion, the understanding of specific revelation is the choice of the Jewish race to climax or bring to birth the revelation of the divine person beyond the stipulation of Jewish laws, institutions, or other innate psychological constitutions of the Jewish religious system, nor is such revelation within the domain of nature or from the innate quest of the human soul to seek for a nobler representation of the divine being. But divine revelation within Christianity is the self-disclosure of God himself in human form, known in history by the name of Jesus Christ. Despite the immanent or ample revelation of the divine being that comes with such special revelation in Jesus Christ, it is still limited since it is not an exhaustive, but rather sufficient avenue of divine revelation that is aimed at guiding the human race towards salvation. It is limited in its description of the inner divine life, the mysteries of divine origin, and other philosophical and theological categories that have consistently challenged human ability to know or comprehend the divine being. In this sense, special revelation is like a map and not a philosophical manual about God and the purpose is salvation and not telling of confidential divine secrets. Consequently, special revelation does not tell us everything about God, only those things that are necessary and sufficient towards the salvation of the world. In this understanding, the inner-working of the Godhead, the self-knowledge of the divine being, and other theological categories are lacking, presupposing the inevitability that God's inner beingness is not exposed because the revelation about God borders ontologically on the basic description of God in relationship to his creation.

The "Scandal of Particularity"

As already highlighted in our preceding discourse about general revelation, we observed that every race, people, and gender could conceive of God. Through the medium of general revelation the possibility of divine revelation within the cosmic or universal sphere is already envisaged and thus gives the entire world the possibility of hosting divine activity or writing of his revelations. In general revelation humanity stood on plain ground and hence it presupposes the justice and fairness of the divine being in offering the partial self-disclosure of himself using this general means. However, even in this theological system of divine revelation priority is given arbitrarily to specific persons, history, places, and genders in the preparation for the specific revelation of Jesus Christ through the selection of the nation of Israel. The restriction of divine plans to a specific people, place, and history raises a serious theological problem as to the fairness of divine election and the rejection of the other equally suitable places, peoples and history to mediate divine specific revelation of himself in Jesus Christ. Considering this problem, the author of the bestselling book, *The End of Science*, John Horgan, in his new work *Rational Mysticism: Dispatches from the Borders between Science and Spirituality* noted, "To my mind, the scandal of particularity is the root of all religious evil. The conviction of certain individuals and peoples that they are divinely chosen leads to religious self-righteousness, fanaticism, intolerance."[11] This recognition or observation becomes important in the light of the contemporary quest for cultural identity by these other different groups of people all over the world, and the opposing quest characterized in the rejection of specification particularly seen in the growing international campaigns for globalization and unity of world governments. Such global trend as typified by the United Nations and other international pressure groups seek to remove all human specifications, national boundaries, ethnic clamoring, and the dawn of global unified political and economical policies. In this context of the world's quest for political and economic unity, inter-penetration of relationships and the mellowing down of religious and sectarian fanaticism, the subject of God's revelation conceived exclusively to a specific place, people, and gender becomes actually repulsive to modern society with their sense of unification. The exclusion of other human societies from such mediation of revelation often is seen as the prejudice and fanaticism of the Judeo-Christian faith. This scandal

11. Horgan, *Rational Mysticism*, 50.

of particularity of revelation has naturally caused reactions against such exclusive claims or monopoly of Christianity in the context of modern pluralism. However, against this modern mindset, the Bible revealed that divine revelation in specific terms was conveyed or revealed in the *particular* history of a *particular* people, and through the medium of a dominant patriarchal society. This revelation was made in divine sovereign freedom and not necessarily based on any pious deeds of the patriarchs of the Israelite race. Philosophically, the feasibility of such divine undertaking is within the reach of human logic since God's plan for human society could not be generally conveyed, mediated, or comprehended to every human society without of necessity a narrowed mediation in a limited and restricted context. If God would have to reveal himself, he could only do so basically by restricting himself to a particular time and place. It cannot occur everywhere, through everybody and in every place. To this end, Thomas Oden observed,

> There remains a "scandal of particularity" in all historical revelation. If God is to become known in history, then that must occur at some time and some place. It cannot occur at every time and in every place. The history of salvation is about those particular times and places and events.[12]

The confinement of divine revelation within a specific human Jewish context is thus primarily born out of necessity and efficiency in the mediation of divine revelation and not a supposedly conception of the superiority of Jewish people in the early period of their religious development since Abraham, the founding father of the Jewish race, came out of the idolatrous religions of the Mesopotamian world. Thus any person or groups of people could have been called as God called Abram and hence suggesting divine freedom or sovereignty in such acts of selection or election. The election of Israel's nation to mediate divine revelation was with divine intention that through Israel divine revelation particularly in special terms will reach the rest of the world. The preparation of Israel to mediate divine revelation was to climax in the self-disclosure of Jesus Christ and with cosmic or universal significance to the people of the world. Through the history of the Israelites, such role of mediation was often characterized by religious and pious pride that has no theological basis since there is nothing in the history of the Israelites that suggested they merited their role as mediator of divine revelation. It is the sheer grace of God from

12. Oden, *The Living God*, 20.

beginning to end. The history of the Israelites is a clear revelation that God's selection of Israelites as opposed to the Canaanites, Egyptians, Sumerians, Phoenicians, and even Africans was not primarily based upon any human achievement, but on the mystery of divine sovereignty, initiative and prerogative that is primarily informed by his loving grace and not the merits of the recipients. Africa could have been selected to mediate God's revelation and their history sovereignly prepared to undertake such a lofty divine responsibility. The high and low ebbs of their spiritual comprehension of the divine being would have been nurtured to accommodate a monotheistic framework, however, the divine choice rested on Israel and it was there that God decided to carry out his program to reach the entire human race.

Apart from the selection of Israel, another scandal of particularity revealed itself in God's revelation of himself in the category of a particular gender and not in a sexless being. In considering such scandal of gender particularity, Oden noted,

> Although God is revealed to both women and men alike, God became fully self-revealed in the life of a particular man born of a particular woman. . . . This particularity is a scandal or offense in the sense that God condescends to become human not generally in all but particularly in one.[13]

Such divine selection or preference of the male gender to express or mediate his self-disclosure has sparked discussion and occasioned the rise of feminist theology. However, such theological reflection or feminist reconstruction often overlooked the fact that God has only two or three choices in respect to gender selection in order to mediate his revelation. Either he conveys his revelation using the female mode, the masculine gender, or a sexless designation. Thus, the Messiah would either have been a man, a woman, or a hermaphrodite. Without apology, the God of the Bible employed the male gender in the disclosure of himself and not the other alternatives available to him. If the scandal of particularity in divine selection of Israel as a people could be overcome by the understanding that Israel never merited such selection, the same theological understanding could also be used to address divine selection of masculinity as the gender mode to express or mediate his revelation. It is not primarily informed from any dehumanizing understanding of the female gender nor it is because of the merits of the male gender, but in light of divine freedom and

13. Ibid., 21.

grace he decided to adopt the male gender in expressing and mediating his revelation. Since God is a spirit, as the Scripture clearly underscored, all the gender alternatives available to him will have been possible to mediate his revelation; however, in the mysteries of his counsel and plans he decided to use the male gender as a representation of his being in his mediation of his revelation (John 5:24). Ontologically, God is neither a male nor female but for the sake of sovereign divine consideration he programmed his being, acts, and words in the category of the male gender. Even at these points of divine self-defined particularities of his revelation we must also stress that the selection of this gender particularly was for universal ends. Thus the scandal of divine revelation as evidenced in divine limitation or restriction of himself in the category of a specific people and a specific gender was basically for a universal purpose.

The universal ministry of the particular selection of the Israelite race is constantly underscored within the Old Testament scriptures. There is provision for non-Israelites to enter into the religious and cultic life of the Jewish people particularly as seen in proselytism. In the Pentateuch laws were given in relation to other nations and despite the harsh tones on the lifestyles of other nations there are consistent commands by Yahweh for humane treatment of these foreigners and their admission into the cultic and spiritual experiences of Jewish temple life. The Wisdom literature captured for Israelites the wisdom sayings, traditions and idioms of other nations. The prophetic genre looked beyond the nation of Israel to address the imperialism, abuse of power, and oppression as perpetuated in international and local contexts particularly those of world powers such as Egypt, Assyria and Babylon. In the New Testament such divine particularity for universal ends becomes visible in the revelation of Jesus Christ, who discloses his mission for global salvation. While the disciples delayed such messages, yet ultimately the book of Acts, the Epistles, and the book of Revelation revealed how the church, starting from a modest and a particular Jewish context, spread to Samaria, Judea, and the outermost parts of the known world. Significantly, the book of Acts ends its story of the early church with the preaching of Paul in Rome, the center of the world at that time. Similarly, the book of Revelation brought the story of God to an end in a universal setting with multitudes moving from every tribe and tongue to the revelation now climaxed in the person of Jesus Christ.

The foregoing discussion generally underscores the thesis that the selection of a specific people, place, and gender to communicate divine revelation was with the sole purpose of reaching out to all humankind. The emphasis on such sacred history as revealed in the Judeo-Christian profession does not rule out the sacredness of other people's faith traditions and their limited comprehension of the divine being. It is this understanding that leads the church fathers to underscore the sacredness of the Greco-Roman philosophies and forms thus interpreting them as prototypes of the climax of revelation now available in Jesus Christ. Such theological respect for other faiths traditions within the confinement of general revelation has theological significance for contemporary inter-faith dialogue. In this persuasion, the particularity of divine selection and activity in the Jewish nation and the ultimate realization of the fulfillment of this divine longing within this particular root does not undermine the understanding that God has witnesses or prophetic institutions or customs, which also reveal dimly the nature of divine activity in these human settings. It is absurd or the height of religious arrogance to presume that God's dealing with the people of Israel preludes a relationship with people of other human contexts. The long history of other people in the world and their diverse religious comprehension must have some preparatory value for the reception of Christianity. Thus, even though God has a primary dealing with Israel yet he also extends his divine activity secondarily within the religious comprehension of other human contexts. The possibility of such understanding becomes pertinent because the Bible itself underscores such possibility in its basic submission that man is the product of the divine image. This presupposes the possibility of a certain degree of divine comprehension and understanding within the spirit of every man or woman. However, a cardinal assumption of the Christian faith is that such a quest is ultimately realized in the advent of Jesus Christ because in such redemptive divine acts in Jesus Christ the universal quest of the human spirit is satisfied.

Divine Revelation and Human Religious Experience

We must pause at the onset of this study to define or conceptualize in simple and clear terms the meaning of religious experience.[14] The difficulty of such definition or the quest to conceptualize religious experience stems from the multiplicity of religious experiences and the subjective nature of these experiences.[15] Complicating further the definition of religious expe-

14. See Evans, *Philosophy of Religion*, 77–95; Geisler, *Philosophy of Religion*, 13–83.

15. See Geivett and Sweetman, *Contemporary Perspectives on Religious Epistemology*.

rience is the tendencies of all the various human religious experiences to vie for justification and legitimacy.[16] Even with the difficulty in defining religious experience, from the similarities shared by all human religious experiences, there is still the quest to relate to the transcendental reality in terms of God or other supernatural absolute forms.[17] From this commonality, we could simply define religious experience as the conscious or unconscious feeling or encounter between a person and a transcendental form. At the heart of religious experience is an awareness or consciousness of a divine being and the quest to engage or relate with such being. It is the discovery or knowledge of a transcendental reality beyond the domain of human senses or within such sensory stipulations. Even though religious experience is conceived beyond the domain of sensory forms it is often charged with human emotion that usually gives the experience its religious appeal. The universal acknowledgement and the thriving of such religious experiential accounts are quite intriguing since it presupposes the universal human quest to comprehend or encounter the divine reality that is perceived to be beyond the human sensory domain.[18]

Revelation is clearly associated with religious experience because such a framework is necessary for its mediation. However, since not every religious experience is credible, the necessity to evaluate their source, nature and goal is to be taken seriously. For example, the so-called religious experiences associated with the supposed encounter between humans and extraterrestrial beings such as the Unidentified Flying Object is universally acknowledged; however, such religious experience, even though having some element of discovery or awareness of a transcendent or unusual being, should be subordinated to other religious experiences.[19] The question at this point is the criterion that calls for the subordination of another religious experience over another. This question is necessary in light of the current ecumenical calls and the pluralistic nature of global religious

---

16. There is an ongoing trend in the contemporary African theological discourse to legitimize some African traditional experiences such as dreams see Mbiti, "Dreams as a Point of Theological Dialogue," 511–22. See also Vincent, "Dreams as an Aid to Personal Development," 31–50, and Hagan, "Divinity and Experience," 146–56. These emerging trends show how religious experiences have become defining centers of theological construction in Africa.

17. On the development of the idea of God see Jurji, *The Phenomenology of Religion*, 70–107.

18. See Clouser, *Knowing with the Heart*.

19. On the arguments of the religious nature of modern society despite its tendencies to claim secularity see Otto, *The Idea of the Holy*, 116ff; Eliade, *The Sacred and the Profane*, 202ff.

institution. Since religious experiences generally go beyond moral, secular, and aesthetic experiences to the uncharted planes of metaphysics as attested in its conscious discovery or awareness of the transcendent being, religious experiences thus moves ultimately from the domain of natural or normal spheres of experience to an altitude that is not within human comprehension. In this metaphysical sphere, it is difficult to subordinate one religious experience to another since both religious experiences are within metaphysical domains that are far beyond normal human experiences, thus making judgment almost impossible. Even though it is within the metaphysical domain, yet religious experience has also a close relationship with the empirical, observable, or sensuous character since after all it is expressively a part of a human experience and not that of the divine being.[20] Such human nature is evident particularly in the possible contradictions of two human religious experiences that are both targeted at understanding the transcendental reality.[21] This kind of contradictory religious experience plausibly reveals the necessity of subordinating religious experiences since the contradiction ultimately suggests that one of the two religious experiences might not be necessarily right and hence, the subordination of one religious experience over another. If among two human religious experiences one of the religious experiences is right and the other wrong as seen in a case of contradiction of religious experience, it shows the necessity of subordinating religious experience in order to guard against the possibility of deception or adhering to a misleading religious conclusion. The origin of such pseudo-religious experiences might not be necessarily an act of intentional deception, but often it has its source from human finitude and frailty which are prominent factors that always militate against the possibility of having an accurate religious experience. Thus, the contradiction in human religious experiences does not arise from the contradiction in the essence of the divine being, but primarily from the inability of the humans to clearly articulate or express these conceived religious experiences. Consequently, the tendencies of self-delusion that are basically in all human religious experiences made it important to assess the falsity or truthfulness of religious experience and hence the ultimate moral necessity to subordinate one religious experience over another. In many cases, such consideration necessitates the moral honesty or responsibility to even dismiss entirely a religious experience as

20. For discourse on two kinds of awareness particularly as expressed in cosmological and ontological forms see Tillich, *Theology of Culture*, 10–29.

21. See James, *The Varieties of Religious Experience*.

erroneous and false. The measure for such evaluation of human religious experience becomes necessary in light of these antecedents. However, before proceeding to such goal let us indulge ourselves with the issues of subordination of religious experiences by making the Bible and African traditional religion a theological frame of reference.

Interestingly, the Bible is indeed a catalogue, a library and documentation of human religious experiences. It documents many religious experiences of the Jewish people. In relationship to revelation, one of those defining religious experiences from the Judeo–Christian perspective are the call of Abraham, the call of Moses, the exodus, the exile, the ministry and death of Jesus Christ, and consequently the proclamation of such events by Paul and other apostles. These religious experiences are central and defining moments in the Bible because of their revelatory value since they provide a historical framework for the revelation or new understanding of the divine being. Similarly, within African traditional religious experiences there are defining religious experiences that also provide footing for divine disclosure. Even though these religious experiences might not be comparable to the biblical ones in detail and goal yet both use the media of dreams, visions, natural and physical encounters in the life of the worshipper, which assumes a framework for revelation. Often, there is a conscious quest for spiritual experiences to help in handling the existential challenges of the African context. The initiative of such experience is taken by the worshipper who visits the shrine or cultic site to find remedy for his existential human needs. It is human existential needs that push the African people to the shrine of the gods and the self-disclosures of the gods in those crisis moments have no teleological value apart from their immediate existential context. Even though at times cultic taboos as revealed by the gods are kept from one generation to another, yet the revelation of the divine being in the dimension of attributes is generally lacking. There are times however when the gods revealed the type of sacrifice or food that they approve to be presented before their altars or shrines, however such revelation of the gods does not transcend these cultic associations between the African gods and the priestly cult to the deeper revelation of divine essence. On the contrary, such revelation of divine essence as good, loving and patient, transcendent, and other divine attributes are conceived not via cultic shrines, but in the context of real life particularly in the existence realms of survival. The context of such revelation is far from the world of diviners, mediums, or African medicine men and women, but it is found in the general interaction of African society in their daily engagement with the human realities of pain and joy. As realities push their existential pangs on them, they discover different aspects of the divine being. It is not a speculative, or prophetic kind of revelation, it is a revelation deeply embedded in the existential struggles of the African people for survival. Thus general revelation extends to their sufferings, pains and struggles because it becomes providentially a living avenue to know and understand the goodness and love of the transcendent being. However, contrary to existential models of explicating divine attributes the biblical models are clearly founded on priestly and prophetic paradigms whereby the priest or prophet revealed an aspect of the divine attributes or part of his essential form. Though we have to point out that such revelation of the divine being is not divorced from the existential context of such revelation. For example, the biblical revelation of Yahweh as redeemer is rooted in the historical event of the exodus. The question worth asking is, why the subordination of African purely existential models of divine revelation to the Jewish overly priestly and prophetic models of divine revelation?

To guide us in answering this question, we must digress and pursue three important propositions at this point. Firstly, we must be clear in our minds that the transcendent being or reality is not ontologically subjective in essence and thus any subjectivity or diversity that follows the experiencing of the divine being is a by-product of human beings as highlighted earlier. The pluralistic and multiplicity of religious experiences are metaphysical devices to comprehend the divine person. As such, ontologically God must be an objective reality that is not subjective in his divine constitution. The second theological proposition lies in the limitation of human experiences to understand and comprehend the transcendent being. Since God or the transcendent reality is within the metaphysical domain that is beyond the natural comprehension of the human imagination or logic the possibility of experiencing or knowing the divine person using these human mystical experiences becomes questionable, and thus the necessity of divine revelation. Divine revelation becomes necessary because of the inability of human religious experience to objectively represent the divine being. Even though such human subjective experiences are considered revelatory since they bring us into the conscious awareness of the divine being, yet they are short of transmitting adequate knowledge about God because of their subjectiveness. For the African people, the comprehension of the divine being via non-metaphysical, but existential realities should be stressed here. It is true Africans believe in metaphysical domains of revelation—such as dreams, visions, and visitation of the diviners—yet their understanding of divine attributes are not fundamentally derived from these metaphysical forms, but are generally the product of their existential interaction with non-metaphysical realities of African society. In this existential sphere, Africans have no "thus says the Lord" as the Jewish prophets or priests in terms of a paradigmatic device to introduce the being or essence of the transcendent realities because the revelation of such categories is already comprehended within the non-metaphysical, the daily existential interaction of the Africans and their environments. Thus African traditional religions do not claim with authority that its practices are a direct revelation from the higher God, but a theological necessity entrenched by the cult of the lower gods.

It is only in the monotheistic religions of Judaism, Christianity, and Islam that such authoritative claims to divine revelation are emphasized. The realization of divine revealed truths within Christianity, Judaism, and Islam presupposes the actualization of divine revelation through the mechanism of human religious events. All these three religions share a common source by which such human-divine encounter took place. Judaism, Christianity, and Islam agree that such divine revelation took place within the purview of Jewish history. The acknowledgement of this dominant singular theological root is significant since it reveals the general agreement by these faiths that something extraordinary had taken place within the monotheistic conception of Jewish religious history. However, the interpretation of the nature, goal, and significance of such events for the universe has been of different kinds. Among these faiths, only Christianity has revealed the significant symbiotic dimensions of divine revelation in the articulation of the human and divine aspects of revelation. Importantly, Christianity based its revelation not on some "good stuff about God," but in the revelation of God himself in a particular person. Thus, for Christianity God did not stay forever in some cosmic transcendence merely revealing his word, as conceived in the pride that Muslims place on the divine revelation of the Quran or the Jewish focus on the Torah revelation. For Christianity it is in the framework of the religious experiences of Jesus Christ that salvation becomes available to the world and ultimately it is based on this same revelation in Jesus Christ that all human experiences or revelations are duly interpreted, evaluated, and judged.

The Consistency of the "Judeo-Christian God" in Revelation

Consistency is the ability by which a form or theological category is without self-contradiction. It is a theological characteristic by which a religious conception is internally harmonious in its basic revelatory proposition or postulations. Internal harmony becomes a standard framework in which divine revelation must be rooted since there is a necessity for the theological comprehension of the divine being to reveal certain harmony or distinct continuity in the mediatory process.[22] It must despite the heterogeneous nature of religious experience reveal a homogeneity or consistency in the transmission of the divine being within the framework of history.

However, by the use of consistency we do not mean mere rationality. Even though rational cohesion is a necessary prerequisite in discussing issues of consistency or harmony, the philosophical category of logic or wooden sophistry is not the meaning underscored by the usage of the term here. This preliminary explanation is very important since logic and rationality is beyond the boundary of revelation because these are concepts outside the perimeters of divine revelation. The basic presupposition of revelation is that it is an act that dwells in the domain of the metaphysical and hence is antithetical in its basic constitution with logic. This is because the functionality or instrumentality of logic lies within the realms of reason, which is the product of senses or sensual empirical observations. Logic or reason reaches its theological conclusions primarily based on deduction or the experimental documentation of data that is carried out in a highly scientific manner. However, revelation presupposes the intrusion of the divine being from the realm that is beyond the grasp or comprehension of the human senses and thus unverifiable using the methodology of scientific experimentation. Consequently, it is impossible for sensuous logic to carry out the basic presupposition of revelation. The incompatibility of logic or rational reasoning with divine revelation does not suggests the understanding that divine revelation is incoherent at such, since divine revelation has some basic sequential forms that are still compatible with human rationality. The sequential divine ordering in the transmission of himself has patterns that should be consistent if the divine person would ever be known. However, even this sequential or systematic ordering of divine revelation in its articulation, composition, and presentation, does not presuppose that divine revelation is in tutelage to reason

22. Francis Schaeffer, "He is There," 99–108.

or logic. Divine revelation has its source and orientation far away from the domain of reason, even though it employs systematic reasoning in its presentation of such revelation of the divine being. Thus, there is a theological fusion of both human and divine dimensions in the articulation and presentation of revelation. God is the source, while humans, through some accepted patterns of logic or culturally-defined mediums, seek to reflect this revelation of the divine person.

On the other hand, if revelation in its basic understanding is beyond the domain of rational confinement or human logic on what basis should we pursue the consistency of the Judeo-Christian understanding of revelation? What becomes the parameter to judge whether a revelation is consistent or not? While the answers to this enquiry might at first seemed problematic yet the answer is indeed simple since the true test of consistency is not rationality but the inner testimony of such divine revelation. This inner testimony consists of the harmonious working of the different constitutions, aspects, or conceptions of the divine being in the history of such revelatory transmission. To the end that it reflects a transcendent and immanent divine person who is nobly high, ethically right and morally consistent in the revelation of his essential being and the relationship of such essential being to the world. The beingness of the divine being must always be consistent in doing right and must also occupy an ethically unquestionable status to warrant the label of consistency. It is this understanding that informed Abraham's question that "Shall not the Judge of all the earth do right?" (Gen 18:25).

From this theological gauge, we proceed to assess the Judeo-Christian God (Heb 1:1–3). The consistent monotheistic depiction of a lofty and ethically conscious divine being is the greatest significant contribution of the Judeo-Christian revelation to humanity. This conscious portrayal of ancient Israel's God sets Israel apart from the idolatrous conception of the gods and goddesses of the polytheistic ancient Near East. This lofty and ethical uncompromising being is also associated with the Christian God since it is the understanding of the New Testament writers that it is the same God of Abraham, Isaac, and Jacob that is at work in their writings or revelation (Heb 1:1–3). The consistent reference to the past heritage of the monotheistic covenant relationship or revelation of God to Israel is always seen at every point of a new divine disclosure of himself. Thus, God revealed himself to the patriarchs and there is a constant reference to such theological continuity between the God revealed in the patriarchal theological or religious consciousness and the mosaic covenant or divine revelation mediated through Moses.

Significantly, God revealed to Moses that "He is the God of your father, the God of Abraham, Isaac, and Jacob." The historical books are rich in the referral of rising Jewish prophetism and declining priesthood to the tenets and demands of the revelation that is strongly conceived to have taken place in the patriarch and mosaic comprehension of the divine being. Always, there is a reference to the "God of your fathers" to elicit moral and spiritual response from the wayward Israelite nation. The revelation in the Mosaic-Sinaitic covenant and the prophetic revivalism that characterized the historical books presupposed that ancient Israel saw the sameness or continuity between God's revelation in the patriarchal and mosaic covenants and the emerging prophetic traditions. The prophets did not create anything new in a particular sense since the dominant theological task of their ministry is to point Israel back to the covenant or revelation that took place in Israel's past particularly in the patriarchal and mosaic covenants. Significantly, their prophetic traditions also looked towards the future to a new covenant or divine revelation of a spiritual kind. Thus, Jeremiah talked about a new covenant that is inwardly in the worshipper's heart (Jer 31:31). Joel revealed the presence of eschatological revelation of God whereby "the young men shall see visions and the old men shall dream dreams" (Joel 2:28). Isaiah also speaks of a time when the knowledge of God will "cover the earth as the waters cover the sea" (Isa 11:9). The anticipation of this divine revelation is already expected in mosaic revelation because Moses desired that all Israel should become prophets, thus receiving unhindered access to God (Num 11:26–30). The New Testament writers believed such a time of ultimate divine revelation prophesied by Joel, Jeremiah, and Isaiah has now come (Acts 2:14–47). The prophetic desire of the New Testament for prophets transcends the modest desire of Moses in the Old Testament and now include the Gentiles, who are seen prophesying within the New Testament church (Acts 13:1). There is now access to God in a way different from the understanding in the Old Testament. In every sense, the New Testament becomes a fulfillment of the Old Testament spiritual yearning and aspiration, thus suggesting the consistency of the revelation of the Judeo-Christian type. Unfortunately, all religions also lay claim to such consistency; however, on close examination, there is a disparity in comprehension of the divine person within the history of such religions. Thus, such a consistency as seen within the Judeo-Christian faith is lacking in other contemporary faiths.

For example, Hinduism makes room for pantheism and does not have the ethical and monotheistic consistencies of the Judeo-Christian revelation. African traditional religion does not have a consistent revelation of the divine being in terms of ethical and monotheistic inclinations as seen within the Judeo-Christian faith. The quest to assert such ethical and monotheistic affirmation by pioneering African works as constructed by Mbiti and Idowu is indeed in this sense a brilliant failure since the African conception of the divine person is riddled with the interfering presence of many divinities and intermediaries that cloud or dim the African revelation of God. Within the Islamic faith, even though based on some kind of monotheistic foundation, it lacks ethical consistency between the lofty conception of God and his deeds in practice because some abrogated texts of the Quran reveal the self-contradictions in the divine nature of Allah and thus presuppose the inconsistency between the lofty divine essence of the Muslim God and his specific deeds in history. From the preceding discourse, one sees the inability of treating the revelations of other faiths as credible forms of revelation and hence, presupposes the impossibility of exploring these religious conceptions as ways to understand the divine being. Even though we recognize that God is without a witness among these religious revelations, such witnesses of the divine voices are not clear enough to call for the salvation of humanity thus compromising their ultimate claims to the divine being.

Traditional African Religious Agents of "Revelation"

In traditional African societies and even in modern times, African people have sought daily guidance by means of consultation of men and women who are traditionally conceived as possessing the power to see the future or to know clairvoyantly the secret behind the problems of the African people. These individuals are known differently as "witchdoctor," "medicine man," "herbalist," or the "diviner." The task of these individuals is to diagnose the problems of their clients and to provide appropriate solutions to them. In the African church, despite its supposedly Christian influence, many church members still patronize these people as agents of spiritual guidance. The reasons for their popularity in recent times are many, however, a few of these reasons can be readily highlighted. First, the missionary churches refused to provide its members with an adequate replacement of the services provided by these institutions of guidance in traditional African society, thus making the members who are given the

Bible as means of guidance to naturally ignore the Scriptures and turn to the shrines for remedies to their human ills. Secondly, the efficacy of the solutions provided by these traditional mediums often overshadows the ministry of the church among Africans. The African people are always vulnerable to a show or manifestation of spiritual powers, and it is a commonly accepted view that the medicine man or witchdoctor has supernatural powers to harm or to make well. This belief normally serves as motivation for troubling African "Christians" who want quick supernatural intervention to their human problems. Unfortunately, these "Christians" do not always see a contradiction between their "Christian beliefs" and their consultation of these traditional religious forms rather they treat them as viable means of seeking divine guidance. Lastly, the African traditionally conceived these traditional forms as the "custodian" of supernatural knowledge or secrets. It is believed that the "herbalist" or "witchdoctor" possesses "supernatural knowledge" of the past, present, and the future," and hence their in-depth knowledge of the condition of their clients and the efficacy of their remedies in eliminating human problems. For example, immediately when a "client" comes to see a "witchdoctor," the witchdoctor has to impress his clients by providing specific knowledge of the events surrounding this client in order to have the total trust of the client; thus the witchdoctor often tells the client the reason for his coming or some personal secret in the life of the client. Even though much of this "revelation" is actually "psychological reading" of his "clients" there are times when "demonic powers" are invoked in order to assist the "witchdoctor" in his quest to impress and dazzle his clients. In contemporary times, the Pentecostal pastors have replaced the traditional role of the witchdoctor because they similarly provide their members with "knowledge" surrounding their lives, and the possible solutions to alleviate their human problems. Thus in this same sense, they are no different from the traditional seer who also engages in similar practices.

In the evangelical churches, sermons upon sermons had criticized the use of these traditional institutions as a medium of guidance for Christians since it is syncretic and un-Christian at best, however, often such criticism has not underscored the reasons for the patronizing of these traditional institutions by "Christian clients." Beyond the reasons highlighted, there is another pertinent reason which is closely related to the first reason. This reason comes from the failure of church's discipleship program to address these issues during discipleship. Often the African churches lack discipleship programs, and thus the converts are left on their own. Such converts never reach spiritual maturity in their Christian life because they lack vital knowledge of the biblical worldview. Consequently, even though they are Christians in names, their worldview is not Christian, but the inherited African pre-Christian worldview. The evangelistic outreaches in Africa often focus on the numerical figures of people turning to Christ, but they spend little time in discipling these converts to adopt the "biblical worldview." The need in the African church is the need for a "biblical worldview" because there are indeed many Christians who are not transformed at the level of their worldview. These Christians take decisions by the dictates of their traditional African worldview rather than the biblical one. The value of these Christians is heavily colored by the cultural determinants of their African communities rather than their new faith in Christ. Thus we have a great number of Christians trooping into the church but little is seen by way of Christian life in the private and public domains. The ethics of these Christians are baptized traditional African ethics, and thus often they are incapable of bringing about the desired transformation in the public and private sectors of African society. In most African churches, the transformational ingredients of the gospel are not duly stressed, and the radical discontinuity between the traditional African forms and the new life in Christ has not found consistent emphasis. This problem could have been averted if the discipleship programs of the African church are tailored to address the traditional African worldview and the expected worldview of the Christian believer. Such interaction, confrontation and dialogue will help to underscore the weakness of the traditional African worldviews, but also underscore particular places whereby its strengths could be harnessed to support the biblical worldview.

Similarly, apart from the consultation of these institutions for guidance, there is also the emphasis on dreams, trances, and visions as accepted media of revelation or guidance in traditional African society. Often the medium of dreams in particular is conceived as sure means for divine guidance. In traditional African society, dreams are conceived as the "vehicle" employed by the gods to reveal to humans their wills. It is often categorized in terms of "good" or "bad" dreams. In most traditional African societies, opposite criteria is employed as means of determining or differentiating a good from a bad one, thus if a man dreams that he is poor, it is conceived that the gods have destined such a person to become rich in the future. On the other hand, if a man dreams he is celebrating or eating, it is conceived traditionally as a sign of a bad omen, hence it is a bad dream. In other African societies, such opposite criteria is not employed, and thus a dream is bad if the events in the dreams are negative and it is good if the events in the dreams are positive and favorable. The world of dreams is often the inward guide by which many African Christians take major life decisions such as marriage, business, journeys, and friendship. Even though the Bible shows cases where dreams were used for revelation of divine will and purpose,[23] the African church must place restrain on the use of dreams as the means of divine guidance or revelation. Such restraints must be emphasized because of the subjective nature of dreams and the temptation of many African Christians to employ the interpretative lenses from their pre-Christian worldview to understand as well as interpret these dreams. Even though God used the means of dreams to reveal his will, there is no guarantee now that he uses the same method to convey his will particularly in the New Testament dispensation when it is expected that God's Spirit is in the heart of every Christian thus providing the needed daily guidance. This emphasis on the inward leading of the Holy Spirit in the life of the believer in Christ must be readily underscored, and it should replace the temptation of consulting with traditional African seers or the temptation to take every dream seriously by many African Christians (See John 14:26; Rom 8:14). Similarly, the leading of the Holy Spirit in the life of the Christian must not replace the need to consult with mature Christians to seek their wealth of wisdom in making critical life decisions. In the same way, the Holy Spirit's daily ministry of guidance in the life of the Christian should not conflict with the words of the Scriptures. The Holy Spirit will not lead us into doing or taking steps that clearly contradict the teachings of the Scriptures. Thus all prompting, inward guidance or inner insight as forms of guidance must never contradict the Bible. This consideration places restriction on the nature of the Holy Spirit's leading. Unfortunately, within the Pentecostal movement the emphasis on the Holy Spirit's leading and guidance have often led to manipulation or exploitation of some Christians by some heretical teachers who employ great eloquence and gimmicks claiming that every selfish inclination or self-centered craving for money is a direct leadership from the Holy Spirit. Such attributed guidance of the Holy Spirit in claims and counter-claims of material things in the life of their members by these "men of God" must be crosschecked in light of the Scriptures (See 1 Thess 5:20–21). Thus the supposed ministry of the "Holy Spirit" in the life of the church must not contradict the teachings expressed in the

23. For example see Gen 20:3–7; 28:12; 31:10–13; 40:5; Judg 7:13–14; Dan 2:45; Matt 1:20; 2:12.

Bible. We must emphasize the place of such daily guidance of the believer in the inward prompting of the Holy Spirit, and providing them with the desired direction for ministry. Such direction often is missed because we are not always in tune with the Holy Spirit, thus our inability to be led by his inward instructions on the course to take. We must also differentiate this leading of the Holy Spirit from the natural human "hunches" or "intuition." Even though the Holy Spirit may bring ideas to our minds in the form of "hunches" or "intuition" the prompting of the Holy Spirit is different from these natural means of discerning divine will in decision making. The difference is that no "hunches" or "intuition" from God should contradict the words of the Scriptures, hence the Bible becomes the gauge to test these "hunches" and "intuition." There is no doubt that the Holy Spirit often could use sanctified or heightened spiritual sensitivity in terms of "hunches" or "intuition" of some Christians in order to offer them some form of guidance in critical times, however, we must subject such "hunches" or "intuition" to the judgment of the Scriptures. On the other hand, we must also realize that the leadership of "hunches" or "intuition" in the life of many Christians is actually the voice of the Holy Spirit in the hearts of Christians who desire to lead and guide Christians towards making the right decisions for their lives. For example, one hears how Christians say that "While I was walking on the road coming back from work 'something' tells me to look back and behold I saw the car moving directly to crush me. If I had not turned immediately I would have been crushed by this car." Similarly, one hears among Christians statements like this: "something told me to pray and then I began to pray . . . it was at the same time that my husband was saved from being run over by a moving trailer." The "something" in the preceding hypothetical statements is nothing but the inward prompting of the "Holy Spirit." However, some people may take such leadership to be mere coincidence or the outcome of the natural psychological need for self-preservation which makes us turn around to check things over and over again, yet for Christians, these promptings are not merely "natural" human inclinations for self-preservation, but a leading from the Holy Spirit who wants to guide and lead us in the daily course of our lives. African Christians must be discipled in these so-called "hunches" or "intuitive" inward messages because they may be the avenue by which the Holy Spirit may make the will and wishes of God known to a people that already presume the efficacy of these sources in the mediation of the divine will. However, we must always emphasize that such promptings of "hunches" or "intuition" must not replace the Bible in the life of

Christian. The Christian must always weigh these inward "messages" with the truths of the Holy Scriptures.

Divine Revelation and Eschatology

There is an intricate relationship between revelation and eschatology particularly as it relates to the understanding of divine revelation in the context of Judeo-Christian faith. Within this theological tradition, there is a preoccupation that divine revelation has some destined divine end in view from the beginning of such divine revelation. It is presumed that divine revelation was designed to reveal certain divine purposes which are conceived in teleological perspectives. It is this dominant motif of the Judeo-Christian revelation that had made Jürgen Moltmann assert the theological thesis that the Judeo-Christian religion is an eschatological faith.[24] In his discourse on "Revelation and Eschatology," Moltmann underscores the forward-looking nature of divine revelation in the Christian tradition suggesting the end points of divine revelation is rooted on some eschatological concerns.[25] Unfortunately, Moltmann, due to his consistent forward-looking theological agenda, neglected the backward-looking nature of the Judeo-Christian faith, particularly in the constant portrayal of divine activity in the past. This reference of divine activity in the past took the forms of warning or reminder to the contemporary times of clearly defined divine activities especially the divine encounter with the patriarchs and the subsequent covenant that such encounter represents. Thus, even the prophetic books are backward looking in this sense, since they look backward to the covenants that God made with the generation of past Israelites and the growing recognition of its implication for the present. The dominance of this backward motif of the Judeo-Christian tradition is also underscored in the Historical books with its consistent reminder of the "God of your fathers." Similarly, such backward looking tendency of the Judeo-Christian faith is reflected in the New Testament through consistent references of the New Testament writers back to the divine activity in the past religious or theological history of the Israelite people. This backward disposition of the New Testament writers took the form of references to prophecies or theological categories that are seen to be in harmony with the new theological emphases of the Christian church. Even though the New Testament saw themselves at a defining place in the history of divine

24. See Moltmann, *The Theology of Hope.*
25. Ibid., 37–94.

revelation, yet they often felt that the phenomenon of divine revelation in the New Testament was merely an extension or fulfillment of the oracles, events and divine phenomenon conceived to have taken place in the Old Testament. Seen in this perspective, the Judeo-Christian faith has historical or backward looking tendencies, which do not bear resemblance to the lofty eschatological generalization forwarded by Moltmann.[26] Similarly, the backward looking nature of the Judeo-Christian faith also breaks in pieces the theological superstructure on which Mbiti made his popular assumption that Africans are backward looking in their understanding of eschatology and thus this theological orientation causes a problem for their comprehension of a linear historical emphases of the Christian faith particularly as reflected in the future-looking tendencies of the Christian religion.[27] However, this perceived problem of conceptual compatibility is easily resolved if the backward nature of the Christian faith is also affirmed since it shows significant continuity with the assumed backward looking tendency of the African people.

Beside this backward tendency of the Judeo-Christian tradition, there is also a commitment towards the present. The Old Testament presupposes that references to the mosaic or patriarchal covenants are within the context of ethical motivation for the present and the forward looking prophecies of the Old Testament are always attached or associated with divine moral imperatives of the moment. It is not an aimless theological adventure into the past but a reference or theological journey that is undertaken with the constant goal to address the ills of the contemporary context of such theological travellers. Thus, the Old Testament is not only eschatology but it has also a salient commitment to the present. Similarly, the New Testament writers also underscored a theological commitment to the present. The theological emphases on eschatology in the New Testament are not an existential or psychological escape from the realities of the moment to the fanciful eschatological imagination rather they are the engagement of the present particularly in their persistent emphases that the present is below the ultimate divine desire and hence the theological painting or revelation of such divinely desired end for the world in eschatological grandeur. Consequently, New Testament eschatology addresses the situations of the moment, even as it looks forward to the future when

26. Concerning other eschatological works by Moltmann see Moltmann, "Hope and History," 369–99; Moltmann, "Politics and the Practice of Hope," 288–91; Moltmann, "Theology as Eschatology," 1–50. See also, Moltmann, *The Experiment of Hope*; Moltmann, "Is the World Coming to an End," 129–38.

27. See Mbiti, *The Akamba and Christianity*.

such problems are solved through divine intervention that is understood to have already started in the present through the revelation and mediation of Jesus Christ. In this perspective, the Judeo-Christian faith entertained and showed a commitment to the past, the present and the future.

On the other hand, even though the Judeo-Christian revelation stresses the tripartite dimensions of time yet there is a propensity within the divine revelation in this context to explore a futuristic framework in order to express the culmination of divine revelation. Consequently, divine revelation has a predisposition for the future since the goal or end of divine revelation already presupposes an eschatological emphasis, which is fundamentally built on the theological presupposition that the divine person revealed himself in relationship to some ultimate, defining purposes or end. For the Christian religion the goal or end of divine revelation is God's redemption. The cosmic redemption consists of the renewal and newness of all creation and the anticipation of the restoration of pristine human dignity as God's image bearer. However, for the Christian faith such resolution of divine manifestation is predicated on one's commitment and faith to the Lordship of Jesus Christ in the present.[28]

Conclusion

The preceding discourse engages the subject of divine revelation particularly as expressed within the sphere of general and special revelation. It also highlights the limitation of general and special revelation, the scandal of particularity, the place of experience, the consistency of the Judeo-Christian revelation and the place of eschatology in the revelatory process. The consideration reveals christocentric emphases since the discussion of general and special revelation, the scandal of particularity, and the consistency of the Judeo-Christian tradition are hyphenated on some form of christocentric foundation, thus presupposing that the christocentric content of special revelation sets the Christian revelation of God apart and consequently such understanding reveals the uniqueness of the Christian message. Similarly, it underscores the place of "divine guidance" among African Christians, and the temptation to seek traditional modes of "guidance" or "revelation" instead of relying on the Scriptures and the inward leading of the Holy Spirit. This chapter emphasizes that every inward prompting of "hunches" or "intuition" must be judged and

28. For an introduction to evangelical understanding of biblical eschatology see Erickson, *A Basic Guide to Eschatology*.

tested by its compatibility to the teachings of the Scriptures. The African church must discourage the temptation among its members to seek traditional modes of seeking "spiritual guidance" or "direction." The church discipleship program must take seriously the challenge or danger that the pre-Christian traditional institutions of "spiritual guidance" poses to the Christian converts who even though professing to be Christian, go about with the traditional African non-Christian worldview that patronize the "witchdoctor," "herbalist," or the "sorcerer." Such discipleship classes must reiterate the place of divine guidance in the Bible and the understanding that the Christian life provides the avenue for seeking guidance in the daily life of the Christian believer. Without such emphases, Christian converts become immature and nominal because their pre-Christian worldview is not yet transformed, and thus he or she is unable to make sense of the Christian faith since from its perspective it lacks the way to know or understand the unknown paths of the future and the needed guidance for the present challenges.

4

The Scriptures

Introduction

EVERY HUMAN SOCIETY HAS often prided itself in some form of religious or metaphysical experience.[1] These metaphysical experiences are closely associated with the origin of religion or the passionate quest of the human spirit to understand the supernatural dimension of mortal existence.[2] The value attached to these kinds of supernatural experiences naturally leads to documentation of this religious phenomenon in written forms, thus contributing to the subsequent transmission and preservation of these cherished religious and theological categories from generation to generation. In Africa, the documentation of these religious experiences of the African people has unfortunately not taken place.[3] This is because of the dominant nature of oral tradition within African society thus hindering the right documentation and the actual description of these religious experiences of the African people. Describing this religious inclination of the African people, Mbiti rightly observed,

> Africans are notoriously religious, and each people has its own
> religious system with a set of beliefs and practices. Religion

1. See Aerthayil, "Interiority," 279–88.

2. On the dominant study of different theories of revelation particularly in the last three centuries see McDonald, *Theories of Revelation.*

3. For the analysis and study on the complexity of this African religious heritage see Turaki, *Christianity and African Gods.* See also Turaki, *Tribal Gods,* and Turaki, *The British Colonial Legacy.*

permeates into all the departments of life so fully that it is not easy or possible always to isolate it. A study of these religious systems is, therefore, ultimately a study of the peoples themselves in all the complexities of both traditional and modern life. Our written knowledge of traditional religions is comparatively little, though increasing, and comes chiefly from anthropologists and sociologists. Practically nothing has been produced by theologians, describing or interpreting these religions theologically.[4]

However, the inability to document or keep account of such mystical or metaphysical experiences of the African people does not necessary presuppose that the African people did not value religion nor does it presuppose that the religious experiences of the African people in pre-Christian times are without coherence or systematic patterns.[5] However, the oral cultural mechanism of African society did not reveal a dominant stimulus to commit such religious experience to writing.[6] As much as this development is a setback towards the understanding or recovery of the African traditional religions, yet even without such literary medium African traditional religions have expressed themselves in continued piety, zeal, and practices throughout the history of the African people.[7] In contemporary times, some of the basic metaphysical experiences of the African people have been extrapolated from African traditional songs, proverbs, myths and other African cultic or ritualistic practices.[8] Contrary to this oral nature of the African traditional religions, the Judeo-Christian faith reached the African people in the category of sacred *writing*. Even though the metaphysical experiences of the Jewish people primarily employed orality within the earlier phase of its development, yet a conscious quest to put it in writing made the Judeo-Christian faith a literate version of "human" religious experiences. It is within this religious heritage of the Jewish people that a significant theological drama took place, which has subsequent universal theological significance for the rest of humanity. In particular, this drama took place in the Scriptures, hence the importance of the Scriptures to the

4. Mbiti, *African Religions and Philosophy*, 1.

5. On the many problems of systematized theology see D'Costa, "The End of Systematic Theology," 324–34.

6. See Mbiti, "Cattle are Born with Ears," 15–25; Hollenweger, "The Theological Challenge," 244–46.

7. This orality of the African traditional setting has always posed serious missiological and theological problems for the Christian message that is received in written form. See Klem, "The Bible as Oral Literature," 479–86.

8. See Mbiti, *Concepts of God in Africa* and *African Religions and Philosophy*.

Christian faith.[9] To underscore such importance, this chapter describes the nature and role of the Christian Scriptures, especially in the context of oral predilection of the traditional African society.

Africans and the Use of the Bible

In traditional African society the concept of a written Scripture is foreign since in the traditional African society Scripture is virtually absent. The words of the gods are not written or documented but spoken verbally by the mouthpiece of the gods from the diviners or the high priest. These verbal spoken words of the gods are conceived as powerful; hence they are respected and revered. The African people in most cases do not fear that the mediators of the messages of the gods could fabricate or manipulate the messages because the integrity of these mouthpieces is often assumed. Such messages of the gods are often existentially related since they deal with the needs and problems within the human society. The gods often speak to address moral, physical, political, social, and spiritual problems of the people, and their diagnosis and remedy are perceived as final in putting to rest a particular problem of a given community. Similarly, the gods speak to settle family problems, reverse a drought or avert a famine. It is always the condition of the African society that is the concerns of the speeches of these gods. Unfortunately, these words from the gods are never documented or put into written form but kept in the memory of the elders, the chief priest or priestess of such gods. In addition, the African people also quote or say incantations from memory as a spiritual defence against the opposing forces or some unpleasant circumstances. It is believed that such incantations have formidable power to check the intrusion of evil powers and to bring about the desired state. Often the words of incantation against a particular undesirable condition are only known to the initiates of a particular cult or shrine. Thus such words said are conceived to be charged with powers in order to bring about the desired outcome. Underscoring the importance of words in traditional African context, Mbiti noted,

9. There is a subtle relationship between the treatment of revelation in the previous chapter and our treatment of Scriptures in the present chapter since Scripture is the authoritative and canonical documentation of divine self–disclosure. The writing of divine revelation and the authority of such writings in the matter of faith and practice is the basic preoccupation of a branch of systematic theology known as bibliology. For the Christian faith the Scripture is not merely words of God, but actually the words of God with a definite article.

> There is a mystical power in words, especially those of a senior person to a junior one, in terms of age, social status or office position. The words of parents, for example, carry "power" when spoken to children: they "cause" good fortune, curse, success, peace, sorrow, or blessings, especially when spoken in moments of crisis. The words of medicine-man works through the medicine he gives, and it is this, perhaps more than the actual herb, which is thought to cause the cure or prevent misfortunes.[10]

For many Africans coming from this background where words are conceived as portents for magical effects it is not surprising the divine words in the Scriptures are also conceived within these traditional definitions. The magical treatment of the Bible is rampant in many parts of Africa. For example, the Bible is often used to find a thief when money or other valued objects are missing. Similarly, in a study by David T. Adamo, the Bible, especially the Psalms, is used among the Yoruba people as a means of incantation.[11]

As already highlighted in passing, in the traditional context of Africa, books are of little value since most of the communication employs oral means. Thus, what does canonicity or the Bible mean in this traditionally defined oral setting? Interestingly, as argued by Mbiti, the Bible has profoundly shaped African Christianity. Bible passages have been committed to memory and had been expressed in songs, prayers, and sermons.[12] It seems African Christian folks have put the Bible back in orality, consequently using oral means to spread its message. Similarly, in Africa, seen as a sacred text, the Bible is often viewed as a charm to ward off evil, thus there are instances of the Bible used to divine or placed under the pillow as a magic potion in order to aid in the protection of the person. Such a magical use of the Bible reveals the influence from traditional African religion whereby things or objects held sacred are also conceived to have the vital force needed for protection or in order to find good luck. Although these kinds of Bible abuse are fairly common, they are an aberration from the norm; generally speaking Africans read the stories of the Bible in order to find the protective promises of God, which are fervently believed in faith to take place in the life of the person involved. Even as an aberration, the magical use of the Bible did not come out of some delusional understanding of the Bible, but from the firm conviction of the power and

10. Mbiti, *African Religions and Philosophy*, 197.
11. Adamo, "The Use of Psalms," 336–49.
12. Mbiti, *Bible and Theology*, 222–34.

authority of the sacred text.[13] In many ways, African Christianity is firmly based on the Bible and richly colored by the cultural worldviews of the African people. The interlacing of these two categories while it reveals the quest of the African people to understand the Bible based on their own distinct cultural forms, it also poses a serious danger since the motivation and basis for such interaction of the two is primarily determined by traditional cultural factors. Nonetheless, these culturally defined presuppositions ultimately reveal the high value that Africans generally attach to the Bible as a religious sacred text, which is pragmatically employed to confront the problems of African society. Often, there is a successful transition or replacement of the power of charms with the powers believed to literally reside in the very words of the Scriptures, thus quoting or chanting of the Scriptures are often common practices, particularly during moments of crisis or unfriendly circumstances. For many Africans, the Bible is the revelation of the divine blueprint for their lives and thus every word of the Scriptures is conceived to inherently contain the divine power of God needed to bring to pass the aspirations or promises of biblical texts. The power of words is traditionally seen in the use of words to bless and to curse, which are chanted magically in order to bring about the state desired. The word of God in the Bible conceived within these culturally defined meanings are common across the African continent. This treatment of the word of God came partly from the dominant understanding of the universe in the religious category.[14]

The Nature of the Divine Word

In the African worldview, as already seen, spoken words are often conceived to have certain mystical power. Thus, often the African herbalist or witchdoctor employs the use of words in order to invoke a blessing or a curse, and to call on the services of good and malevolent spirits. This power of the spoken word is assumed because human words are presumed to be

13. See Adamo, "The Use of Psalms," 336–49.

14. Describing this instinctive religious inclination of the African people, Mbiti observed, "for Africans, the whole of existence is a religious phenomenon; man is a deeply religious being living in a religious universe" (Mbiti, *African Religions and Philosophy*, 15). Unfortunately, "Failure to realize and appreciate this starting point, has led missionaries, anthropologists, colonial administrators and other foreign writers on African religion to misunderstand not only the religions as such but the peoples of Africa" (ibid.). The word of God in this highly religious environment is normally treated with a certain degree of mystical or magical importance.

the means by which spiritual realities are brought into physical being. In this understanding, spoken words are the mediators of spiritual realities. Even though human touch could be employed in order to transfer such spiritual reality into being, priority of place is always given to the power of spoken words. Thus the African children look to their parents for orally worded blessing and the aged people are generally conceived to have the power to bless or curse by the utterance of their words. In this persuasion, spoken words are highly respected and African men and women often manipulate or persuade the aged by way of gifts or good behavior in order to get or secure for themselves good words of blessing from their parents.

In the same sense, words are highly conceived to be mediators of divine blessing in the Bible. The story of Jacob and Esau is a good example because both Jacob and Esau seek to battle for the words of blessing from their father Isaac (Gen 27:1–40). From the Bible story, these orally pronounced words from the lips of Isaac are conceived in magic form to determine the destiny of the person who happens to have them. In this particular instance, human spoken words from the lips of one's parent were conceived as magical since they are powerful enough to determine one's destiny on earth.

On the other hand, the revelation of God in the Bible also uses or understood words in other different ways. Some of the basic ways in which words are conceived in the Bible could be easily illustrated. The first understanding of the word is in the category of a person, hence some passages of the Scriptures refer to Jesus as the "Word of God" (See John 1:1, 14, 1 John 1:1). The labeling of Jesus Christ as the "Word of God" is directly linked to his prominent role as the revelator of the divine will. In Jesus, the divine purpose and will is disclosed for the World to see. The Scriptures also use the label, "Word of God" to describe "speeches made by God," particularly in God's decrees that cause events to happen or program things into existence (Gen 1:3, 24; Ps 33:6). These speeches made by God might not be decrees, but might also describe friendly talks or a personal address that God gives to humans (Gen 2:16–17; Exod 20:1–3; Matt 3:17). But beyond these direct speeches from the lips of God himself, speeches made by God could also include speeches made through human lips (Deut 18:18–20; Jer 1:7, Exod 4:12; Num 22:38; 1 Sam 15:3, 18, 23; 1 Kgs 20:36; Isa 30: 12–14). The designation "Word of God" is also used in the Bible to describe the written word of God (Exod 31:18; 32:16; 4:1, 28; 31:9–13, 24–26; Josh 24:26; Jer 30:2; 36:2–4, 27–31; 51:60; John 14:26; 1 Cor 14:37; 2 Pet 3:2). The written word of God was for preservation and transmission to other generations of divine dealings with his people in history. It was aimed at generating better study of God's word for the subsequent necessity of obedience. It was also written to facilitate easy access to the divine word rather than making references to God's word from memory. Similarly, it was written down for the sake of accuracy and the necessity to guard against unorthodox or heretical teachings since written copies of God's word serve as a standard to check all doctrinal errors. In Africa, the "words of the gods" are transmitted to the people via the spiritual office of the medicine man, diviner or the herbalist. It is not written. It is preserved by the medium of orality.

The Canonicity of the Scriptures

The concept of an authoritative oral or written text is strange in Africa, thus the concept of a canon of authority in terms of Scripture is also in this sense foreign. However, Africans have some authoritative canon of oral beliefs or ethos which guides their moral and religious systems. But since these beliefs are oral in nature there is room for easy manipulation, reinterpretation, or even absolute displacement. In this sense, there is little rigidity in the oral canon of beliefs or religious observances since a persuasive religious representative could maneuver or manipulate these oral religious beliefs for cultural and political ends. Often existential exigencies determine how such oral beliefs are interpreted or used. In this sense, the oral canon remains fluid, but also elastic since it can accommodate the shifting changes of the contexts of human society. In this significant role, the oral canon of beliefs is easily framed or reframed for the generally conceived good of society by the religious representatives or practitioners. The advantage of this oral canonical system of authority is that it is easily redefined or reframed in the light of unforeseen challenges in human society. However, one defining disadvantage is the potential for abuse since the religious representative or custodian of the canon could largely manipulate or exploit such orally defined canon for their selfish ends. On the other hand, even though the written canon can also be abused in the phase of interpretation, it has the stability of authority since every reader can easily see the boundaries of former canonical authority and the newer changes incorporated into the written text.

Generally, every religious movement moves from the phase of an oral canon to a written one. This is also true of Christianity, which employed the use of an oral canon before sectarian necessity imposed on it the need to define its beliefs and revelation in written form. This is also true of the Old Testament religion. The Old Testament religion develops first with some orally defined canon of authority before the crystallization of its beliefs or authority in a written document. Unfortunately for the African people their religious expression and experiences did not evolve from this oral phase to a written one, thus rendering the religious beliefs of the African people credulous and even dubious.

For now, let us turn to the subject of the Christian canon. As already highlighted to guard against unorthodox rendering, understanding or interpretation of God's word, the words of God were put into writing. However, other writings also developed that assumed sacred status (in the sense that they were religious documents) but which were not included in the Jewish and Christian canons. The term, "canon" is used to describe the standardization or the systematic organization of the books into the sacred library we now call the Bible. While the divine authority of some books was disputed, others were readily accepted to be part of the sacred Scriptures of both Jews and Christians. Thus, canonicity deals with the theological processes or steps taken in the course of Jewish and Christian history by which the books of the Bible come to assume sacred ecclesiastical authority. In Israel there were many religious books that were not included into the Jewish canon because of the understanding by the Jewish faith community of their non-divine origin. Such books as the book of Jashar (Josh 10:13; 1 Sam. 1:18), or the War of the Lord (Num 21:14), the Chronicles of Samuel the Seer, Nathan the prophet and Gad the prophet (1 Chr 29:29), and the Oracles of Jehu the son of Hanani (2 Chr 20:34 and 1 Kgs 16:7). Even though quoted within the Old Testament canonical books, were denied entrance into the Old Testament canon because of the understanding of their non-divine origin or authority. After the exiles and the events described in Ezra, Nehemiah, and Esther, the books of the Old Testament were closed. Even though during the inter-testamental period writings in the name of Yahweh or other prophets of the Old Testament continued, however they were not accepted as part of the Jewish canon and thus subsequently tagged the "Apocrypha." The Apocryphal texts spoke to the religious and turbulent nature of the inter-testamental period. They were creative theological efforts to keep the faith alive in the midst of divine silence. Thus, they were theological forgeries using the label of ancient characters to speak to the yearnings and aspirations of the Jewish community at this period. The Roman Catholics include the Apocrypha in their canon following the Jerome's Vulgate inclusion of the same. This inclusion by the Roman Catholic Council of Trent in 1546 was not merely a reaction against the Protestant rejection of these books. For the Roman Catholics, the defense of these books became very important because of the theological justification it gives to some doctrines of the Roman Catholic Church that are not found in the Protestant canon and thus they are not defensible using the mainstream Jewish canon. Bishop Melito of Sardis and Bishop Athanasius of Alexandria writing in 170 AD and 367 AD acknowledged all the books of the Old Testament by giving a list of them. However, they omitted the book of Esther. This arises from the Jewish early misgiving about the divine origin of Esther because of its glaring omission of the divine name.

The foundation for the New Testament writings came from Jesus' admission that the Holy Spirit will come on the apostles thereby leading them to know spiritual truths that are not comprehensible to them now during his advent (John 14:26; 16:13–14). Similarly, the office of the apostles shouldered the responsibility of divine mediation of his revelation in the same fashion as those of the Old Testament prophets (2 Pet 3:2; Acts 5:2–4; 1 Cor 2:9, 13.). The apostles assumed a certain divine unction to speak on God's behalf to the different issues which they addressed (1 Cor 14:37; 2 Cor 13:3; Gal 1:8–9; Rom 2:16; 2 Thess 3:6, 14. See also 2 Pet 3:15–16 and 1 Tim 5:17–18; cf. Deut 25:4; Luke 10:7). Apart from the apostles that wrote the New Testament, there are also other individuals that were also conceived of as having the divine unction to pen down his words for humanity. These non-apostles were the writers of Mark, Luke, Acts, Hebrews and Jude. These books were accepted into the New Testament canon because of their close association with the apostles and the assumption by the early church that their writings were equally authoritative thus giving them the same status as the divine mouthpiece. As early as the fourth century, the twenty-seven books of the New Testament were accepted in the Eastern and the Western parts of the Mediterranean world. This is evidence in Athanasius Paschal's letter of 367 AD and the Council of Carthage in 397 AD respectively.[15]

The Characteristics of the Divine Word

Apart from the issues of canonicity, there is also to be considered in this section, the divine features of the Scriptures which set it apart from any form of human documents or writings. Five characteristics of the

15. See Grudem, *Systematic Theology*, 63–64.

Scriptures are worth considering in this section. The first characteristic of the Scriptures that set it apart from any human documents or books is the authority of the Scriptures. Even though other human books such as constitutions also claim to have authority, the validity of such claim could easily be put to the test by recognizing that the authority of the constitution lies heavily in the domain of human authority; however, the Scriptures derives its authority absolutely on the divine. The authority of the Scriptures is based on the certainty that the Bible is actually the word of God and that rejecting or accepting its words is tantamount to accepting or rejecting divine words. The Bible generally asserted that all the words found within its pages are authoritative words of God (See Num 22:38; Deut 18:18–20; Jer 1:9; 14:14; 23:16–22. See also 2 Tim 3: 16.). Thus, the Scripture is its sole basis to ascertain or define its own authority. To say that the Scripture is the divine word does not mean a straight-jacket dictation, even though there are instances of divine dictations in both the Old and New Testament (See Rev 2:1; 2:12; Isa 38:4–6.). However, there are indications that the normal process of transmission is usually not direct dictation, but employs diverse of mediums (Luke 1:1–3; John 14:26; Heb 1:1). The second characteristic of the Scripture lies in the concept of inerrancy. The understanding of inerrancy asserts that the Bible in its original manuscript prior to the myriad translations is a document that is free from error and also free from contradiction. The authority of the Scripture comes also from the recognition that God cannot lie or speak falsely (Num 23:19; Heb 6:18; Titus 1:2; Prov 30:5; Ps 119:89; Matt 24:35). Thus, all the words of the Scriptures are completely true and without error, falsehood or dishonesty.[16] From this understanding of the veracity of the Scriptures, the Bible becomes God's ultimate standard for truth and thus the basis for all matters of faith and practice (John 17:17). Beyond the domain of faith and practice, the Bible is equally infallible in matters of history, scientific presentation, and philosophy as found in its most sacred pages. The theological implication of the biblical teaching of inerrancy is that it encourages trust and comfort in the reader of the Bible. It also presupposes that the Bible rightly provides direction and guides to various issues of human existence. Without the infallibility of the Scripture, the Bible becomes another human book deprived of authority and hence unable to serve as the

16. For a detailed study on the subject of biblical authority and inspiration see Packer, *Fundamentalism*; Packer, "Infallibility," 337–39; Packer, "Scripture," 627–31; Carson and Woodbridge, eds. *Hermeneutics*; Helm, *The Divine Revelation*; Geisler, *Inerrancy*; Pinnock, *Biblical Revelation*.

absolute authority of morality and ethics.[17] The third characteristic of the Scriptures is its clarity. Even though the Scriptures do have some aspects that are hard to understand,[18] generally the Scripture affirms its absolute clarity (See Deut 6:6–7; Ps 19:7; 119:130; Matt 12:3, 5; 22:29). The Scripture was not written to the scholar or the academic community; instead the Scripture was written to the congregation of faith. Similarly, it was not written to church leaders or shepherds of the church, rather it was written to the members of the body of Christ, or to the faithful in each generation (See Phil 1:1; 1 Cor 1:1; Gal 1:2; Col 4:16; John 20:30–31; Jas 1:1, 22–25; 1 John 5:13). However, since the contemporary readers of the Bible are distant from the world of the Bible in language, time, culture and beliefs, there is need for scholars to aid in the process of rediscovering the meaning and purpose of divine revelation in the pages of the Scriptures so that the community of faith will adequately understand the divine voice across time, culture, and language.[19] The fourth characteristic of the Scriptures is the theological necessity of the Scriptures. The Bible is cardinal or primary in knowing the gospel, understanding the prerequisites of spiritual life and the divine will. Without the Bible all knowledge of humans on such matters is riddled with problems since it does not relate these categories under divine consideration. This does not suggest that God's nature or attributes could not be known outside of the Bible; however it presupposes that the fullness of the divine nature or attributes is made known clearly within the sacred pages of the Scriptures.[20] The last characteristic of the Scriptures is the sufficiency of the Scriptures. This biblical teaching assumes that God at each stage in redemption revealed himself progressively and all that we now need to know about salvation, ethics in the present times and even the knowledge of the hereafter are adequately given or revealed within the pages of the Scriptures (See 2 Tim 3:15; Jas 1:18; 1 Pet 1:23; 2 Tim 3:16–17. See also Deut 4:2; 12:32; Prov 30:5–6; Rev 22:18–19). The general implication of this last characteristic of the Scriptures is that it presupposes that the Scriptures can be trusted in every matter that pertains to its general

17. See Warfield, *Limited Inspiration*; Haley, *Alleged Discrepancies of the Bible*; Geisler, ed. *Biblical Inerrancy*; Feinberg, "Inerrancy," 141–45.

18. For example see 2 Pet 3:15–16.

19. See Fee and Stuart, *How to Read the Bible*; Carson, *Exegetical Fallacies*; Barr, *The Semantics*; Hirsch Jr., *The Aims of Interpretation*; Dockery, *Biblical Interpretation*; Berkhof, *Principles of Biblical Interpretation*.

20. Concerning the necessity of the Scriptures in relationship to the gospel, cultivating a spiritual life and knowing God's will see Acts 4:12; Rom 10:13–17; 1 Tim 2:5–6; Deut 8:3; 32:47; 1 Pet 2:2; 1:23–25; Deut 29:29; 1 John 5:3.

preoccupation of salvation, development of spiritual life and godly living in the present world and also the hopes and anticipation of the next.

Conclusion

The chapter outlines the basic issues pertaining to the subject of the Bible or God's word. It reveals the nature, the characteristics, and the issues of canonicity. The cardinal presupposition behind the study is the recognition of the inerrant nature of divine word and the translation of such lofty conceptions of the divine word in the context of the daily experiences of the believer. Despite the radical criticism launched against the Bible the contemporary world reveals an unabated reverence and regard for the Bible as God's divine word for the salvation of humanity. In Africa, such lofty regard of the Bible is often seen in the magical treatment of the Bible and the use of it in order to confront the many ills of African society. The simple presuppositions behind such use of the Bible lie in the culturally conceived understanding that there is a vital force that lies behind words when such words are magically recited or chanted. The chapter places the cultural understanding of the Bible within the matrix of theological discussion of the subject of bibliology or the study of the Bible. It seeks to underscore the relationship between the nature of divine words as conceived in the Bible and the traditional conceptions of the words of the gods in traditional African societies.

5

The Existence of God

Introduction

THE EXISTENCE OF GOD has been a contentious subject throughout the history of religion and philosophy. The reason for such controversy on this subject lies simply in the invisibility of God and thus his intangibility as the world of matter around us. Thus, scientific scrutiny of God has come out without none empirical conclusions on the existence of God. With the contemporary adventurous spirit of science which by the help of powerful satellites has successfully scanned the farthest space and has clearly dislodged the fictitious remnant of medieval superstition concerning the existence of God above the layer of the skies, there is now a clear certainty among science and its practitioners about the non-existence of God. However, as Africans the existence of God to us is not an academic subject because since childhood we are consciously and unconsciously taught about his existence. To Africans, God is a living reality and his existence is consciously affirmed in everyday interactions. In prayers, ceremonies, songs, proverbs and moral lessons, Africans generally call upon or make reference to the Supreme Being who controls and directs events in the world. In the traditional African sense and setting, there are no atheists, but rather polytheists who assume not only the existence of God, but the existence of many of his kind. Significantly, it is also such religious acceptance of the existence of God and other beings in the category of the supernatural that is the distinctive mark of Semitic religious inclinations, of which the Jewish religious understanding becomes a heir. There is no systematic thesis within the pages of the Bible in defence of God's existence, instead the biblical writers assume that such a being exists and proceed from such a premise to underscore his relationship with the world. This chapter reveals and critiques the basic arguments on the existence of God, evaluates the nature of divine ontology and issues of the divine attributes. It places this discussion within the purview of traditional African worldview.

Classical Discourse on the Existence of God

One of the first places to begin the discourse on the existence of God is a reference to the inner testimony of God's existence in the human breast. There are scriptural indications that the human mind actually entertains or recognizes the existence of the divine being (Rom 1:18–21; Ps 14:1). The scriptures also affirm the existence of God as derived from human contemplations of nature (Ps 19:1–2; Acts 14:17).The presence of design and conceivable laws or patterns in nature is normally employed as an argument for the existence of a maker or designer. Traditionally, many forms of theological arguments have been posited to stress the existence of God.[1] Thus, it is necessary to highlight these traditional "proofs" of the existence of God. In this direction, four arguments have often been underscored. The first argument has been described as the cosmological argument. The cosmological argument lies in the philosophical presupposition that every known effect has a cause. Thus, since the world must have a cause, the cause must have its causation in a greater being, that is far beyond human causation. However, this argument is flawed since the argument could still be carried to its logical conclusion by also asking the cause of God since everything must have a cause. The second argument is teleological. From the design and conceived harmony in creation particularly as seen in its order and laws, this argument presupposes that there is an intelligent purpose behind such design, harmony and concord in nature and thus assumes that such purposeful design must come from God. However, the flaw of this argument is that patterns or harmony in creation are subjectively defined since where one sees harmony another might not necessary sees harmony but disorder and chaos. The fallen state of our world often does not allow humanity to see the intelligence in the

---

1. On the discussion concerning the existence of God see McDowell, *Evidence That Demands a Verdict*; Geisler, *Christian Apologetics*; Geisler and Feinberg, *Introduction to Philosophy*; Charnock, *The Existence and Attributes of God*, 11–67.

world and hence the modern school of thought such as existentialism has generally refused to see meaning or purpose in the world. Consequently, this despair, frustration and anxiety of the modern world as revealed in war, diseases and natural disasters have normally made many to question the validity of intelligence or meaning behind the pain and confusion of the modern period. The third argument is an ontological argument which presupposes that there must be a being who is the sum total of beingness and beyond whom nothing can be imagined. The assumption of the ontological argument is that such a being must exist whose existence is merely imagined to exist. The flaw of this argument is that there is the possibility of imagining a being or concept that has no concrete and tangible existence. Thus one can imagine of the greatest of all goats, strong and with a hundred heads, yet the concrete existence of such a being is in doubt, it merely exist in the imagination of the one imagining it. The last argument of the proof of God is the moral argument which presupposes that the general recognition of right and wrong naturally underscores the existence of a law giver. To the credit of this argument, there is a general recognition among human society of categories designated right and other moral categories labeled wrong. However, the flaw of this argument is that there is relativity to the conception of right and wrong. It is true that different human society acknowledge the moral fields of right and wrong yet these human societies conceive differently the nature of the conception and definition of right and wrong, hence revealing the moral fluidity among the human community which is not a formidable basis to argue for a divine law giver. Even though the validity of these arguments is questioned, these arguments are necessary steps towards accounting for the presence or existence of God. Africans accept the fact of God's existence without these philosophical or academic arguments. This is not to disparage Africans as not thinking philosophically, but to affirm that African philosophy is fundamentally based on strong religious understandings which make its basic presupposition not to question the existence of God, but the unquestioned acceptance of his existence. We accept the existence of God as Africans not because we are foolish, but because it is reasonable to do so because the world could not be reasonably understood without such reference to the existence of a supreme being, thus the Africans begin with an assumption similar to those of the biblical world and continue from there to understand the claims of the Christian faith. In this way, the African non-Christian populace are at a higher plane comparable to their counterpart within the secularism and scientific mindset of the West.

God in Intellectual and Popular Theological Discourse

God has been defined variously according to the assumptions and conclusions of different religious systems. In his intensive study, *No One Like Him*, John S. Feinberg had generally underscores the three dominant contemporary views about God.[2] Firstly, he engages Ludwig Feuerbach's hypothesis that God is not an independent reality, but a projection of human infinite extension of his limited attributes. For Feuerbach, man created god in his own image instead of the biblical understanding that God created man in his image and likeness. In his work, *Essence of Christianity*, Feuerbach noted, "The divine being is nothing else than . . . human nature purified, freed from . . . limits . . . made objective . . . and revered."[3] The second consideration by Feinberg is Paul Tillich postulation that God is "Being-itself" or "the ground of Being."[4] To understand Tillich, a prelude into his thought is necessary. Tillich began his systematic theology by presupposing that the "object of theology is what concerns us ultimately."[5] He asserted that the ultimate concern of human existence borders on "our being or non-being,"[6] that is, the meaning or meaninglessness of our existence. For Tillich, anything outside these philosophical and theological domains is irrelevant to theology since it is external to our ultimate concern of beingness or non-beingness. In this persuasion, God becomes for Tillich the absolute and symbolic representation of our being. He represents the ultimate in our highest human yearning for existence. With this summation, God is not a being but a symbolic illustration of our human quest for meaning. In a sense, he is existence itself. The logical conclusion of Tillich's philosophical proposition is that God in this theological scheme becomes merely a representation, concept or label that has no actual existence. On the other hand, Feinberg's last consideration is the view that argued actually for the existence of God and the possibility of rational interactive relationship with Him.

In the theological reflection such as the ones briefly outlined in the preceding discourse there are two presuppositions about God that are often pushed forward. These two presuppositions are namely a course of thinking that defines God in impersonal forms and another one that

---

2. See Feinberg, *No One Like Him*, 41–55.

3. Feuerbach, *The Essence of Christianity*, 14.

4. Tillich, *Systematic Theology*, 235.

5. *Ibid.*, 12.

6. *Ibid.*, 14.

projects personality to the divine being. For the first category, God is a concept, or principle or psychical phenomenon that is within the domain of a force which lacks personality and thus ontologically he is designated to hold sway in the sphere of inanimate realities or partial inanimate existence.[7] In assigning God to the realm of inanimate existence such thinking resolves the theological problem that arises when God is assigned personhood or predicated some self-consciousness. For example, a being within the sphere of inanimate objects or force could hold no one accountable for moral or ethical concerns or conclusions. Within this definition, God could not exercise any responsible relationship with humans and thus, humans are free from any disguise or real suggestion necessitating accountability to him. Such pantheistic inclinations reduce the subject of right and wrong to subjective human conclusions and not from just divine decrees.[8] The limitation of such projections of impersonality on the divine person results also in fictitious spirituality, which seeks to manipulative spiritual categories for the selfish well-being of the worshipper. Magically inclined philosophy and self-centered religiosities are often the product of a way of human thinking which conceives of God in category of the impersonality. Within such framework, God is merely a sub-human entity since he is robbed of personhood and hence is incapable of a rational interactive relationship. The rejection of divine selfhood or personhood is closely related to the human quest to satisfy his or her insatiable religious longings without the pain of accountability to the divine being. Personhood connotes relationship and identity, but it also connotes divine self-consciousness which becomes illusive within theological or religious systems that deny the divine being such a category. In the final analyses, the divine being becomes a toy of manipulation and the product of such religion becomes primarily human-centered. In this postmodern context, there is an alluring temptation to move the divine being from the realm of personhood to non-person and engendering the talk of God that places the divine being within the realm of "it" and other labels of non-conscious selfhood.

7. For the critique of Rudolf Bultmann, Karl Barth and Immanuel Kant as perpetuating the "unreality of God" in theological and philosophical discourse see Bockmuehl, *The Unreal God of Modern Theology*.

8. Contrary to the impersonal nature of Asian religious beliefs, African traditional religions conceive of a "High God" who no doubt is perceived in the category of person rather than a force. For such studies on the conception of the 'High God' in traditional African religions see Bews, "The Concept of the 'High God,'" 315–321. See also Ada and Isichei, "Perceptions of God," 165–73.

The lapses of this kind of understanding reveal the theological aberration of the modern context. It is certainly a 'delicate bridge' between full-fledged atheism and irresponsible spirituality. However, ascribing personhood to God connotes the idea that the divine being is a person who exercises all the faculties that such inferences of personhood connote. This way of ascribing personhood to the divine being does not merely place God within the sphere of a noun since a noun in definition is used to define a person, place or thing, however it went ahead to conceive of the divine being in terms of a proper noun. Thus even within the designation of God as a person we must move from ascribing to him the mere luxury of a common noun since God has no class, hence he is not to be comprehended within such a class, rather God is a personal noun just as we have human nomenclature to define or describe us. For example, names such as Samuel, Joseph, Thomas and other human names are within the sphere of personal nouns because these names do not merely suggest existence, but they also assign unique personhood to the person described with such labels of names. Understood in this line of thought, God becomes a personal being who has uniqueness of personhood and is ontologically different in his essence and attributes. The personhood of God imposes culturally on human society the inevitable conclusion of responsibility and accountability to his unique personhood and thus in the long run, places human beings on the plane of obedience and faith in the awesomeness of such a unique personality as God.

In popular African thought, the existence of God is taken for granted since there are indications from proverbs, stories, myths and cultic practices that assume divine existence and presence. Similar assumptions form the basic presuppositions of the Bible since there are no laid out theoretical definitions, citations or references to some cogent arguments in defense of divine existence. Instead, the Bible begins with the theological assumption of the existence of the divine being and uses this theological metaphysical framework to assert and present the divine activities, revelations and beingness.

In the general African context, such understanding of God within the African church is fuzzy and often it is an inadequate representation of the divine being since it derived its origin from the popular affirmation or recognition of the existence of God within the African traditional conception or African popular Christianity.[9] Often, when talking about God

9. For the understanding of God as conceived within the western missionary tradition and the African traditional society see Loewen, "Which God," 3–19. See also

various Sunday school images come to mind. Dominant in this picture is the Sunday school portrayal of God as the "Wise Old Man," who is sitting on a throne and always ready to punish our acts of foolishness or bless some of our wise decisions. This strict picture of God is often devoid of laughter or smiles. Unfortunately, many adults go through life with such a Sunday school kind of image of God and hence it is often the reason why many adults lack relationship with this outdated "Old Man" who is un-related to modernity whether as expressed in the technological-scientific advancement or the pop culture of the contemporary time. This "Old Wise Man" representation of God significantly places the divine being in the past and hence divorcing him from the dominant trends within the pres-ent and the future worlds. The idea of an "Old Wise Man" as a representa-tion of God in Africa may come from the respect and prestige ascribed to the aged and the cultural understanding that they are the custodians of communal wisdom and morality. Complementing this image of God in popular African Christianity is still another Sunday school picture of God as "Father." Even though this picture of God as father bears justification from the scriptures yet the excessive imposition or drawing a father image of God using the physical fatherly attributes from reality often creates a fundamental theological problem since such a picture of God as a father only makes sense to a person who has a nice and loving father, however, those with a bully father finds almost nothing exciting in a portrayal of God as a father. Thus, the failure or absence of the human father is duly imposed on the divine, hence fundamentally distorting the understanding of God as a father. This paternalistic conception of divine fatherhood often creates gender tension for a person that has a loving mother rather than a loving father. Normally, the adult Bible study expounds or explores similar childhood portraits of God and never really makes any significant theo-logical departure or theological progress from childhood mental images about the divine being. Thus, divine beingness and attributes are vaguely conceived and the ignorance of the divine being is hidden under religious piety and emotional attachments to divine mental objects or caricatures of the divine being. In many ways, there is biblical justification for the rep-resentation of God as an "Old Wise Man" and as a "Father." Since often by describing him, as an "Old Wise Man" is a metaphoric description of his wisdom and eternality and also by the description of God as a "Father" we are expressing his loving and caring nature. However, such descriptions

---

Bosch, "God in Africa," 3–20; Demerest, "The Quest for God," 99–101 and Daneel, "The Encounter," 36–51.

are only theological labels that actually do not reflect divine ontology and hence provide no blueprint for understanding the nature of the divine being since the understanding of divine wisdom, eternality, love and care could be expressed differently using other theological metaphors or expressions. But most importantly, these divine metaphors as shown raise serious theological problems to individuals who associate such divine mental images with mainstream realities as evidenced in their own father or the logical implication of surrendering one's life to an "Old Wise Man" in the context of modernity with its unjustifiable discrimination against the elderly and the aged. The problem with such catechistic or Sunday school portrayal of the divine being is that it ignores divine ontology and has projected largely human categories on the divine being, thus making the divine being essentially a dignified father or a wise old man. Even though such projections of human categories on the divine person has the advantage of bringing the divine being closer, they blur the constituents of divine ontology and hence reveal a lack of understanding of the divine being who is excessively clothed in human frailty by the imposition of such human categories.

Discourse on Divine Ontology

The impossibility of understanding the nature of the divine being has often generated unhealthy theological speculation on the constituents, essence and goal of the divine being. Such theological speculation has birth in the contemporary 'process theology' which asserts that the essence of the divine being such as omniscience and omnicausality are on the process of assuming such traditionally designated functions.[10] Hence, God as reasoned by process theology is a dignified human being limited in knowledge particularly the knowledge of the outcomes of different courses of actions. In this process line of thinking God is conceived to have only the capability to actualize Godhood in the long run since ontologically he is in the process of becoming God.[11] Consequently, the evolving divine person

10. For a theological discussion that underscores and employs a process theological grid or framework see Hartshorne, *The Divine Relativity*, 31–32. See also Gragg, *Charles Hartshorne*; Peters, *Hartshorne*, 66–68; and Surin, "The Self–Existence of God," 28–29. In response to process theology see Ware, "An Exposition," 175–95.

11. For example, Clark Pinnock underscoring the process or open theism agenda has noted, "History is not the playing out of a tirelessly fixed decree but a theater where the divine purposes are being worked out by the resourcefulness of God in dealing with the surprises of a significant creation. History is neither random nor

in such a system of theology is short–sighted, limited and a pre-divine being in the process of becoming divine. Such a divine being uses the historical environment as a learning process targeted towards the deification of God in the real traditional sense.[12] The limitedness of this divine person is actually a human projection of mortal finitude on the divine person and only shows the great ignorance surrounding the theology of divine ontology particularly the description of God in his inner self. Traditionally, discussion of the divine has often explored the theological domain of his attributes especially in the categories of communicable and incommunicable divine attributes. At other times, it is an illusive investigation into the mysteries and intrigues of trinity with a corresponding relationship to the sociological, philosophical and theological implications of such intimate divine relationships as expressed in the triune persons of the Godhead. However, it is possible even while highlighting these traditional ideas to also discuss the divine being without necessarily making reference to the traditionally fashioned theological designations. Since God transcends the borders of finitude, it presupposes that his ontology is indeed incomprehensible. The traditional theological discussion of divine ontology in the domain of attributes is in this sense merely descriptive and primarily based on the heightening of human virtues to speak of God and the use of analogy to describe God.[13] In both cases, human forms are projected onto God in order to discuss about God, thus even at the beginning; discussion of God is flawed with human limitations. Within these limitations, such discussion does not precisely engage the inner or self-understanding of the divine being, but merely articulates external features of the divine being as expressed within the confines of his acts which is also defined and expressed in human terms. Underscoring the relational dimension of divine attributes, Stanley Grenz had observed,

> Many theologians appeal to the concept of divine attributes in an attempt to pierce through the veil of mystery to the one, eternal divine essence. However, because God is triune—the Father, Son, and Spirit in eternal relationship—our quest to speak of the being and attributes of God actually constitutes an

---

predetermined." See Pinnock, *Flame of Love*, 56.

12. On the problem of divine ontology in the Old Testament and Jewish rabbinic traditions see Abrams, "The Boundaries," 291–321.

13. On the traditional study of divine attributes see Chafer, "Trinitarinism," 137–165. See also Erickson, *God the Father Almighty*; Frame, *The Doctrine of God*; Bavinck, *Doctrine of God*.

attempt to characterize the relational nature of God—God in relationship.[14]

Consequently, beingness of God must be separated from his *doing* since the former comes before the latter. For example, when we say that a man is good or loving we imply by such a statement that through our observation that man or woman is doing or acting good. Thus, good or love cannot be discussed speculatively without reference to acts or deeds because they are in themselves a description of deeds that we call good or deeds that we call loving. If these antecedents are right, saying that the divine being is good or loving is within the characteristics that relate to his interaction with external factors and thus these virtues do not define the essence of the divine person. Since even among humans, the term good or love, are acts and they do not always tell us the essence or nature of the human person. They only succeed in telling us the relationship that exists between the person called good or loving to external forms around him. Consequently, human kindness, goodness, or love as well as divine corresponding expressions of these virtues, even though having some ontological relationship in the beingness of God and the human person, fall short of revealing the actual beingness of these entities. From this premise, theological discussion on divine ontology with a focus on divine attributes and even the trinitarian descriptions are merely representations of the divine persons in acts of relationship within himself or other external entities and do not necessarily reveal the divine person in his beingness. For example, the divine attribute of omniscience that is the divine person is all knowing also is not a description of the ontology of God since it takes pride in knowledge and hence such knowledge consists of knowing forms outside of one's self or other inward references. Consequently, such divine knowledge is clearly predicated or defined by its relationship to external or internal forms which should also assume an independent reality for the knowledge to be valid. Similarly, the quick reference to divine omnipresence as a description of the constitution of divine ontology also is problematic since omnipresence connotes God's presence everywhere and thus suggests the presence of God in relationship to things or other objective realities. One close description of divine being in his essence is a reference to his self-existence. However, even such self-existence is only possible because it is understood as an existence in reference to external forms. It is still a dependency on himself and the inner or outer expressions of his selfhood. This feature of the divine being is understood in terms of relationship and does not really

14. Grenz, *Theology for the Community*, 77.

describe the ontology of God since it presupposes the divine dependence or relationship to himself, thus it merely describe the relationship within the divine being and not necessary the divine person himself. Since relationship is secondary and beingness is primary and being comes before doing, it presupposes that God has to be in order to have relationship with himself. Consequently the teaching of divine self-existence does not provide us with the being of God rather it merely expresses the doing of God particularly in his relationship to himself. The problem surrounding the ontological discussion of the divine being is that it becomes nearly impossible to discuss the divine being without reference or relationship to external or inward divine forms. This problem arises because divine revelations in world religions have focused mainly on divine ontology as expressed within the confinement of space and time. All divine revelations, and Christianity is not an exception, are rooted in divine relationship with forms or objects outside of the divine self.[15]

To move forward from this theological impasse we must leave behind the traditional discussion on divine attributes or trinitarian constitutions of the divine person and discuss God within the framework of the expression of his beingness, thus attributes such as self-existence are the expression of his beingness but they are not actually the beingness of God since, as already highlighted, such attributes emphasize inner relationship and being must of necessity come before relationship. In this understanding, while using the traditional nomenclature of divine attributes we are using them with the understanding that they are expressions of divine beingness but they are not to represent in any way divine essence in itself. In discussion of this expression of divine being, we must be ready to have the humility to recognize that the divine essence is beyond the comprehension of humans and that all the talk of divine attributes are merely expressions and not the essence of God.

On the other hand, since according to the biblical emphases there is no inconsistency between the divine essence and the expression of such divine being in the category of attributes, there is the necessity to explore this biblical consideration. As the preceding discourse had generally

---

15. John H. Walton has underscored the functionality of the understanding of divine ontology in ancient Near East. He observed that a god exists in ancient Near Eastern conceptual thought ". . . when it was separated out as a distinct entity, given a function, and given a name." Thus, the mere presence of a god does not represent existence until such god has a functional role to play among the gods or within the domain of the human world. For a study of the divine ontology and attributes of deities in the ancient Near Eastern world see Walton, *Ancient Near Eastern Thought*, 87–112.

argues that the traditional discussion on divine attributes are misplaced since they are not primarily a reflection of divine essence. However, this conclusion raises a serious problem because it seeks to divorce or set a dichotomy between divine beingness and divine deeds as expressed in the dimension of divine attributes. There should not be a dichotomy or inconsistencies between God's deeds and the basic constitution of his being, thus if the Bible reveals his attributes, they are therefore a reflection of his essence which must not contradicts his deeds. While humans show a polarity between the constitutions of their being and the expression of their deeds, for the divine, the possibility of such contradictions in the personhood of the divine being will lead to 'divine hypocrisy' whereby the divine person betrays his essential being because it is incompatible with his deeds. The moral impossibility of such endeavour makes it necessary to speak of divine attributes as compatible to his essential being thus justifying the traditional usage of such a label.

Piecing together the arguments so far presented, we could say that the traditional usage of divine attributes to describe the beingness of the divine person is founded on the theological assumption that the beingness of God is consistent with his deeds because a God with contradictions in this central thesis or foundation becomes morally dubious and cannot be trusted or obeyed.

Within these expressions of divine essence or using the traditional label of divine attributes the following discourse now turns.[16] Beginning with divine *self-existence*, the term presupposes the ability of the divine person to live or exist without making reference to any external activity or form[17]. As already highlighted in the preceding discourse, the possibility of divine dependence on himself clearly necessitates the discussion of divine relationship within himself. However, God in his self-existence has no reference or dependence on an outside category from his self. Thus, all other existences are dependent and only exist by reference to external factors or categories, but God is existence since he is the source and life of all there is and all that will ever be. He is uncreated and maintains himself without the support or necessity of other beings or forms. Similarly, the divine being has expressed his beingness in the form of a person and not in some vagueness or cosmic impersonal force or energy. Contrary to

---

16. Elwell has rightly observed that divine attributes "are essential characteristics of His being. Without these qualities God would not be what He is—God." See Elwell, *Evangelical Dictionary*, 451.

17. See Charnock, *Discourses*, 2:368.

pantheistic persuasion, the divine ontology has employed the media of a person to express his being. The basic idea of divine personhood connotes the ability or expression of divine beingness in the category of rational agent that has a unique identity, expressive freewill and the capacity to enter into meaningful interactive relationships with forms within or outside his being. Within the Judeo-Christian profession, the divine ontology is conceived in masculinity. As already stated, the divine being is ontological spirit by nature and hence has no gender preference in the primary constitution of his being. However, in mediating revelation he assumed a masculine mode and revealed himself using the male gender. The male gender preference of the divine being may have been primarily informed by the patriarchal nature of the cultural context of the Judeo-Christian revelation.

In the same vein, another distinctive expression of the divine ontology is the designation of the divine being as the *eternal spirit*. God is ontologically a spirit that is not within the created order, thus he is not influenced by time or space since he is the one that created time. As eternal spirit, he is immaterial in composition, however his spiritual or invisible bodily composition does not presuppose that he is unable to interact with matter. The eternity is a prerequisite for a divine being because without such attribute God becomes mortal and hence susceptible to death and other existential forms that confronts and reveal the frailty of humanity. However, in Jesus Christ, God did *temporarily* die since Jesus Christ is taken to be the incarnation of God. The mystery of such suspension of divine eternity in the person of Jesus and the succumbing of the divine person to the powers of death is unfathomable because it challenged the divine eternity and suggested divine identification with human frailty in Jesus Christ. More so, such dying of the divine person is only possible because of the temporary kenosis or emptying of some divine attributes in the person of Jesus Christ. This suspension of divine eternity also raises another serious problem in relationship to the divine attributes of *immutability* or the *unchangeability* of the divine being. Ronald Nash has rightly observed that "Of all the current debates about the divine attributes, the disagreement over the property of immutability is the most heated."[18] Divine immutability is the biblical teaching that God is unchangeable in his essence, promises and plans because changes connote mistakes, imperfection and the inability of one to have foresight as to the outcome of a given course of action. A divine being that changes could not be trusted since it is not

18. Nash, *The Concept of God*, 99.

possible for such a being to keep to his word, plans or promises. Divine immutability is the heart of the divine attributes since it presupposes that God will be consistent in his being and deeds. The understanding of divine immutability holds God's attributes together. In the long run, the biblical teaching on divine unchangeability has the merit of engendering trust and confidence in the immutability of God's essence, purpose and promises thus necessitating absolute faith that God will continue to be God as in the past, through the present and also the future.

But how could God be immutable and still undergo the transformation or the metamorphosis of incarnation? In another way, since the incarnation presupposes change or translation of God into the human person does this understanding not go contrary to the unchangeability of God? As noted earlier even though God is spirit he could manifest himself within the dimension of matter, hence the adoption of a human body and the expression of his humanness within the world of matter does not suggest change *per se* but reveals his intimate relationship with matter and the manifestation of his humanhood through material reality. Related to the subject of divine unchangeability are two contentions, namely whether it is possible for the divine being to change his mind or whether the divine being has emotion. Concerning the first, there are scriptural passages that seem to suggest on the surface that the divine being has the ability to change his mind by persuasion and prayers. Often to underscore this theological stance, reference is made to Old Testament passages that are conceived to show divine changeability. On close examination of these passages they do not reveal divine changeability rather these passages often employ anthropomorphic language to speak of God and his activity (See Jonah 3:4, 10; Isa 38:1–6; Exod 32:9–10; Gen 6:6 and 1 Sam 15:10). They also reveal divine freedom to act and feel differently in response to different situations or circumstances. For example, Hezekiah's intercession for the divine sentence of death brings about a new situation which necessitates a divine response to these new situations and not necessarily a change in the divine being. It is a consideration of a new event that results in the prayer of Hezekiah. In this regard, prayer is a contingent human action that introduced a new situation which requires a new divine response.

On the other hand, there is a concern about divine impassibility or the understanding that the divine being does not have or show emotion. Even though God did not have or express sinful human passion the contention that he is impassible goes against the teaching of the Bible since there are various passages of scripture that reveal divine expressions of human emotions (See Exod 32:10; Ps 78:40; 103:13; Isa 54:8; 62:5; Eph 4:30). The product of such thinking in respect to divine impassibility comes from the Gnostic platonic philosophies which associated expressions of passion or emotion with the body and thus evil from their own point of view.[19] However, such is not the case since human emotions are God-given and should be expressed in their sanctified form in the worship of God and in the context of human interpersonal relationships. As a result of the Greek philosophical influence on the Christian Church, throughout the history of the Church there are theological emphases that underscore divine impassibility. Such understanding could be readily illustrated by a referral to Church history. In the patristic work of Cyril, there was a theological persuasion that is suggestive of divine impassibility, thus, Cyril wrote that when . . .

> we say that he 'suffered and rose again.' We do not mean that God the Word suffered in his Deity . . . for the Deity is impassible because it is incorporeal. But the body which had become his own body suffered these things, and therefore he himself is said to have suffered them for us. The impassible [God] was in the body which suffered.[20]

Anselm in his work, *Cur Deus Homo* noted, "For without doubt we maintain that the divine nature is impassible—that it cannot at all be brought down from its exaltation . . ."[21] John Calvin also supported some degree of divine impassibility when he observed in his discourse on divine repentance that "whenever we hear that God is angered, we ought not to imagine any emotion [i.e., passion] in him, but rather to consider that this expression has been taken from our own human experience."[22] Contrary to these theological emphases, there is the theological and practical necessity of divine passion. In refuting divine impassibility, Oliver Buswell affirmed the theological necessity of divine passion, thus he noted,

> The schoolmen and often the philosophical theologians tell us that there is no feeling in God. This, they say, would imply

19. Abraham J. Heschel has done an excellent study on the philosophical root behind divine pathos or the tendencies to think in theological circles in terms of divine impassibility. It traces the rabbinic and Greek roots of such philosophical understanding. He also reveals the nature of divine pathos or emotion within the scriptures. See Heschel, *The Prophets*, 25–86.

20. Bettenson, *Documents*, 67.

21. Anselm, *Anselm of Canterbury*, 58, 59.

22. Calvin, *Institutes*, xvii, 13.

passivity or susceptibility of impression from without, which, it is assumed, is incompatible with the nature of God . . . [But] such a view is in real contradiction to the representations of God in the Old Testament and . . . the New Testament. . . . here again we have to choose between a mere philosophical speculation and the clear testimony of the Bible, and of our own moral and religious nature. Love, of necessity, involves feeling, and if there be no feeling in God, there can be no love.[23]

To deny passion in the constitution of divine essence is definitely a denial of the realistic nature or content of such attributes of love, grace, mercy, and goodness because in human expressions of these attributes the instrumentality of emotions is often employed in order to bring about the right desired effects as means of showing compassion. For Africans who are people of emotion, the necessity of expressing these emotions becomes very important. It must also have its motivation and origin from God. From an African point of view, a God without emotions becomes indeed ridiculous and thus impossible for the African to share with such deity the complexities of their emotions.[24] Reasserting a similar thesis to Buswell, Thiessen also revealed,

Philosophers frequently deny feeling to God, saying that feeling implies passivity and susceptibility of impression from without, and that such a possibility is incompatible with the idea of the immutability of God. But immutability does not mean immobility. True love necessarily involves feeling, and if there be no feeling in God, then there is no love of God.[25]

Moving away from the preceding discourse on divine emotion or passion to its related category of divine suffering, one realizes the dominance of philosophical and theological understanding which also challenges the possibility of divine suffering. For us in Africa, the problem that divine impassibility in the category of suffering raises for us are twofold, firstly, it sabotages our quest to understand a higher divine purpose in the midst

23. Buswell, *A Systematic Theology*, 55–57.

24. Ali Mazrui described as myth the label that Africans are emotional beings. He saw this presupposition as clearly laid out in Negritude to be faulty since it subjectively predisposed that Africans are not able to think rationally and thus incapable of comprehending the Greco-Roman intellectual legacies of the West. Even though Mazrui's thesis should be taken seriously however, the denial of emotionality to the Africans in the quest of conforming them to the Greco-Roman heritage of the West is also problematic. See Mazrui, *Political Values*, 81–102.

25. Thiessen, *Lectures*, 130–131.

of sufferings since the divine person himself does not suffer. Secondly, it makes all talk on prayer and piety that suggests that God is with us at the moment of suffering hollow and unrealistic since the divine person himself has no capacity to suffer. For at the heart of Christian theology is the theological proposition that the divine person has suffered in the passion and death of Jesus Christ. To what degree did God the father share or have the potential to share in the suffering of Jesus Christ? St. Hilary of Portiers of the Western Church has, in the fourth century, noted, "If any man hearing that the only Son of God was crucified, says that His divinity suffered corruption, or pain, or change, or diminution, or destruction: let him be anathema."[26] John of Damascus adding his voice to such theological persuasion noted,

> For since the one Christ, Who is a compound of divinity and humanity, and exists in divinity and humanity, truly suffered, that part which is capable of passion suffered as it was natural it should, but that part which was void of passion did not share in the suffering. For the soul, indeed, since it is capable of passion shares in the pain and suffering of a bodily cut, though it is not cut itself but only the body: but the divine part which is void of passion does not share in the suffering of the body . . . we say that God suffered in the flesh, but never that His divinity suffered in the flesh, or that God suffered through the flesh.[27]

After some examples to illustrate the impossibility of such divine suffering, John of Damascus further remarked, "much more, then, when the flesh suffered . . . His only passionless divinity escape all passion although abiding inseparable from it."[28] For these ancient Christian writers and their subsequent theological heirs, God is not to be associated with suffering since, as generally argued, his constitution forbids such experience of pain or suffering. However, such a way of thinking is a direct affront to the harmony and unity of the divine Godhead since in a true relationship or union the experience of any person within the Godhead should be shared by the other members of the Godhead. Thus, making divine suffering on the cross merely a peculiar experience of the Son and not that of the Father and the Holy Spirit is to deny and also negate the interrelational and empathic experience or union within the Godhead. In this understanding a 'divine isolationism' exists within the Godhead that tends

26. St. Hilary of Poitiers, "On the Council," 15.

27. John of Damascus, "Exposition of the Orthodox Faith," 71.

28. Ibid., 71.

to separate the experiences of each individual person constituting the divine union. However, if the divine union is opened to some form of interconnectedness that moves beyond the singular honor of sharing the same essence to the fundamental place of also sharing similar experiences, then the members of the Holy Trinity each is directly or indirectly partaking in the experience of each member. Therefore the deeper level of communion actually has a communal form or disposition whereby the divine persons are mutually affected by the passion, desire and experiences of each of the godhead members. Unfortunately, due to the influence of Western individualism, often excessive individualism is projected onto the Godhead that made each member of the Godhead like three individuals living in a room, but each separated and unaffected by the passion and experiences of the other. Such individualistic trinitarianism often views the divine union as a collaboration of individuals in a binding relationship without underscoring the communal implication of such a union as it affects each of the members of the divine union. However, contrary to this individualistic trinitarinism, communalistic understanding of the union of the Godhead has the inherent potential to stress the common inter-penetration of the divine persons in a relationship that allows equal or similar symbiotic influence on each of the members of the divine Godhead. Communalistic trinitarianism also opens the possibility of sharing the pains, the experiences and joys of divinehood. It also allows the divine suffering of the Son to be expressed, shared and felt by each of the individual members of the divine Godhead.[29]

The continuous conceptualizations of God in Greek philosophical forms have become a perennial concern as this preceding discourse on divine impassibility reveals. In his work, "Must God Remain Greek" Robert E. Hood noted the tutelage and general control of Christian theology by Greek Philosophy, and thus he observed,

> Greek is . . . descriptive of the way Christians think about God intellectually and talk about God theologically, for that thought and discourse have been shaped and defined by ancient Greek philosophical thought. To this extent, we can say that Christian theology has given God an 'ethnic' or 'ethnocentric' character that is Greek.[30]

29. See Horrell, "Towards a Biblical Model of Social Trinity," 399–421. See also Macleod, *Shared Life*; Fatula, *The Triune God*; Hodgson, *The Doctrine of the Trinity*.

30. Hood, "Must God Remain Greek," 462.

Furthermore, Hood noted the implication of this Hellenization of God on the African Christianity, thus he revealed, "The latter's hegemony in preserving and shaping Christian theology and doctrine has in effect rendered these African and African–based cultures intellectually homeless, even though they are well represented demographically in the church."[31] Hood underscored that the Christian theology of God was a "descendants of Graeco-Roman thought."[32] He proceeded further to also note the". . . Graeco-Roman packaging of Christian theology, dogmatics, languages, and traditions . . ."[33] Significantly, he opined that such cultural control over theology now viewed as "cultural imperialism" "raises acute issues of cultural and religious hegemony" because "Western Christians continue to exercise exclusive guardianship over the shape of Christian theology and over the debate about the meaning of Jesus Christ for a multicultural church and world; this is an especially crucial matter in Afro cultures, such as Africa . . . where the church is growing rapidly."[34] He also noted,

> . . . the critical issue is whether Christianity within the traditions of these Third World cultures, where the Christian faith is going from strength to strength in contrast to the West and the East where it is in a state of 'suspended animation,' must be filtered through Graeco–Roman religious thought and patterns in order to be considered legitimate and authentically Christian.[35]

"In other words" noted Hood, "Do Christians from Third World cultures have to become imitation of European or imitation of North Americans before they can be considered fitting contributors to the formation and shaping of Christian thought?" By the same token,

> can there be a diversity of theological concepts about God's revelation that allows for alternatives to the Greek model, certainly for Afro cultures? Can the theological treasure house of Christianity open up yet another account with African . . . cultures, an account in which those cultures are contributors rather than merely being recipients of the inheritances of Europe and North America?[36]

---

31. Ibid., 463.
32. Ibid., 462.
33. Ibid., 465.
34. Ibid.
35. Ibid., 466.
36. Ibid.

The credibility of such reconceptualization of God within an African cultural category becomes not only legitimate but a necessity particularly in the overall tendency of the cited works which seem to explore Greek philosophical terminologies that deny the passibility of God. We must explore theological alternatives from this dominant feature of Western theological discourse on divine impassibility in order to underscore the necessity and theological legitimacy of a passible God.

Another incommunicable divine attribute is the attribute of omnipresence. The omnipresent nature of the divine being connotes the understanding that the divine being does not have size or other spatial features; however he is present everywhere with his entire being, though acting differently in different places or different settings (See Ps 139:7–10; Jer 23:23–24; Isa 66:1–2; 1 Kgs 8:27; Acts 7:48; 17:28). The biblical teaching of divine omnipresence should encourage the understanding of God's presence to bless, comfort and protect his people in every conceivable circumstance or place on the face of the earth whether in the desert, air, sea or land. This understanding of divine presence should also extend to places such as prisons, hospitals, schools, streets, war zones, conflict areas and other places of deep human need. On the other hand, divine omnipresence should also encourage the understanding that the divine presence is everywhere to punish those who do not conform to his divine will and standards (Amos 9:1–4).

Apart from these incommunicable attributes there are also divine communicable attributes. These attributes consist of spirituality, knowledge, wisdom, goodness, holiness. There are also other divine communicable attributes such as peace, righteousness, jealousy, wrath, will, freedom and power. However, because of the limited scope of study our attention will be on the first category of divine communicable attributes. Beginning with the divine attributes of spirituality or invisibility, the scriptures teach that God is spirit and that we share in this basic composition of the divine being (John 4:24; 1 Thess 4:23). Concerning the mental attributes of *knowledge or omniscience*, the Bible teaches that God knows and understands everything. This knowledge of God is not partial or knowledge that comes with the sequential revelation of events, but a knowledge that is exact, detailed and complete.[37] It is a knowledge that is based on the

---

37. Many contemporary theologians argue that divine knowledge is incomplete since the future is not yet an actual event, thus God has the knowledge of the past, the present, but not the future. For the theological discussion that is in favor of this and similar views on divine omniscience see Sanders, *The God Who Risks*; Basinger, *The Case for Freewill Theism*; Boyd, *God of the Possible*; Hasker, "The Openness of God,"

comprehension and understanding of everything in one eternal act (See 1 John 3:20; 1 Cor 2:10–11; Heb 4:13; Matt 6:8; Job 37:16; Isa 46:9–19; 42:8–9; 55:9; Ps 139:6). The knowledge of God did not come from the wealth of experience he gathered from his interaction with the outside world, but it is a product of knowledge that is inherently with him before the creation of the world. To even say that God increases in knowledge is to miss the point since he is a being that is already perfect in knowledge of the past, present and future events and thus he does not need to increase in knowledge or gather knowledge from his relationship with the world. He sees eternally all events whether in the past, present and the future in one simple context of knowledge. Similarly, the understanding of divine omniscience also presupposes that God knows the direction of unacted or uninitiated possible course of action (See 1 Sam 23:11–13; Matt 11:21, 23; 1 Kgs 13:19). Related to this divine mental attribute is the attribute of divine wisdom. The biblical teaching on *divine wisdom* could be paraphrased as the divine ability to use the best methods possible in his own understanding and self-knowledge in order to achieve his divine purposes. God in the Bible is described as the perfection of wisdom. Such divine wisdom is clearly expressed in creation, redemption and the daily activities in the life of his people (See Job 9:4; Ps 104:24; Rom 11:33; 16:27; 8:28; 1 Cor 1:18–20, 24, 30; Jas 1:5; Ps 111:10; Prov 9:10). Thus, a proper understanding of the biblical teaching on divine wisdom will ultimately lead to a peaceful disposition and trust in divine wisdom particularly in the midst of life's problems.

Within the moral divine attributes are the attributes of divine goodness and divine holiness.[38] Concerning the former, the biblical teaching on

---

111–39; Pinnock, "God Limits His Knowledge," 141–62; Rice, "Divine Knowledge and Free-Will Theism," 121–39; *idem, God's Foreknowledge*; Swinburne, *The Coherence of Theism*, 162–78 and Pinnock *et al.*, *The Openness of God*. For a theological and philosophical response to this understanding of limitation in divine omniscience see Nash, *The Concept of God*, 83–104; Morris, *Our Idea of God*, 51–72; Craig, *The Only Wise God*; Wierenga, *Review of The Openness of God*, 248–52; Freddoso, *Review of God*, 105–6 and *idem*, "The 'Openness of God,'"124–33.

38. In his unpublished work, "God's Universal Moral Laws: Ordering Human Life and Creation," Turaki used divine moral attributes as a dynamic theological category which could be used to address social, civil and political abnormalities in human society. This is against the traditional theological attitude that merely treats divine attributes without reference to their societal implications. Significantly, his quest for the theistic transformation of human society via the exploration of divine moral attributes is a significant contribution to the theological subject of change since most often the advocates of change in human society humanly placed this quest for change within philosophical, sociological and psychological parameters. However, Turaki's approach

divine goodness underscores that God is the ultimate standard of whatever is designated or labeled good. It also teaches that God's deeds are without flaw and thus commendable (See Gen 1:31; Ps 34:8; 100:5; 106:1; 107:1). Humanly speaking when we say that God is good this is often associated with human goodness. Thus by such label we mean that God is benevolent in his acts or deeds that we humanly consider to be good. We quickly assume that divine goodness is somehow related or similar to the idea of goodness as conceived in human evaluation and descriptions. However, we fail to see that goodness is intrinsically an aspect of the divine nature or attribute by which we could say of the divine person that he is good in essence and goal. This same understanding is not true in the case of human acts that we consider to be good since often the essence and goal of certain actions are primarily determined by personal considerations and communal definitions of what is generally considered as good or goodness. If divine goodness transcends the goodness conceived among humans than it throws into doubt the possibility of the human person attaining such lofty virtue of divine goodness. For example, what do we mean when we say God is love, or has a nature that is good and kind? Since even though God ontologically has such human expressions of the conception of love, goodness or kindness in himself yet these divine attributes are not actually found in human persons as they are fully expressed or represented in God. Hence, human vocabulary should have respected the difference between divine goodness and the other kind of goodness as practiced by humans since they differ not only in degree as often presupposed but also in essence and goal. In this persuasion the difference is not merely the label of 'extra-goodness' to show the heightening of divine goodness, but it should

---

placed rightly the quest to change the human society on God and his disclosed moral attributes. This theistic approach presupposes that no change is good enough that does not have significant relationship with the divine attributes. In his evolving thought on "Universal moral laws," there is a conscious quest to assert these theological propositions within a universal application. The basis for a universal application grows largely from the understanding that human beings are universally accountable to God and the entire universe is within the purview of his presence. Thus, whether pagan or Christian, Jew or Muslim, the divine attributes of love, goodness, compassion, sovereignty and other constitutions of the divine being are benevolently the theoretical basis by which we can build and impact society. Despite the many merits of this work, the problem of the work lies in its ambivalent Christological agenda particularly the theological hypothesis that seeks to change human society in Theocentric terms. In the long run, is it possible to change human society without reference to Jesus? Is such a shift from special revelation to natural theology not an indication of our partial commitment to Christology? Also, is this not a quest to change human society without Jesus? See Turaki, "God's Universal Moral Laws."

be described as 'essential and teleological goodness.' The two terms taken together describe, humanly speaking, the faint idea of divine goodness, which is by essence good and also good when considered apart from the perception of inward divine motivation. If human and divine goodness are different at such crucial points of essence and goal thereby assuming that what we describe as good is not necessarily divine goodness, on what grounds should we pursue goodness or consider ourselves good? If the goodness of God is at variance with human goodness and it is suggested that they are not the same in essence and goal, there is the tendency that such divine goodness is not attainable since humans within such understanding will lack the capacity to practice or realize such lofty conception of divine goodness. If this is the case, then on what basis is the divine command to be good? The answer to this question is simple in the light of the Bible since the Bible presupposes that even though divine goodness and human goodness are at different levels yet they are also similar since as bearers of the image of God we have a conception of goodness that faintly captures the divine type of goodness in the acts or deeds considered humanly speaking as good. Despite the fall, which has distorted the goal and nature of human goodness to make it selfish and at variance with divine goodness, human beings have the capacity to be good or to do good since they are by nature created with some divine nature of goodness as the embodiment of the divine image. It is to this end that Plutarch noted,

> . . . by nature man neither is nor becomes a wild or unsocial creature; it is rather the case that the habit of vice makes him become something which by nature he is not, and on the other hand he can be made civilized again by precept and example and by a change of place and of occupation; in fact even wild beasts, given a measure of gentle treatment, lose their savage and intractable qualities.[39]

Even though the Bible did not support the humanistic optimism of Plutarch, there is a consistent biblical emphasis on the capacity of the human person to carry out some defined goodness in spite of the fall. At creation, God created man as 'exceedingly good.' Such aesthetic comment of the divine being is not merely a product of the human physical nature but it also consists of some moral dimension particularly in the capacity and potential of the human person to practice goodness that is within the divine type. At the fall, such goodness becomes marred hence the perversion of human goodness to human parameters and standards. In this way, the fall

39. Plutarch, *Fall of the Roman Republic*, 186.

makes every act of human goodness a selfish venture that is predicated on the benefit it gives to the one exercising such goodness and not necessarily the divine kind of goodness. If for example, someone gives his fortune to the poor or donates his or her blood to the sick as an act of goodness, humanly speaking, he or she is considered good. However, consideration is not extended to include the goodness of the motive for such humanly labeled acts of "goodness." It is possible that such goodness is merely an extension of human selfish ego which extends alms to the poor or blood to the sick while considering the prestige that such acts fetch for him or her within human society. In this understanding even though the act itself is considered good the motives that go along with the action are not actually good since they make people tools or means of getting society's prestige or a way of enhancing ones' status. Consequently the act is good but the motive behind the act flaws the act itself. Goodness in this way is not practiced for goodness' sake but for other benefits that good deeds bring to the one doing such acts of "goodness." Unfortunately, it is these parameters that make human goodness always to fall short of divine goodness.

Similarly, in discussing another communicable divine moral attribute of holiness, there is also the understanding of the idea that divine holiness differs also from the human conception of the term.[40] The biblical understanding of divine holiness teaches that God is totally separated from any form of sin or evil and totally committed towards the seeking of his glory.[41] There is a divine necessity to separate from sin in order for God to have the moral credibility to enforce his moral stipulations. Consequently, holiness is not merely moral purity or the ability to do good but the inner and outward manifestations of this special ability to separate or be elevated from the contamination of things that are "finite and imperfect." The Bible makes this understanding of divine holiness the basis for human life and thus presupposes the human capacity to live God's designed form of life.[42] However, the New Testament revelation underscores that without commitment to Christ and regeneration of the Holy Spirit such a lofty divine life of holiness becomes illusive of the human race because of the fall.[43]

---

40. For passages that reveal the holiness of God see Psalms 22:3; 71:22; 78:41; 89:18; 99:3, 9; Isaiah 1:4; 5:19, 24; 6:3.

41. Grudem, *Systematic Theology*, 201–2; Chafer, "Biblical Theism," 5–37.

42. See Exodus 19:4–6; Leviticus 11:44–45; 19:2; 20:26; 1 Peter 1:16; Hebrews 12:10, 14; 2 Corinthians 6:14–18; Ephesians 2:21.

43. Still, "Holiness of God," 15–40. See also Coppedge, *Portraits of God*.

Divine Attributes and the African Context of Suffering

There is a shocking oversight in traditional theological discussions on the divine attributes.[44] The oversight lies in the inability to discuss divine attributes in relationship to the context of suffering and pain.[45] In such theological scheme, God's divine attributes become a mere academic reflection and does not serve as an adequate engagement of human predicaments that constantly challenge the understanding of these divine attributes. It often ignores the obvious human tendency to question the divine attributes of God particularly in the context of suffering. Significantly, it is the context of suffering and pain that usually sets the theological agenda, the understanding and comprehension of the divine being. For Africans, even though situations of pain and suffering exist in other parts of the world, the African continents seem to have a monopoly of human problems. Thus, a discourse on divine ontology or attributes must relate divine attributes to the despicable human conditions that presently characterize the African continent.

Even without reference to the dehumanizing conditions of life in Africa, human problems anywhere always pose a serious concern to divine attributes. For example, problems, particularly about unjust suffering in the world, have often provoked questions such as "Where is God?" Even though such a question seems simple and innocent such a question is a direct response to the omnipresent attribute of the divine being. Similarly, in the context of pain many question the wisdom, knowledge, love and the omnipotence of God. Many people in moments of pain and sorrow have asked, "does God actually know what I am passing through?" This question is a direct challenge to divine omniscient knowledge and underscores the inadequate comprehension of divine love or a reappraisal of divine knowledge in the context of pain or suffering. In other circumstances many have asked what is the need of passing through such and such a problem?

---

44. In his work, *When Bad Things Happen to Good People*, Harold S. Kushner sees the problem particularly in the book of Job as the tension between two attributes of God, namely divine goodness and divine omnipotence. To this end, Kushner observed, "God would like people to get what they deserve in life, but He cannot always arrange it. Forced to choose between a good God who is not totally powerful, or a powerful God who is not totally good, the author of the book of Job chooses to believe in God's goodness." Interestingly, this study reveals that theological reflection on human problems must be predicated on the tension its raises for divine attributes. See Kushner, *When Bad Things*, 42–43.

45. On the general problem of human suffering as it relates to God see Hall, *God and Human Suffering*.

Or what is the divine purpose for going through pain and suffering? In such moments, the person asking the question is directly questioning the wisdom of God, that is, his ability to use the best possible means to obtain the best desired divine results. In this moment of pain or crises in our life, there is also the human tendency to question divine omnipotence, that is, whether God is indeed able to deliver us from the undesirable human predicament we find ourselves. Apart from these highlighted questions, many have posed sober questions that have to do with divine. If the love of God is indeed true, we humanly speaking reasoned, why the presence of pain and suffering in our life? Thus suffering and pain more than anything else often provoke us to ask serious questions pertaining to the love of God. Does God actually love us by allowing us to go through these painful circumstances? In the introduction to his work, *The Problem of Pain*, C. S. Lewis connected the entire concern of his discussion on the problem of human suffering to the attribute of divine love, when he observed,

> For the far higher task of teaching fortitude and patience I was never fool enough to suppose myself qualified, nor have I anything to offer my readers except my conviction that when pain is to be borne, a little courage helps more than much knowledge, a little human sympathy more than much courage, and the last tincture of the love of God more than all.[46]

Furthermore, Lewis underscores the possibility of reconciling human suffering to the understanding of a loving God. Thus he notes, "The problem of reconciling human suffering with the existence of a God who loves is only insoluble as long as we attach a trivial meaning to the word 'love' and look on things as if man were the centre of them."[47] But since God is the center, reasoned Lewis there is the possibility of reconciling human suffering and the divine attribute of love. In Africa, as a result of the immeasurably painful experiences of many Christians the possibility of asking such questions is not only common but it is familiar. Africans generally throw themselves on God in prayers with soul–searching questions about divine love and justice within the disparity of the world and the general inability of most Africans to actualize their humanity because of hostile economic and political environments. Thus, Africans, more than any single group of people in the modern world, have the awesome temptation to question the wisdom, love, knowledge and power of God. However, such self-questioning is healthy because it critically reflects the tension

46. Lewis, *The Problem of Pain*, 10.

47. Ibid., 36.

between the existential realities and the accepted religious conceptions of the divine being. It is ultimately rooted in the quest to translate the conception of God into engaging the existential forms in real life. Thus, it removes theology from its abstract or philosophical character in the traditional discussion of divine attributes by allowing the discussion of divine attributes now to take place in the context of suffering and pains. Some reasoned that this quest to understand or evaluate traditional discourse on divine attributes in a new context of suffering and pain poses a serious problem because there is the possibility that such discourse will lead to emotionally-conditioned theological responses which are based upon the existential realities and not the biblical revelation. However, such should not be the case since Africans and the universal questioning of the divine attributes are important steps towards a better understanding of biblical revelation since the Bible revelation of divine attributes takes place very often in the same locus of pain, suffering and oppression.[48] Significantly, most Africans have inwardly resolved these existential struggles to reconcile the divine essence and their existential predicaments thus manifesting a faith in God that transcends the imposing limitations of their human existential context.[49]

Conclusion

For the majority of Africans, the existence of God is taken for granted since the rich cultural and religious context of the African worldview provided the theological basis for such understanding. God is understood to be a living reality and immanently works in the life of the individual and community in order to providentially attend to their varying needs. Even though at times his transcendence is often acknowledged particularly as reflected in the different cultural and religious myths or folktales, such understanding does not rule out the conception of God in immanent terms. From this understanding, the motivation to argue for the existence of God within African society becomes needless. However, with the current globalization and the intrusion of modernity, particularly Western secularism and the scientific mindset, it should be expected that these modern

48. For example, the biblical revelation of God as holy, loving, omnipotent, omnipresent, and omniscient often than not takes place in the context of human troubles and suffering.

49. For theological construction in human contexts of suffering see Sobrino, "Theology in a Suffering World," 153–78.

contexts will put African understandings of God to the test. It is from such a view point that discourses on the existence of God become essential as the African continent undergoes the process of modern technical and scientific transitions.

6

Angels, Spirits, and Demons

Introduction

Tʜᴇ ᴇɴʟɪɢʜᴛᴇɴᴍᴇɴᴛ ᴀɴᴅ sᴄɪᴇɴᴛɪғɪᴄ probing launched an attack against the supernatural. This resulted in the demise of the subject of angels or other categories that pertain to the supernatural. Even though the discourse on God generally continued, the discussion did not include the subject of angels. Consequently, the subject of angels became seemingly out-dated and a residue of medieval superstitions.[1] To counteract this neglect, systematic writings sought to reimpose on the subject of the supernatural the auxiliary theme of angels. The characteristic of this systematic redress is often a wooden presentation of the biblical teachings surrounding angels which normally made them the subject of academic curiosity rather than a convincing reality. However, contrary to these academic treatments of the subject of angelology, the modern context is once again captivated with the subject of angels.[2] In the popular modern context, there is a resurgence of the subject of angelology as expressed in countless fictional books, pseudo–scientific fictional movies and modern

---

1. David Keck, *Angels and Angelology*.

2. There are medieval descriptions of angels that persist within popular Christian thought. As late as the seventeenth century, John Milton in his classic, *Paradise Lost*, reveals such angelology in his unorthodox representation of angels as having powers to eat and to make love. See West, "Milton's Angelological Heresies," 116–23; Allen, "Milton and the Love of Angels," 489–90.

art celebrating the existence of the world of angels.[3] *Hollywood* movies in particular have screened fantasized stories on the reality of angelic personalities or superhuman beings. It has fanned the public imagination and presented tales of angels falling in love with humans, angelic or superhuman intervention, extraterrestrial beings and fictional stories of angelic or celestial battles of good and evil with angelic and demonic personalities involved. Interestingly, some of these fictional plots about angels have successfully won awards and become bestsellers. It appears the *Hollywood* industry is booming by the exploitation of this modern fascination for the angelic world. Similarly, for example, the Nigerian movie industry, *Nollywood*, often presents or translates the reality of these angelic or demonic beings on the movie screens, thus exploring the fascination and fears that many Nigerians and Africans have for the Angelic world or the world of spirits. This chapter investigates the characteristics of the spirit world and the basic biblical teachings on angels and demons.

Angels and Spirits in the African Worldview

Angels or spirits hold a special place for many Africans. The fascination of the angelic world does not come as a surprise because of the affinity Africans generally have for the spirit world. The majority of Africans saw the similarity between their traditional understanding of the spirit world and that emphasized by their new faith in Jesus Christ. The familiarity arises from the entrenched understanding of the mediating spirits or divinities who serve as messengers of the Supreme Being. These groups of spirits are conceived to bridge the gap between God and humanity and they are often shouldered with the task of perpetuating or replicating the will of the Supreme deity among human people. The affinity of the African conception of these supernatural beings and biblical teaching on angels has greatly influenced the dominance of angels in the prayers, sermons, cultic and sacramental observances of the African Independent Churches. The phenomenon of African Independent Churches could be seen as a merger of the African and biblical worldviews and thus resulting in a worldview that is significantly dominated by an emphasis on angels and spirit beings. In traditional African society, the spirits are often depicted in realistically or portrayed in imaginative ways. Thus, there is the recognition of tall

3. See Carroll, "Nightmare and the Horror Film," 16–25; Freeland, *The Naked and the Undead*; Harrington, "Ghoulies and Ghosties," 191–202; Lucano, *Them or Us*; Twitchell, *Dreadful Pleasures*.

and short spirits, good and bad, ugly and fair spirit beings. Even though most African worldviews are greatly divided on the nature or forms of these spirits, there is a general consensus as to their characteristics. Seven defining characteristics of spirits in traditional African society could be stated here. First, there is the general acceptance of the existence of these spiritual beings. They are not merely a traditional fictional creation that lacks a basis in reality, but they are conceived as concrete realities that are presumably perceived to co-inhabit the world of humans. There are endless stories of men and women who attest to seeing and even talking with these spiritual personalities. These spirits for many African societies are not a force or energy, but beings with distinctive personalities. Secondly, spirits according to the traditional ethics of most African societies, are fundamentally divided into two broad camps namely good and bad spirits. The cause of the evil or goodness of some spirits is not always accounted for; however there is a recognition that evil spirits exist to haunt people and good spirits to bless people. Often they are believed to dwell in specified areas or come out at certain specified times of the day. Thirdly, Africans often perceive the spirits as closely related to the traditional medicine man or cultic leader. The knowledge of the demand or wishes of spirits are investigated through consultation of the diviner or seer. Thus, he or she is the custodian of esoteric knowledge pertaining to the realm feared by most Africans. In this way, he or she is accorded great prestige because of his or her cultic prowess in dealing with the spiritual beings. Fourthly, African people believe that spiritual beings can intervene at will in the physical order. The two realms of the spiritual and the physical, terrestrial and the celestial, the seen and unseen, have no defined borders since these spirits are expected to manifest or reveal their presence to the world of humans. There are many African myths about spirits turning into human beings and going to the market or even seeking marriage or partaking of any other human activity. Similarly, the Africans have always affirmed the extraordinary powers of spiritual beings. They are conceived as the embodiment of power which can be used to haunt or bless, thus the need to seek a protective shield against the activities of malevolent spirits and to seek alliance with the good ones. Also, most Africans understand the mediating roles of spiritual beings as messengers of the Supreme God. There is the acknowledgement of their role as emissaries of God who are saddled with the task of controlling a certain sphere or other assigned functions. However, the divine function is often obliterated as is often seen in these spiritual beings accepting sacrifices and other cultic rituals, thus they are not merely a channel or means to God as often argued, but they are also an end in themselves. Lastly, the majority of Africans maintain the belief that spirits are not subject to human limitations or restrictions. Thus they can go through walls, live in water, stay in trees, fly through the air, take animal or human forms, dwell in rocks or mountains and even possess people.[4]

Biblical Teachings on Angels and Demons

From these characteristics of spirits in traditional African society, the African understanding of the spirit world is not the same as the biblical conception. Even though there are converging similarities, there are equally differences. In a particular sense, Africans have no angelology, if by angelology we mean a catalogue and array of spirit beings with names and distinctive roles, working in a monotheistic framework. Instead, the activities of these spirit beings under traditional African beliefs are often capricious and within the framework of polytheism.[5] Thus contrary to the African traditional conception of spirit beings and the modern versions of fictitious angelic stories and plots, the Bible presents the reality of these angelic beings without the exaggerations that normally accompany the presentation by African traditional societies and the ghost films or angelic movies of the modern entertainment industries.[6] Biblical angelology affirmed that angels and other spiritual beings are a direct creation of the Supreme God and thus work ultimately under his divine control despite the seeming opposition of his plans by some of these spirits (See Neh 9:6; Ps 148:2, 3; Col 1:16). The biblical accounts conceive of the angels as highly intelligent beings, immaterial and clearly organized in hierarchy (See Matt 28:5; Acts 12:6–11). However, even though they are spiritual and invisible beings angels can also take bodily material form in certain special occasions (Matt 28:5; Heb 13:2). Similarly the Bible calls angels by several names such as "holy ones" (Ps 89: 5, 7), "sons of God" (Job 1:6; 2:1), "watchers" (Dan 4:13, 17, 23), "spirits" (Heb 1:14, "thrones," "dominions," "principalities," "authorities," and "powers" (Col 1:16; Eph 1:21.). Within these angelic beings are angelic personalities such as cherubim (Gen 3:24; Ps 18:10; Exod

4. For a study of demonology and redemption in the African context see Ferdinando, *The Triumph of Christ*. See also Daneel, "African Independent Church Pneumatology," 35–55; Oosthuizen, "Interpretation of Demonic Powers," 3–22.

5. See Langton, *The Ministries of Angelic Powers*.

6. For the biblical teachings on angels see Graham, *Angels*; McComiskey, "Angel of the Lord," 47–48; Bromiley, "Angel," 46–47; Dickason, *Angels*.

10:1–22; 25:22; 18–21), seraphim (Isa 6:2–7), and other fearful looking angelic creatures mentioned in Ezekiel and Revelation (Ezek 1:5–14; Rev 4:6–8). The Bible describes the angels as uncountable and thus numerous (Deut 33:2; Ps 68:17; Heb 12:22; Rev 5:11). Even though only the names of two angels were mentioned in the scriptures there is the possibility that the ones not mentioned also have names (Dan 8:16; 9:21; 10:13, 21; Jude 9; Rev 12:7–8; Luke 1:19, 26–27). Going through the pages of the scriptures, some basic functions for the creation of angels are given. Four salient reasons for the creations of angels are hereby underscored. First, angels are created to glorify God and to carry out some of his plans and purposes. Often in the Bible angels are found in the context of the worship of God and the execution of divine plans (See Ps 103:20; Rev 4:8; Luke 2:14; Heb 1:6; Luke 15:10. See also Luke 1:11–19; Acts 8:26; 10:3–8, 22; 27: 23–24; 2 Chr 32:21; Matt 16:27; Luke 9:26; 2 Thess 1:7; Zech 1:10–11; Dan 10:13; 12:7–8; 20:1–3). Secondly, the Bible reveals that angels are made to show the greatness of divine love and his plan for us.[7] Similarly, they are created to serve us by offering protection and care to the entirety of human and, by implication, non–human creations (See Ps 91:11–12; Matt 18:10; Acts 12:15; 2 Kgs 6:17). Lastly, creation of the angelic world provides us with a model for the pursuit of holiness and righteousness (See Rev 5:11–12; Isa 6:3). The Christian person must live in consciousness of the angelic world since it presupposes the existence of another world that is different to the world of matter. In relating with angels or recognizing their presence in our daily human experiences, we must not worship angels or receive doctrines from them since these practices could open us to demonic manipulation (See Rev 19:10; 1 Tim 2:5. See also Gal 1:18; 2 Cor 11:14; 1 Kgs 13:9, 18).

From the discourse on good angels, we must also highlight biblical teaching on demonic spirits and their diabolic leader, Satan. Our modern world has undergone a radical religious revolution particularly in the areas of the reality of demonic beings and personalities. In denying the existence of demonic beings, the modern psychology for example have sought to explain away demonic possession with terms such as "multi-personality" disorder, schizophrenia and other high sounding psychological labels. As already seen in our discourse on angels, contrary to this scientific approach, the reality of demonic beings and personalities is a common feature of our movie industries especially as seen in modern fascination for horror movies.

---

7. For human superiority over angels see Gen 1:26–27; 1 Cor 6:3; 2 Peter 2:4; Matt 22:30; Luke 20:34–36.

Apart from classical horror movies such as *Frankenstein, Dracula* or the modern day horror movie such as *Warsaw Texas Massacre*, there are now different brands of horror movies depicting the reality of powers or evil personalities that are beyond the domain of humans. Often some of these popular movies depict graphically on our screen the horrific and terrible nature of these evil demonic beings with imaginative creation that have no credence from the vantage of biblical revelation. Contrary to this popular presentation, the Bible speaks of the origin, activity and fate of these demonic personalities.[8]

For the Bible, demonic beings are not forces which exist in some form of impersonal existence. On the contrary, the Bible reveals their personality and their role and destiny within the framework of God's purpose and plans. There is need in this discussion to briefly reflect a concise biblical teaching on this subject. The Bible teaches that the existence of demonic beings came as a result of celestial rebellion that took place in Adamic times, particularly between Genesis 1:31 and Genesis 3. The Bible in the former text noted the goodness of creation, but somehow between this pristine good creation and the presence of evil in chapter 3, there seems to be a silent rebellion that took place here, which the Bible in different other places makes references to (See 2 Pet 2:4; Jude 9; Isa 14:12–15; Ezek 28:11–19). Some have opined that the celestial rebellion took place in pre-Adamic times, that is, before the creation of the human race. Even though the point of this rebellion was not specifically given, yet the occurrence and certainty of this rebellion was directly and indirectly implied within the scriptural traditions.[9] The head of this celestial rebellion against God was named Satan and his pristine beauty, pride and subsequent diabolic activities have been reflected greatly within biblical thought. For biblical thought, there is centrality given to the activity and personality of Satan because the imperfections of the world and the presence of evil within its social and political networks or relationships are all understood within the category of satanic activity. In this sense, Satan is not a footnote neither

8. On the understanding of fallen angels in Jewish traditions and other faiths see Jung, "Fallen Angels," 287–336; See Kuhn, "Angelology," 217–32; Caldwell, "The Doctrine of Satan,"29–33; *idem*, "The Doctrine of Satan," 98–102.

9. See Job 1:6–2:7; 1 Chronicles 21:1; Zechariah 3:1; Matthew 4:10; Luke 10:18. Satan which literally means the "accuser" is also known with many other names such as the serpent (Gen 3:1, 14; 2 Cor 11:3; Rev 12:9; 20:2), the ruler of this world (John 12:31; 14:30; 16:11), the evil one (Matt 13:19; 1 John 2:13), Beelzebul (Matt 10:25; 12:24, 27; Luke 11:15), the prince of the power of air (Eph 2:2) and the devil (Matt 4:1; 13:39; 25:41; Rev 12:9; 20:2).

does he merely occupy the margin of biblical revelation or serve as an appendage of biblical thought, instead Satan is a dominant character in biblical thinking, without him, the biblical revelation would definitely be incomplete in the explanation and causation of evil, but also in the necessity of redemption. There are two basic activities of Satan and his demonic cohorts namely the causation of sin and thus evil, and secondly, a strict opposition to God and his creation.[10] Even within such pronounced hostility between God and Satan there is recognition of the limitation of Satan and the understanding that his activities are within the purview of God's sovereign control (See Job 1:12; 2:6; Jude 9 and James 4:7). Since one cardinal activity of Satan is to sabotage the purposes and plans of God, similarly one preoccupation of Jesus Christ during his earthly ministry was exorcism and the promise of deliverance from the fear and activities of demons. For the Johannine community, "The reason the Son of God appeared was to destroy the devil's work" (John 3:8; See also Hebrews 2: 14). Similarly, such power to dislodge or destroy demonic activity is given by Jesus Christ to the individual Christian and the constitution of his body, the Church (See Luke 9:1; Luke 10:17, 19; Acts 8:7; 16:18; 2 Cor 10:3–4; Eph 6:10–18; 1 Pet 5:8–9; Heb 2:14; Col 2:15; 1 John 4:4). Such victory and deliverance that is given to the Church is often not stressed within mainline denominations, however the Pentecostals and African Independent Churches have generally expressed the victory obtained through Christ's redemption in order to offer freedom and deliverance to their members. The importance of rediscovering the basic New Testament belief concerning power encounter or spiritual warfare is made pertinent by our African context, where the existence, presence and activities of these demonic personalities have cultural credence. Refusing to recognize and explore the challenge of our African context will only lead to much confusion and irresponsibility on the part of clergy because the biblical assumption on the reality and continuous activities of these personalities are graphically reflected within the passages of the scriptures and from the experiences of our African context. In particular, African Christians must be pointed back to the mighty power of Jesus in his ability to protect the believer from the powers of witchcraft and evil spirits. As Christ of the gospels, the book of Acts and the Epistles, teaching on power encounter must reiterate or present a triumphant Jesus who has won the victory over the forces

10. For scriptural passages revealing his causation of sin see Genesis 3; 2 Cor 11:3; John 8:441 John 3:8. See also passages that talk about his opposition to divine plans and programs such as Matthew 4:1–11; 2 Corinthians 4:4 and Revelation 19–20.

of evil and thus given the same authority and power to the Christian believer to exercise in his name (See Matt 10:7–8; 28:18–20; Luke 10:17–20;
John 14:12–14; Acts 4:7, 10; Eph 1:19–23; Phil 2:6–11; Col 2:15). In this
understanding, the African Christian believer is called to act in the same
authority that Jesus exercised during his earthly ministry. The exercise of
this same authority by African Christian believers places them on a higher
realm above the forces of witchcraft, evil spirits and all other spiritual
forces that have continually harassed and oppressed the African people.
These spiritual beings are constantly the fears of most African people, and
Christian theology must relate the victory of Jesus Christ in order to address these fears of the African people.

Conclusion

Tite Tiénou observed rightly that, "A sound theology, particularly in our
African setting, must maintain the mysterious and the supernatural without becoming absurd and ridiculous."[11] This is true especially in the light
of the African fascinations and obsessions with the world of the spirits.
In African rural and urban areas, demons or angelic beings are beings
that are real and they are considered to be part of the human spiritual
habitat. In many places in Africa, the presence of these spiritual beings
are conceived to be looming around that they are often pacified through
the means of sacrifices, rituals and other cultic observances. The belief in
these superhuman beings normally creates fear or paranoia about their
presence and activities among African communities. Thus, every calamity that befalls African society or individuals could be traced back to
these spiritual personalities. On the other hand, even though the Bible
acknowledges the existence and activities of these superhuman entities,
the Bible guards against cultural or religious obsession with these spiritual
beings by acknowledging the sovereignty of God. Since God is sovereign,
the activities of the demonic angels are perceived to be under his control
or power, thus they do not act independently of divine plans or descriptions. Within this understanding, the demonic and the angelic community
are creatures of God and thus can only exist or act within the purview
of divine will and control. The African church needs more emphasis on
the divine sovereignty of God when teaching about these demonic powers
since there is already a tendency in the traditional African worldview to
exaggerate the powers and activities of these fallen spirits. In the same way,

11. Tiénou, *The Theological Task*, 35.

the African church must also emphasize the victory of Jesus Christ over the forces of evil which have been given to the believer now in Christ.[12] Such understanding of Christ's victory over the forces of evil should help to annul the fears of these spiritual powers and to grant the African Christian confidence to live each day of his life in trust of the divine ability to protect.

12. For example see Ephesians 1:19–23 and Colossians 1:13.

7

The Nature of the Human Person

Introduction

do we even know

IN MOST NON-WESTERN SOCIETIES, personhood is an idea that lacks precise definition because often it is conceived as shifting, changing and even transferrable. In this way of thinking, personhood is not an entity that comes automatically because one is a member of the human race, but it is something that one could acquire, lost or fail to acquire.[1] In this perspective, it is possible to be a human being and still be considered a non-person or placed socially within the category of the non-persons. For many non-western people, there is no contradiction between being a human being and still entertaining or acknowledging the cultural understanding that some persons could still be found within the domain of the non-persons. The quasi or semi-status of these human beings is not only openly acknowledged but it is largely ridiculed as unacceptable. Consequently, the most important thing in these non-western communities is to attain or acquire personhood and thus the greatest achievement is to be conferred or recognized as a "person" in these defined traditional ways.

On the other hand, there are non-western communities that are generous with the idea of personhood and extend the same to everything

1. For example, Susan R. Hemer has shown the intricate relationship between personhood and places among the Lihir people of Papua New Guinea, and how mobility affects the relational and individualistic conceptions of personhood among these people. See Hemer, "*Piot,* Personhood, Place, and Mobility," 109–25.

within the environment. Such generous understanding of personhood does not conceived personhood as primarily the sole monopoly of the human race, but extends this attribute to animal or things within nature, thus in this perspective the environment is culturally assumed to be animated or inhabited by personified entities. Describing this similar understanding of personhood among the Hoti of Venezuelan Guiana, Robert Storrie observed,

> Hoti ideas of the person, and of what it is to be human, are central to any attempt to understand their ways of relating. For the Hoti, the boundaries between interior and exterior, and self and other are neither sharply drawn nor immovable. The distinction between body and mind (or soul) is clearly not marked by the same ontological discontinuity that has often prevailed in Western thought. The notions of humanity which define and generate persons are inclusive of the whole environment. Thus the moral sphere includes all beings of the cosmos, so that household pets, family members, and the powerful masters of animals all hold the same moral understandings.[2]

According to Storrie, the Hoti culturally assumed the "essential equivalence of all beings," hence personhood is generously extended to the entire constituents of the environment.[3] Within this same generous tradition, in modern times, there is now increasingly recognition of the intricate relationship between personhood to properties that one has acquired. In particular, Margaret J. Radin has noted the influence of acquired possessions on personhood. For Radin, some material possessions are "bound up with personhood because they are part of the way we constitute ourselves as continuing personal entities," and hence they should be treated differently in legal matters.[4] Similarly, in his study of the correlation between personhood and places, Konstantinos Retsikas has shown the intriguing relationship between personhood and places among the Indonesian people of Eastern Java.[5] This same kind of correlation between personhood and

2. Storrie, "Equivalence, Personhood, and Relationality," 414.

3. Ibid.

4. Radin, *Reinterpreting Property*, 37.

5. In the conclusion of this study of Alas Niser, Retsikas noted, "The case of Alas Niser exemplifies in a highly specific manner the way in which an attachment to place is generated. Such an attachment is radically different from our understandings of it as primordial and given. As I have shown, neither persons nor places are conceived as static. Furthermore, I have argued that the fundamental correspondence between persons and place as of a particular kind is not rooted in deep histories of sedentary

places is also reflected in the writing of Lisa M. Austin who also notes the powerful role of places upon individual's sense of personhood.[6]

It was in the light of the preceding diverse conceptions of personhood in non-western world that led Lynn Morgan to observe that personhood is generally a social construct which is largely determined by each community in its own way. In particular, Morgan noted, even though "[p]ersonhood is a highly contested category, but the answers to 'what it is' will not be found in factors external to society" because "all practices of personhood are political gestures, played out in a social matrix in which power is unevenly distributed."[7] It is also primarily from these socially in-formed and diverse understandings of personhood that Valerie Hartouni observed, "Who or what is called person is, among other things, a highly contingent historical formation. It is both the site and the source of ongoing cultural contests and always under construction as a self-evident fact of nature."[8] Noting also the place of social factors in the construction of personhood, Clinton R. Sanders observed,

> Personhood is, then, an elemental social designation that may be acquired or forfeited, given or taken away. It is a matter of social identity that determines how a being is treated, the rights and freedoms he/she/it possesses, and even whether and under what conditions the being is allowed to live. Therefore, it is in the close examination of the process by which this key social status is acquired, achieved, afforded, or removed and the inter-actional consequences of its possession that we may gain central insights into the exchanges that constitute social life.[9]

Unfortunately, despite the imposing nature of these various non–western descriptions and definitions of personhood, Christian systematic theology, in its chief obsession with issues and concerns of the Western world, has not primarily given attention to this subject in its discourses. Accordingly, this chapter seeks to reposition Christian systematic theology in order to address these theological concerns. To this end, the chapter

---

habitation. Rather, it is predicated on short histories of mobility and a facility of domesticating *particular* instances of difference. This domestication is facilitated by the transformability of persons and place. By means of their mutual engagement through, with, and in place, Madurese and Javanese have become the very places they helped constitute; they are of the same House." See Retsikas, "Being and Places," 983.

6. Austin, "Person, Place or Things?," 445–65.

7. Morgan, "Life Begins When They Steal your Bicycle," 13–14.

8. Hartouni, "Reflections on Abortion Politics," 300.

9. See Sanders, "Killing with Kindness," 210.

describes the differences between the Western autonomous conception of personhood and the acquired personhood of the African cultural traditions. It observes the inability of the systematic theology to recognize the significance of these cultural two systems.

Western Autonomous Sense of Personhood

The western world narrowly defined personhood generally in terms of an autonomous category that is often independent of external or communal factor. This understanding of personhood arrogates or defined the human person as basically an autonomous being whose personhood is inherently located in the person and not outside him. Even though the nature of this autonomous category that defines a person is highly debated but there is a general consensus in western thought that it is a category that is fully embedded in the human person and it constitutes the inalienable part of his being. This inward category is believed to confer on the human person its personhood and it is generally accepted that every 'normal' human person is inherently and innately endowed with this personhood. It is considered to be inborn and not acquired or conferred on the human person. Even though there are dissident thoughts who often challenged the established western beliefs on the human person, the general constitutions of the western world is founded on the idea that human beings are born innately with a sense of personhood and the constitutions acknowledged and respected these personhood. Significantly, it extends personhood to the unborn and duly acknowledged the personhood of the dying and the aged. Consequently, it constitutional framework thrives on the understanding that the human beings are born with personhood and this personhood is neither conferred nor acquired but comes from our membership of the *homo sapiens*.

In contemporary times, this understanding of personhood has been questioned in various ways. For example, modern discourse on personhood in the western world has entertained the possibility of extending personhood to animals. It is from this frame of reference that Paul Singer based on the criteria of "sentience" has extended personhood to animals.[10] He also dubbed anybody that refuses to respect and protect the rights and

---

10. See Paul Singer, *Animal Liberation: A New Ethics for our Treatment of Animals* (New York Review/Random House, 1975); *Idem*, "Equality for animals?" *Ethics, Human and Other Animals: An Introduction with Readings*, ed. R. Hursthouse (London: Routledge, 2000).

personhood of animal as "speciesist."[11] Extending further this mode of reasoning, Marjorie Spiegel has tacitly acknowledged the personhood of the animal world by making a comparison between the enslavement of animals to the Atlantic slave trade.[12] Nancy R. Howell extends personhood to the Chimpanzees because these primates show a great degree of language, spirituality and intellectual life that has resonating resemblance to those of the human persons. She also observes that such realization will send out of balance the whole anthropocentric talk on sin, image of God and salvation because it will lead to the "de-centering of humans as the focus of the God-world relationship."[13] Sanders has also observed the need to treat pets as "virtual persons" because of the emotional attachment of their owners to them particularly during the time of pain or death.[14] D. Scott Bennett has also largely argued for the need to recognize and treat human-animal chimera as persons under the constitution since human-animal chimeras are the product of human stem cells injected to an animal host.[15] In particular response to animal rights' advocates, David MacDonald has noted as problematic the common attribution of "personhood" to animals through a direct comparison of the everyday slaughtering of animals to the holocaust.[16] Similarly, Christopher Fisher has also dismissed this optimism in the quest to find personhood among the Chimpanzees and shows clearly the uniqueness of human personhood against the scientific

---

11. Describing the new coined word, "speciesist," Singer observed, "Racists violate the principle of equality by giving greater weight to the interests of members of their own race when there is a clash between their interests and those of another race. Racists of European descent typically have not accepted that pain matters as much when it is felt by Africans, for example as when it is felt by Europeans. Similarly those I would call "speciesists" give greater weight to the interests of members of their own species . . . Human speciesists do not accept that pain is as bad when it is felt by pigs or mice as when it is felt by humans." See Singer, "Equality for animals?" 170.

12. See Spiegel, *The Dreaded Comparison*.

13. See Howell, "The importance of Being Chimpanzee," 179–91.

14. Describing this reality among pet owners, Sanders noted, "Pet owners commonly regard their animal companions as virtual persons. Rather relegating them to generic species categories, these caregivers relate to their nonhuman companions as individuals with whom they enjoy authentic social relationships bounded by shared histories and encompassing direct knowledge of the animal's personal attributes . . . In short, they see their pets as subjects, as friends or members of their families whose pain and illnesses are matter of regret . . ." See Sanders, "Killing with Kindness," 209.

15. See Scott D. Bennett, "Chimera and the Continuum of Humanity: Erasing the Line of Constitutional Personhood," *Emory Law Journal* 55 (2006): 347–87.

16. See MacDonald, "Pushing the Limits of Humanity?" 417–37.

findings of language, intelligence, spirituality, and social skills among the primates.[17]

In addition, the modern thinking in the discourse of personhood has also questioned the attribution of personhood to dementia patients or individuals in coma. Concerning the status of dementia patients as persons, Janis Moody noted,

> The ongoing destruction of the brain and the effect of this on the individual can ultimately leads to questions about whether individuals with dementia can be considered [as] person ... All of which has ramifications for people with dementia and their personhood status.[18]

Similarly, this modern discourse on personhood has also sought to understand the status of personhood particularly in mentally retard individuals. Attributing personhood to consciousness, Ronald E. Cranford and David Randolph Smith had reasoned that an individual ceases to be a person when he or she loses consciousness and become unresponsive to his environment.[19] Underscoring this perception, they noted, "permanently unconscious patients lack personhood."[20] On the other hand, Sophia I. Wong has described the moral personhood of individuals who are considered mentally challenged.[21] She observes that there is need for "a robust inclusion of people with disabilities" as moral persons, which is primarily based on sound theories of justice for all.[22] Wong notably observed,

> Theories of justice remind us we must structure our social institutions so that they include people with disabilities in every aspect of our daily life, because they are moral persons and they are owed a place at the table as a matter of justice. In so doing, theories of justice are the key to robust inclusion, because there are many things that virtuous and benevolent individuals cannot accomplish without social coordination.[23]

On cognitive disabilities and personhood, Eva F. Kittay has also described the exclusion of individual with mental or any other type of disabilities as

17. See Fisher, "Animals, Humans, and X-Men," 291–314.

18. Moody, "Dementia and Personhood," 19.

19. Cranford and Smith, "Consciousness," 233–48.

20. Ibid., 248.

21. Wong, "The Moral Personhood," 579–94.

22. Ibid., 581

23. Ibid.

"morally repugnant as earlier exclusions based on sex, race, and physical ability have been."[24] In disillusion, modern neuroscience has dismissed the quest for personhood as a modern illusion since all the criteria of personhood has been readily challenged and proved inadequate of becoming a universal basis or standard that could be used to ascertain one's possession of personhood. In particular Martha J. Farah and Andreas S. Heberlein has shown that the human conception of itself as a person is primarily the product of a mental trick played by the brain on the mind which makes the human being to see or conceive itself as persons while in actual reality this personhood has no neurological existence. Underscoring this mental trick, Farah and Heberlein observed,

> The weight of the evidence, from a sizable literature only sampled here, clearly supports the conclusion that the human brain represents the appearance, actions, and thoughts of people in a distinct set of regions, different from those used to represent the appearance, movements and properties of other entities. These regions together form a network that is sometimes referred to as 'the social brain' . . . but could equally well be termed a network for person representation.[25]

For Farah and Heberlein, "personhood is illusory, constructed by our brains and projected onto the world."[26] Interestingly, John Banja, in his response to Farah and Heberlein, has acknowledged that even though the idea of personhood is in many ways elusive, yet it should not be regarded as an illusion.[27] For Banja, there is a "personhood prototype" in each human being that help us to think in terms of "personhood" in spite of the absence of a concrete "essence" which backs up this "neural personhood."[28] It is such neural networks that trigger cognitively "in memory every time we encounter the things our society commonly calls 'persons.'"[29] These networks of neural operations also help us in recognizing "an individual with an amputated limb as a person," but we "would

---

24. Eva Feder Kittay, "At the Margins of Moral Personhood," *Ethics* 116 (2005), 100.

25. Farah and Heberlein, "Personhood and Neuroscience," 42.

26. Ibid., 37.

27. Banja, "Personhood: Elusive, but not Illusory," 60–62.

28. Ibid., 61.

29. Ibid.

be left in a quandary about the personhood status of someone who was walking around headless."[30] Accordingly Banja observed,

> Although 'personhood' turns out to be an extremely important (and sometimes tragically divisive) word in our society's vocabulary, I do not believe that we can dismiss it as illusory. Indeed, I think that to call it so is to misunderstand its real significance or function.[31]

For some individuals, there is tacit acceptance of human personhood but there is no consensus whether human personhood begins at the start of life or at the end of it. This contention has also led to endless debates in clinical studies on the blurring of borders between self and personhood. Similarly, the various contentions on human personhood in the western discourse have also take into cognizance moral tone and undertones particularly in the different shades of debates in according pre-embryonic and embryonic fetus personhood. In retrospection, the overall impressions in popular and academic discourses on human personhood are that the western world generally treats and accords personhood to every member of the *Homo sapiens*. Even though there are different opinions whether all human being possess personhood in various philosophical, ethical and scientific school of thoughts, there is the general acceptance that personhood is generally an element that is inherently possessed by all human people. This is the bedrock of western morality and its perennial obsession to extend helps and charities to other members of the *Homo sapiens*, which are deemed to be persons and part of the human race even though they are not directly a part of the western racial stocks.

Personhood in Traditional Christian Systematic Texts

Looking at church history, the discourses on "personhood" began early in the history of the Christian church. These discourses on "personhood" were primarily to define, describe or present theological arguments in defence of the divine and human nature of Jesus Christ. Similarly, such discourses on personhood also engage the controversial issues of the "three persons" of the trinity. The motivations for these discourses largely come from the increasingly Hellenistic orientation of Christianity and the need to redefine or re-express Christianity in philosophical templates, thoughts

30. Ibid.
31. Ibid.

and idioms of the Greco-Roman world. Unfortunately, despite the imposing nature of "personhood" in these early Christological discourses of the Church Fathers, however, these discourses did not translated into the descriptions of the general nature of the human person and the complications of the terms especially when applied to the diversity of the human race.[32] In particular, it takes for granted that personhood is a contested category that is largely denied, even at this time, to people at the fringe of the Greco-Roman society such as the slaves, the prisoners and the barbarians whom are deemed less than human being because they are not accorded fully the treatment due to persons.

Traditionally, the discourse on the human person is naturally treated in systematic theology under the subject of anthropology or the biblical teaching on the human nature or person. Unfortunately, this same discourse often too takes for granted the description on personhood and merely assume that the understanding of human personhood is the same all over the world. Significantly, the discourse on the human nature largely ignores the diverse understandings in the different cultural conceptions of the human personhood and narrowly defined the human nature in terms of its constitutions whether the human beings have one, two or three elements in their physical-spiritual makeup. The trichotomy, dichotomy, or monism debate in defining human nature in standard systematic texts comes as no surprise because of the predictable turn Christian theology took in the course of its history to satisfy enlightenment critique and scrutiny which largely denied the immaterial constitutions of the human being. Consequently, Christian theology obsessively preoccupies itself with presenting arguments whether the human person is essentially tripartite or trichotomy in character, that is, three essential aspects of his being, or dichotomy, that is, having two essential constitutions to his being, or even monism, that is, having only one aspect to his essential makeup as human being. Often much ink is spent to show or proof that the human nature is essentially defined within these stated categories. Unfortunately, this way of thinking did not engage or take into its theological discourse the various traditional conceptions of human nature in other non-western societies which have no serious problems with the mathematics of human

---

32. Kelly rightly observed, "[it was] in the fourth and fifth centuries that the doctrine of human nature became an issue of prime importance in the Church." He also noted that "[i]n both East and West alike it was taken for granted that man is a composite being made up out of body and soul. He is a 'rational animal' . . . with a foot in the higher intellectual, as well as the lower, or sensible, world." See Kelly, *Early Christian Doctrines*, 344.

constitutions whether one, two or three, but have problems with basis, nature or methods for acquiring human personhood. Regretfully, Christian theology has refused to move ahead from mere stale discourse on the constitutions of the human being to complicated nature of defining the basis for human personhood in both the Western and non-western cultural traditions. This transition is necessary because of the contemporary identity crisis, genocide, ethnic-cleansing, bioethical concerns, scientific advancements, cultural beliefs and religious fanaticism which often arbitrarily assigned other human beings in the category of non-persons. Even though traditional systematic texts have address these ills by its emphasis on the universality of the *imago dei* in all human beings, there is now need to know whether human personhood is an aspect of *imago dei* or whether *imago dei* is a Hebraic idiom for human personhood. Unfortunately, we will not immediately pursue this line of thought here, because in its history, discourses on *imago dei* often takes the predictable turns into windings and endless debates on the actual category or categories which constitute the divine likeness or image in the human race. We look briefly how systematic texts have traditionally asserted the "personhood" of the human beings without directly engaging the subject of personhood or taken into cognizance the non-western understanding of the same.

Beginning with the *Systematic Theology* by Charles Hodge, one sees his persistent quest to assert the "humanity" of all races. Even though he approached Christology in terms of the "persons" of Christ, his treatment of the nature of the human being did not employ this category, but merely describes constitutions of the human being and proffers cogent argument to ascertain the humanity of the various races. Hodge was so much convinced of the "humanity" of all races that he observed, "All men are of the same blood, of the same race, of the same order of creation."[33] He also emphasized this sameness of the human race even to the point of anatomy. For example, Hodge observed,

> The Caucasian, the Mongolian, the African, have each their peculiarities by which the one is easily distinguished from the other, and which descend from generation to generation without alteration. With regard to these peculiarities, however, it is to be remarked, first, that they are less important and less conspicuous than those which distinguish the different varieties of domestic animals all belonging to the same species. No two men, or no men of different races, differ from each other so

33. Hodge, Charles. *Systematic Theology*, 88.

much as the little Italian greyhound and the powerful mastiff or bull-dog . . . Such is the sameness of all the varieties of mankind as to their corporeal structure, that a system of anatomy of European exclusively, would be as applicable in Asia, Africa, and Australia, as in Europe itself.[34]

In Hodge, the language of personhood is glaringly absent; however he rightly acknowledges the "humanity" shared by all races. Hodge observes that there is a physiological, psychological, philological and moral sameness that cuts across the human race and sets the human race above the animal world. For Hodge, this sameness serves primarily as the standards by which entities are admitted or refused admittance as members of the human race. Significantly, Hodge also extended this sameness to include spiritual relationship which he presumed is shared by all members of the human race. Describing this common spiritual bond, Hodge observed,

> Wherever we meet a man, no matter of what name or nation, we not only find that he has the same nature with ourselves; that he has the same organs, the same senses, the same instincts, the same feelings, the same faculties, the same understanding, will, and conscience, and the same capacity for religious culture, but that he has the same guilty and polluted nature, and needs the same redemption.[35]

In Hodge, the term "personhood" is not use, but the idea is reflected in his quest to extend "humanness" to every member of the human race. It appears the idea of "personhood" is readily implied and underlies his discourse on the sameness of the human species in every race. Consequently, if this reasoning is right, for Hodge, personhood appears to be defined in physiological, psychological, philological, moral and spiritual categories which humanity commonly shares. They are the attributes that make each human being a member of the same species and not another. It is these common same characteristics that inherently define and classify one as a member of the human race. Even though he recognizes the inherent diversities of human race, Hodge's quest to unify the entire human race on the theme of our commonness, did not allow him to rightly acknowledge the importance of these diversities. His emphasis on the sameness of human race in general dismisses the local perceptions of our humanness especially in terms of the human quest for authenticate personhood. To be fair to Hodge, several factors are particularly responsible for this

34. Ibid., 86.

35. Ibid., 90.

unifying framework by which he approached the human nature. One of these important factors is the universal disposition of Christian theology and the gospel especially in its readiness to speak to every context whether near or far, as seen in its vision of moving from Jerusalem, Samaria, and then to the uttermost part of the world. Though the "humanness" of Jesus Christ is defined in terms of a "person" and his divinity in the same category, however, in defining human nature, traditional systematic texts ignored the use of "person" and concentrate primarily on the constitutions of the human nature, *imago dei* and our common humanity. The emphasis on these highlighted categories is also seen in the *Systematic Theology* by Louis Berkhof.[36] Like in the writing of Hodge, these same arguments in history, philology, psychology, natural science, physiology and scriptures were briefly expressed in defence of the unity of the human race.[37] This by implication means that human race shares a bond especially as reflected in the highlighted categories. Wayne Grudem comes close to highlighting the place of personhood in human relationship. In his discourse on "Equality in Personhood and Importance," Grudem describes the equality between the female and male genders especially as reflected in Genesis 1:27. Emphasizing equality in the personhood of the sexes, Grudem observed,

> The fact that both men and women are said by Scripture to be 'in the image of God' should exclude all feelings of pride or inferiority and any idea that one sex is 'better' or 'worse' than the other. In particular, in contrast to many non-Christian cultures and religions, no one should feel proud or superior because he is a man, and no one should feel disappointed or inferior because she is a woman. If God thinks us to be equal in value, then that settles the question, for God's evaluation is the true standard of personal value for all eternity.[38]

This equality in personhood is briefly extended in practical terms to "a man or woman, employer or employee, Jew or Gentile, black or white, rich or poor, healthy or ill, strong or weak, attractive or unattractive, extremely intelligent or slow to learn . . ."[39] It appears Grudem is tailoring discourse in systematic text to particularly engage specific areas of inequality or where often the personhood of other members of the human being is denied. This development in Grudem shows progress in the movement of

36. Berkhof, *Systematic Theology*, 188–90.

37. Ibid.

38. Grudem, *Systematic*, 456–71.

39. Ibid., 459.

systematic text from the general acceptance of the humanity of all human beings particularly as seen in Hodge and Berkhof to describing the playing out of this same thesis concretely in grey areas of inequality where most human beings are denied personhood. In these particular interests, *Christian Theology* by Millard Erickson shows a new sensitivity to acknowledge the personhood of people in the grey areas of nonpersons. Erickson extended the discussions on human nature or *imago dei* to deal with the personhood and humanity of these people. In the chapter entitled, "the Universality of Humanity," Erickson particularly mapped out and addressed the humanity of all races, both sexes, people of all economic statuses, the aged, the unborn and the unmarried. In extending personhood or underscoring the humanity of all human being, Erickson observed,

> . . . there are some incidental variations among humans that do sometimes affect, at least in practice, society's regard of their humanity. While the fact that people who differ in some way are, nevertheless, fully human, may not be rejected in theory, society tends to treat them as being somewhat less than others . . . It will be observed that the special status that God accorded to Adam and Eve by making them, in distinction from the animals, in God's own image, is extended to all members of the human race.[40]

In Erickson and Grudem, one sees the desire to address and give personhood to the human race especially in the specific quest to assert the personhood of individuals that are often culturally assumed to reside within the category of the nonpersons. This development in modern systematic texts is important, however, this concern most also move ahead to address in details the local understandings of personhood particularly as expressed in communities that are non-western in their cultural and religious orientations. Consequently, there is the need for the bulk of humanity in non-western world who lives daily in the grey area of nonpersons to fully rediscover their humanity via the interaction of Christian theology with the local cultural understandings of personhoods. There is also the need for a new template for systematic theology that takes into cognizance the persons and issues in these grey areas which will lead to better understanding of our humanity from the local contexts of our existence and in mutual dialogue with mainstream Christian theology. This again will redress the one–sided treatments of the human nature or personhood in idioms of the Western world that clearly did not resonate with the different

---

40. Erickson, *Christian Theology*, 559.

perceptions of personhood in other communities. The issue here is not to superficially judge whether one understanding of personhood is valid or not, but to emphasize the need to allow the expressions of other diverse understandings of personhoods to dialogue with Christian theology in order to create views on personhoods that are clearly grounded in biblical traditions.

The African Understanding of Personhood

The African idea of personhood is totally different from the Western perspective whereby personhood is closely associated with the thought of rationality, will, and memory.[41] Underscoring this difference, Ifeanyi A. Menkiti noted, "A crucial distinction thus exists between the African view of man and the view of man found in Western thought: in the African view it is the community which defines the person as person, not some isolated static quality of rationality, will, or memory."[42] Similarly, personhood is not defined in metaphysical categories such the body, mind, soul, and spirit.[43] In traditional African society personhood is something somebody acquired rather than something that one inherently possesses.[44] In

41. According to Godfrey Tangwa, "Western philosophy has a perennial obsession on person, and more importantly with criteria for personhood that would clearly segregate those entities worthy of moral consideration from those without or with less moral worth" [See Godfrey Tangwa, "The Traditional African Perception of a Person," 40]. For critical remarks on the understanding of personhood in western philosophy see Hubbeling, "Some Remarks on the Concept of Person," 9–24.

42. Menkiti, "Person and Community," 172.

43. Speaking of the inherent problem in associating the African understanding of personhood with the Western body and mind-soul dichotomy, Kwasi Wiredu observed, "The differences between this ontology of personhood and certain wellknown Western ones are obscured when what we have called the life principle is," for example, "identified with the Western notion of the soul. This translation was initiated by Western scholars, but now many Africans vie with them in sponsoring it. Yet, by this one act of assimilation, the African brings upon herself all the intellectual perplexities of the body-and-soul enigma of Western philosophy. The soul, in Western discourse, is indeed supposed to be the life principle of the human system. But it is also conceived as the seat of thought. Descartes speaks of mind and soul interchangeably. But none of the ontological inventories of personhood offered by the African peoples . . ." "assigns both the animating and the thinking functions to any one constituent. It follows that the soul cannot be identified with any of them." See Wiredu, "An Oral Philosophy of Personhood," 13.

44. On different perspectives and reactions to this thesis see Paul Riesman, "The Person and the Life Cycle," 71–138.

this traditional African setting, personhood is a state attained by fulfilling certain community expectations which are conceived to define personhood.[45] These community expectations are basically prescribed obligations, responsibilities, norms, and achievements which are communally recognized as pertinent to the conception of personhood.[46] Describing this understanding of personhood, L. Lungile Pato observed,

> The underlying thinking here is that an individual is never born whole and fully human. The family, the clan, the community or the nation to which one belongs enables the individual to become a mature human person. A person is socialised and occasionally resocialised and, in the process, given an identity, a place of belonging, human dignity and personhood.[47]

In fact, in Africa, one hears of people saying, "he is not a real man" or a person because such a person is either impotent, disabled, or even poor. In the same sense, one could also hear of people talking about a barren women that "she is not a woman," thus technically denying such a barren individual personhood. It is in this perspective that Wiredu has observed,

> [A]n individual may be said to be a person or not to be a person. Or, in a slightly more elaborate commentary, he might be said to be very much a person or not a person *at all*.[48]

In particular, this notion of personhood often defines personhood in terms of communal determinants. African society directly confers personhood on its individuals based on certain personal achievements that are accorded social or community importance. It is these defining accomplishments that warrant the possessing of personhood. In this communal understanding of personhood, Menkiti further observed,

---

45. The Bantu term *Ubuntu* has also being used to describe the unique understanding of a human person by Africans. Using this term, M. Mnyandu observed, "Ubuntu is not merely *positive human virtues* but the very human essence itself, which lures and enables human beings to become Abantu or humanized beings, living in daily self expressive works of love and efforts to create harmonious relationships in the community and the world beyond" [Mnyandu, "Ubuntu as the Basis of Authentic Humanity," 81]. In this perspective, Ubuntu or African conception of humanness needs the community in order to operate or function.

46. For the material and immaterial components of the human person in traditional African belief systems see Kagame, "The Problem of 'Man,'" 35–40; Gbadegesin, *African Philosophy*.

47. Pato, "Being Fully Human Being," 56.

48 See Wiredu, "An Oral Philosophy of Personhood," 15.

> The first contrast worth noting is that, whereas most Western views of man abstract this or that feature of the lone individual and then proceed to make it the defining or essential characteristic which entities aspiring to the description 'man' must have, the African view of man denies that persons can be defined by focusing on this or that physical or psychological characteristic of the lone individual. Rather, man is defined by reference to the environing community.[49]

Even though ideally African people believe that all human beings are "human," the society assumes that the degree of human personhood depends upon some distinguished characteristics or traits. The task of most African people in the long run is to possess these enviable characteristics in order to affirm their personhood. Thus young people or youths generally are deemed not technically "persons" because they have not taken the cherished responsibility of married life. In this understanding, to remain unmarried is a sign of unrealized personhood, and often African people conceive the unmarried as "incomplete individuals" or even "nonpersons" in the technical sense. In particular, Menkiti opined that, according to the African understanding, personhood is absent at the beginning or youthful stage of life, but he underscored the attribution of personhood to the aged, hence he noted, Africans often believed that "full personhood is not perceived as simply given at the very beginning of one's life, but is attained after one is well along in society, indicates straight away that the older an individual gets the more of a person he becomes."[50] In addition, Menkiti also observed,

> What we have here then is both a claim that a qualitative difference exists between old and young, and a claim that some sort of ontological progression exists between infancy and ripening old age. One does not just take on additional features, one also undergoes fundamental changes at the very core of one's being.[51]

Consequently, for example, most youths rush into married life without adequate preparation just because they want the respect, prestige and personhood ascribed to the married individual. In fact, in most African communities, the unmarried person is described with many derogatory terms which show the societal displeasure and disdain for his unmarried status.

49. Menkiti, "Person and Community," 171.

50. Ibid, 173.

51. Ibid.

In modern and Western conceptions of personhood often personhood is viewed as an inherent component of the human being which we possess from birth.[52] It is the common denominator that makes us human. This understanding presupposes that humans have no basic contribution to their becoming of human persons because it is what they innately possess before any acts of either good or bad on their own part. Thus in this peculiar Western thinking, personhood is a characteristic or quality that is metaphysically tied to our humanness. It is the direct constituent of our humanity, thus it is within the philosophical category of our "being" rather than our "doing."[53] By placing personhood within the category of our "being," we mean that personhood is an essential quality that comes naturally from our classification as human beings. It is what God has bestowed intrinsically in our being as human beings. It is neither acquired nor conferred on one by a human community because it is intricately connected to our description as human beings. Contrary to this understanding, the African society generally believed that it is in our "doing" of the accepted norms or obligations of the society that we attain certain degree of personhood. Thus personhood is outside the sphere of "being" and categorized as part of "doing." In this way of thinking, the "being" of human beings becomes worthless without a corresponding quest to attain "personhood" in the defined and accepted mores of human society. In this perspective, Wiredu is right to note that "to be called a person is to be commended" by the African community.[54] Significantly, this conception of personhood is closely tied to African communal ideology which often ignored or even annihilates the individuality of the persons for the sake of communal solidarity. This overarching communal conception often blurs the individual in order to assert a corporate function. To this end, Kapolyo rightly noted, "[i]n African anthropology it is impossible to deal with human beings apart from their cultural surroundings or identity."[55]

---

52 In particular, rationality is often described as this common denominator which defined the personhood of humanity; however, this assumption has become suspect since this category is largely deficient in speaking of human dignity. For example, John F. Cosby has made an insightful treatment of the subject of human dignity in reference to the "incommunicably" and "irreplaceably" component of the human personhood rather than the commonality of rationality. See Cosby, "The Twofold Source," 292–306.

53. This dominant understanding of personhood in western philosophy has being challenged. For example, Alistair McFadyen has spoken "against the individualistic claim that persons precede relations" [See McFadyen, *The Call to Personhood*, 107].

54. See Wiredu, "An Oral Philosophy of Personhood," 15.

55. Kapolyo, *The Human Condition*, 117.

In particular, the underlying corporate identity of the African worldview places emphasis on the corporate at the expense of the individual. Thus at the core of this communal thinking, it is human society that gives "personhood" to individuals, and thus the fate of each individual within such community hangs in the balance because his acceptance and recognition as a "person" depends on the vested interests of the community.[56] Consequently, human individuals in African society strive in every way possible to attain, possess or achieve "personhood" in his lifetime because failure to attain "personhood" places one eternally within the class of the obscure, nonentities and faceless individuals of African society. To evade such a horrible fate, most often African people strive to attain "personhood" in the constructed traditional descriptions. This striving to attain "personhood" can be a healthy exercise since it makes each individual member of African society accountable to the community because his "personhood" is tied to collective approval, recognition or acceptance of the community, however, the quest to possess such "personhood" often degenerates to a kind of insatiable desire to possess material things or the needed affluence which often are key to the attainment of one's status as a "person." Inevitably, corruption and excessive greed become a sure way to procure or assert one's personhood and general importance. Even though traditional African people frowned at corruption or other vices, the existential necessity to attain "personhood" often overrides this ethical predilection, thus placing emphasis on one's ability to attain personhood. Consequently, it is not surprising that most African communities would still identify with a corrupt leader as long as he or she seeks to attain personhood in the prescribed traditional ways.

Within this general conception of "personhood," Africans drive to attain prestigious sense of "personhood" often leads to the compromise of ethical standards and bringing the entire drive for personhood into disrepute. In contemporary time, this drive to fulfill or attain "personhood" is expressed in several ways. For example, the quest for flashy cars, exquisite building, elaborate marriage ceremonies, expensive social functions, polygamous relationships, many children, importation and use of foreign goods and the continuous temptation of African leaders to permanently stay in public office can all be traced to the quest or drive for personhood

---

56. It is from this communal orientation of the African society that Desmond Tutu observed, "We say in our African idiom a person is a person through other persons. A totally self sufficient human being is ultimately subhuman. We are made for complementarity . . . So we need each other to become fully human." See Tutu, *An African Prayer*, xiv.

that most Africans want to satisfy by means of these channels. Consequently, almost everything on the African continent that is wrong could be connected to the "psychological incompleteness" that most Africans feel which comes as a result of their inability to attain "personhood" in the prescribed mode, that is, in accordance to the African traditional worldview. This idea of personhood as already seen is different from "self-hood" since the community plays a significant role in the attainment of such status. In this setting, selfhood becomes a strange concept because people's personhood is conferred on them by the community, and thus the human person actually seeks the community to warrant him or her such recognition. In this defining nature of the African community, the dictum by Mbiti is right that African people conceive of themselves in terms of a cohesive community with each individual affirming that "I am because we are, and we are because I am."[57]

On the other hand, despite its communal tone as readily seen in the defining way the society ascribes personhood to the individual members of the community, the attainment of such personhood is clearly an individual thing because each individual is expected to work at achieving or attaining "personhood."[58] The failure to attain the desired or enviable sense of personhood is not a failure of the community but of the individual, hence the individual is often blamed for his inability to attain this status.

In addition, despite this ingrained or entrenched understanding of personhood, the African people also recognize the physical differences between human persons and non-persons such as objects or non-human things. Ironically, they chose to categorize human persons who fail to attain personhood in the category of non-persons.[59]

Interestingly, "personhood" in traditional African understanding can be acquired as well as lost. Menkiti has already alluded to the possibility of African people losing their personhood at the time of death, when it is expected that the dead gradually loses his personhood as he or she now joins the impersonal congregation of the dead ancestors.[60] However, even before then, one could lose his "personhood" by failing to carry out

57. Mbiti, *African Religions and Philosophy*, 141.

58. In this perspective, Kapolyo rightly observed that in Africa "[t]he prominence or primacy of community does not mean that individuality is abhorred or obliterated" (Kapolyo, *The Human Condition*, 41). Consequently, one's individuality is truly respected in the quest to achieve personhood.

59. For the contemporary discussions on the subject of human dignity in relationship to non-human objects see Linville, "A Defense of Human Dignity," 320–32.

60. Menkiti, "Person and Community." 174–75.

to the end the prescribed obligations of the human community.[61] Despite the excellent description of the acquisitional nature of personhood in the traditional African society, the weakness of Menkiti's position is his treatment of the attainment of "personhood" as a onetime act which when gotten cannot be lost until the time of death.[62] However, contrary to this position, it is commonly accepted that one can lost his personhood since it is the community that confers "personhood" and thus it is also possible that the community can also take such "personhood" at will. Wiredu rightly observed, "personhood," under this African understanding, "is something that one can gain and later lose."[63]

Unfortunately, it is this fear of losing their hard earned sense of "personhood" that often pushes African leaders to stay in continuous power because leaving office is a signal of a corresponding demise in their conceived "personhood." Thus, at all costs, African leaders stick to power because their offices are not merely "offices" in the Western sense, but places that aid their attainment of personhood, and therefore, resignation, retirement or vacating of the office is a heavy blow on their "personhood." Consequently, since the office becomes part and parcel of their sense of personhood, they find it impossible to relinquish or step down from their office. This understanding of personhood inevitably has grave consequences for governance in African society because most Africans want to carry on in their offices to the grave, hence retirement, resignation or stepping down becomes undesirable because it destroys their sense of personhood. This largely contributes to the difficulty encountered by African leaders as they seek to go or move out of public offices. The threat of losing "personhood" is a threat of annihilation since the loss of personhood renders extinct the human persons and also contributes to his transition

---

61. Indirectly Menkiti noted this possibility when he said, "As far as African societies are concerned, personhood is something at which individuals could fail, at which they could be competent or ineffective, better or worse. Hence, the African emphasized the rituals of incorporation and the overarching necessity of learning the social rules by which the community lives, so that what was initially biologically . . . become a person with all the inbuilt excellencies implied by the term." See Menkiti, "Person and Community," 173.

62. Menkiti implied the possibility of losing one's personhood when he observed, ""personhood is something which has to be achieved, and is not given simply because one is born of human seed. . . . As far as African societies are concerned, personhood is something at which individuals could fail, at which they could be competent or ineffective, better or worse" (See Menkiti, "Person and Community,"172).

63. See Wiredu, "An Oral Philosophy of Personhood," 16.

to a non–person. Noting the Western discomfort with this African understanding of person, Wiredu added,

> Despite some momentum in the career of the normative view of personhood . . . , there is still among many English speaking people, to say the least, a discomfort with the notion that a human being could be supposed to be less than a person. This discomfort arises, I suggest, from a clash of oral intuitions reflecting the deep difference between African communalism and Western individualism.[64]

Significantly, this understanding naturally keeps the African people constantly on their toes whether in their quest to attain personhood or their quest to preserve such highly valued personhood. It is cogent that Christian theology should address this conception of personhood in the traditional African worldview which often spills over into the life of most Christians. It will also help in providing Christian direction to the common mystical association of public offices to personhood. This is a formidable problem because the art of governance is often less productive and ineffective as a result of people's association of their "personhood" to the offices which they occupy. It is wrong to presume that "my continuous importance as a person" or "my personhood" is tied to the office which I hold." Christian theology must provide biblical understanding of the human person, and use the biblical framework in critical engagement with the traditional acquistional nature of personhood in African society.

Biblical Teaching on the Human Personhood

Within the Bible the origin of the human person is not found in some evolutionary process as general underscored by present scientific guesses rather the origin of the human race is depicted as decisively the initiative of God.[65] Almost all the creation stories and myths in Africa recognize that the creation of the human race was directly or indirectly connected to God. Even though often they conceive of an intermediary being or animal as directly causing the existence of the human being, yet there is the overall recognition that God was the creator of the human race. The reason for assigning creation to an intermediary being or animal might

---

64. Ibid., 16.

65. For a description on biblical anthropology in sensitivity to some aspects of African cultural perspectives see Kapolyo, *The Human Condition*, 46–170.

be to disassociate God from the state of the world as occasioned by evil, problems and suffering. Thus the myths often refuse to identify God with such a creation, even though ultimately they recognize the Supreme Being as the creator of the human race. Contrary to this understanding, the Bible underscores that the human race was a direct creation of God. The biblical account depicted God as actively involved in the making of the first human couple. The Bible speaks of the human person as created in the "image and likeness of God."[66] This description conspicuously defined the biblical sense of personhood since the essence of the human being is closely tied to God rather than the human community. The human being is a person because he or she draws innately his beingness from God. The environment or surrounding has no contribution to add to his essential quality as a person. This theocentric nature of biblical personhood is contrary to the dominant role of the African community in conferring personhood. The divine declaration to create a being in his own *image* and *likeness* constitutes a declaration to confer on man among other things a unique sense of personhood. While the *imago dei* has been variously described in substantive, relational, functional and conditional terms, it must with these preceding descriptions or meanings carries the unique sense of human personhood because it is the characteristics that set the human being above the animal and vegetable world. In a sense, the *imago dei* appears to be a unique Hebraic idiom that describes the unique status of the human being above the rest of creation. Consequently, human personhood becomes an aspect or expression of the *imago dei* without exhausting the other possible meanings that the terms might have conjured in the minds of the ancient Jewish people. In addition, this biblical conferment of personhood to the human race clearly places the different members of the human race on the same pedestal and thus goes against any cultural assumption of the superiority of another human race over the other, or the political, biological and cultural persuasions that assign sub-human status to some species of the human race through some pseudo-scientific conclusions, cultural worldviews, political ideologies and economic parameters. In Africa, for example, sub-human status is ascribed to unmarried persons or the uninitiated of a particular community cult. In other places in Africa, it is the man in a monogamous relationship or those physically challenged such as the blind, the lame, or the dumb. In some other places,

66. See Genesis 1:26–28. For the understanding of the "image of God" as the extension and manifestation of the deity rather than just mere representation of the deity see Herring, "A Transubstantiated Humanity," 480–94.

it is the female gender or families which are descended from slaves; while in other places, it is the poor masses of struggling humanity. Similarly, those of influential status such as the rich, the aged, those of royal family and people of magic crafts, or even people of polygamous unions are often conceived of as superhuman or of enviable status. In the Western world, it is the educated, the celebrity, the young and the rich that are the valued persons within the society. Consequently, disregard or contempt for the illiterate, the fat person, the aged and the ugly persons are often common. Similarly, outward artistic beauty is also given some degree of consideration particularly as revealed in the general dislike and contempt for the unattractive or short people. Such cultural methods of adding value or demeaning the worth of the human person runs contrary to the biblical declaration that the human race with its diverse social, cultural, economic and physical constitutions are all the product of the divine image and likeness. In this biblical orientation lies the cure for such hideous cultural or political ideologies of the superiority of a race and the devilish human tendencies to demean members of its own species as sub-human or non-human.

At the heart of biblical teaching stands a dominant emphasis on the fall, however before considering the fall of the human race in relationship to our personhood, we must in passing highlight the purpose, goal and the significance of the divine creation of the human race in his own image. As to the reason for the creation of man, there is one biblical answer namely that the human race was created for the glory of his Maker (Isa 43:7; Eph1:11–12; 1 Cor 10:31). When we say we are created for the glory of God are we not merely repeating some already taught Sunday School answer or boring lines from our catechism or baptismal classes? It is true that the word, "glory" is not an everyday term. It is often used within the religious setting to describe God or other hallowed beings. However, the usage of glory to describe the whole duty or existence of humans to God bears this same understanding and much more. Even though we will not occupy ourselves with the intricacies of this term, in Pauline thought it connotes absolute obedience and submission to the divine revealed will (1 Cor 10:31; 2 Cor 4:4; Eph 1:12; 1 Thess 2:12). Using the analogy of a maker and the object made or for example a carpenter and the chair he made, the item created or made reveals the glory of the maker without any work on its part whether good or bad. The glory derived in this case is seen without any activity on the part of the object. Thus, the chair or table of the carpenter in question reveals the glory or artistry of the carpenter without any participation by the chair or table. Is it also possible to say that without any activity on the part of creation that there is passively the revelation of the glory of God within creation? Such a thesis has biblical approval particularly in the general descriptions by the biblical writers that nature reveals the glory of its Maker (See Ps 19:1). Consequently, while nature and the human race reveal passively the glory of God as seen in his intellectual and physical endowments, in Pauline thought such glory is much more reflected in human activity undertaken to obey and submit to divinely revealed purposes and will.

It was the inability of the first couple to obey or submit to the divine revealed will that led to the fall and the imputation of the sinful nature on all their subsequent descendants. The story of the fall emphasized this basic presupposition that the human race lost paradise because of their inability to obey or submit to the divine injunction.[67] The Edenic rebellion of the human race brought about the biblical doctrine of inherited sin or genealogical corruption of the human race (Gen 3:1–19). It also presupposes that our personhoods were variously affected by the corruptions that came with the fall. We could trace the origin of inferiority complexes, poor self-image and distortions of our personhoods to this event. We could also trace the origin of human cultural taboos, religious practices, and political ideologies which deny personhood to the members of the human race to this same event. Similarly, the fall begins the sorrowful tales of human plots and schemes to sabotage or disfranchise his fellow human beings of his sense of personhood. In the story of the fall lies the beginning of the obsessive quest by the human powers and communities which everyday seek to deny the worth, value and dignity of the human persons.

Significantly, in the imputation of the sinful nature on the entire human race lies the paradox of biblical revelation, and this presupposes the necessity of human salvation through Jesus Christ.[68] It also underscores the need of salvation or restoration of our human personhoods in order to reflect even though dimly the original worth conferred on us by God as his image bearers. Salvation in this sense will consists of the holistic redemption of our entire being and thereby offering us the freedom to serve God in the newness of the spirit that is no longer enslaved to the cultural ideologies that claim to denies or confers personhood.[69] In this

67. Genesis 3:1–19.

68. On the edenic relationship between the sexes and some theological responses to feminism see Cotterell, *Feminism and the Bible;* Foh, *Women and the Word of God;* Clark, *Man and Woman in Christ;* Mickelsen, ed. *Women, Authority, and the Bible;* Piper, *What's the Difference?.*

69. The theology of divine imputation raises a serious theological problem for

newness of life in Christ, our personhood is not merely an identity we acquire from our changing human communities, but it an enduring sense of personhood that is based on the belief and acceptance of Jesus' sacrifice on the cross which sets us free from deep-sated ills that had marred our worth and value as human being. In this sense, salvation is not merely the redemption of the soul or spirit, but the repositioning of the entire human personhood totally in conforming to the person and works of Jesus Christ. In this later understanding, the Christian sense of personhood is not only theocentric but Christocentric because it is renewed in the image of Jesus Christ and commissioned daily to follow in his very steps. It is this image of a renewed humanity whose identity or personhood is now Christ-centered that we see in the book of Acts working on behalf of Jesus Christ and conferring on men and women power for authentic living. It is this renewed humanity and with a sense of transformed personhood that actually turned the Greco-Roman world upside down. The New Testament vision of this renewed humanity is clearly climaxed in the calling of Christians now as the "sons and daughters" of God who are now empowered with the power of the Holy Spirit to live this new authentic life

---

Christian theology because it is not humanly comprehensible for the crime committed by the people we do not know such as Adam and Eve to have rippling effects on the entirety of the human race. The rippling or relational effects of sin are evident in our world today. The sin of the mother has a way of affecting the unborn child, the sin of the father has a way of destroying the social life of the son, the sin of a family has a way of ruining a community, and the sin of a community has a way of ruining the entirety of a state or a nation [On the general problem of sin and evil see Feinberg, *The Many Faces of Evil*; idem, *Theologies and Evil*; Peterson, *Evil and the Creation*; Plantinga, *God, Freedom and Evil*; Carson, *How Long, O Lord?*; Geisler, *The Roots of Evil*]. In this way, the rippling effects of sin could be used to argue for the transference of sin to the entire human race. For example, the terrorist acts of Osama Bin Ladin on September 11th 2001 have affected not only American attitudes towards the Arab race, but have fundamentally affected American foreign policies and relationship to other nations of the world. Every Arab or black is seen as a potential Osama Bin Ladin and thus such phobia and suspicion has led to maltreatment and often the unjust treatment of innocent people. The unleashing of wrath on people in the aftermath of September 11 is a psychological transference of the wrath against Osama Bin Ladin on anything or persons that have some close or distant relationship to the said culprit. This illustration even though helpful might not necessarily answer the deep seated theological question that impinges on the theology of divine imputation. Thus somehow, through the disobedience of Adam and Eve, mysteriously the sin nature which all of us closely know became a part of our being or nature. Fundamentally, it was this change of nature or the imputation of divine righteousness in Jesus Christ that becomes the good news revealed in the advent of the New Testament. Through the death of Jesus Christ on the cross and his subsequent resurrection, the New Testament underscores that such imputation of righteousness has taken place in our spirit.

of God in Christ. By this theology of adoption, the Christian believer is now a member of God's family and fully endowed with the needed power and new identity to change the world. Like Jesus, the Christian believer is not only human but also divine and has everything necessary to live the authentic life of God as Jesus did.

Conclusion

The crisis of the modern world is a crisis of personhood which has revealed itself continually in form of identity crisis and other forms of internal confusions and mental dislocations. This feeling of dis-personalization at home and in workplace is not really new. In the modern era, even though it has its origins largely during the industrial revolution and the introduction of machines into homes and the office place, a kind of chronic-depersonalized living has continually characterized the adoption and use of computers and gadgets of science both at home and the working place. In addition to these technological revolutions are political, social, religious and cultural factors which further fanned the loss of personhood in the modern world. For example, the ineffectiveness of political powers in democratic terms has largely affected the people ruled who often compromised their humanity or give away all forms of person-ness in order to meet their existential needs. The failure of modern political structures has ultimately led to the annihilation of human personhood, compromised of its presence and the negotiation of its terms. This failure largely accounts for the continuous presence of many groups of dehumanized or depersonalized people loitering the streets of our cities begging and sleeping under the bridges as a means of fending off the harsh political and economic realities which seek to annihilate their humanness and personhood. For these people, the quest to survive has caused the erosion of their humanity which also affected their personhood. With such eroded personhood they became social outcasts which sense of personhood is denied or remotely entertained. In Africa, this depersonalized existence is further complicated by the disappearance and collapse of the extending family systems and the falling apart of tribal and ethnic solidarity fronts. These cultural factors also directly attack the sense of personhood, thus further contributing to the inability to secure and attain personhood. In addition, the shifting and changing natures of modern religions and it continuous impersonal dispositions have brought about fanatic and fundamental religious groups who seek a return back to the closely-knitted faith communities of persons that began these religions. The quest to return to the communities sons whether back to the religious times of Mohammed or the time early church and Jesus Christ is a quest to return to a time which these religious traditions is commonly idolized as a time of pure au͟ _......͟ faith that help people to live or attain an authentic sense of personhood. In this regard, the renewed violence by Islamic terrorist sects, for example, is a quest to find the eluded community of faithful persons which exists at the time of the prophet. Hence the promotion of Sharia and its attending legislations is intended to create a community of faithful persons which will usher in a time like the one of the prophet.

In these perspectives, almost everything that is now wrong in the modern world could be readily traced back to failure of the unrealized self or the annihilation of human personhood whether in religion, politics or within the socio-cultural arena. This understanding makes "personhood" a crucial subject for theology because ultimately theology is the quest to discover, find and realized the authentic human life which was originally given by God, but was lost through the fall. Seen in this perspective, Christian theology must help the realization of the authentic self or personhood which now largely has eluded our world. It is here the task of theology must begin and end because it is in rediscovering our authentic personhood and living by the blueprints of this new identity in Christ that we directly fulfill all the ethical requirements of the Bible.

The preceding discourses observe that authentic personhood whether in Western and African point of views are grossly inadequate to base our identities. It notes that our personhoods must come from the biblical vision of a new community. This new community is a renewed humanity where lies the image of God *par excellence*. The New Testament vision of this new community in Christ is the Christian and biblical answer for the innate human quest for authentic personhood and fulfillment. Accordingly, the power to live the authentic human life and to affect and touch the world lies in the discovery of the Christ-centered kind of personhood. It is the power from this new identity that helped the early church to transform the society, and it is also in this same new identity or new personhood that will come the continuous impact of the Christian faith on the human society.

Consequently, Christian theology in systematic texts must give this concern a pivotal centre and not merely as a topic or sub-topics at the fringe of its theological reflections. Past systematic texts have noted in passing the humanity of the human race, but this must extend specifically now to people or persons in the grey areas of nonpersons. It must particularly help them to come to the full knowledge of the New Testament's concept of a new humanity in Christ whom are divinely commissioned to change the world. The good news of the New Testament is that God has found a new community of persons which is not based on race, color and creeds and conferred on this same community the power to live the authentic life. Christian theology must make this biblical emphasis and help to see that the non-persons of the human society are offer the opportunity for this new personhood and train to live daily in the power and self-understanding of this new life and Christ-transformed personhood.

8

The Person of Christ

Introduction

THE CENTRALITY OF JESUS Christ to the Christian faith cannot be overstated since the Christian faith derives its essence in the person of Jesus Christ. Without right emphasis on the centrality of Christ, the Christian faith loses its essence and hence becomes truly meaningless. Unfortunately, peripheral concerns have taken the attention of the church, which often define the centrality of the Christian faith around other things rather than on the person of Christ. Underscoring the importance of Jesus Christ to Christianity, John F. Walvoord rightly notes,

> Christianity by its very name has always honored Jesus Christ as its historical and theological center. No person has been more essential to its origination and subsequent History and no set of doctrines has been more determinative than the doctrines and of the work and person of Jesus Christ. In approaching a study of Christology, one is therefore concerned with central rather than peripheral theological matters.[1]

For many Africans, the person of Jesus Christ is such a center and a point of constant fascination. This is easily reflected in the centrality of Christology in their songs, prayers, sermons and various religious observances. Jesus Christ is indeed the centre of African Christianity. At the heart of African Christianity despite its cultural orientation as seen within the

---

1. Walvoord, "Christ in Contemporary Theology," 11.

expression of African Independent Churches, African Christianity is in every aspect Christocentric in profession. Its basic message is that Jesus Christ saves. Consequently, the discussion of this chapter sets contextual Christology within the purview of classical Christological discussions by affirming the humanity and deity of Jesus Christ and also acknowledging the various aspects of redemption particularly as reflected in its application. It also highlights some theological problems especially in the Christological proposals by the African theological discourse.

The Historical Jesus

Unfortunately, despite the benevolent and peaceful portraits of Jesus Christ within the pages of the scriptures, the person of Jesus Christ has through church history engendered endless controversies and debates. Through such controversies, the claims of Jesus Christ to Godhood have been put to scientific and historical scrutiny. The search for a historical Jesus has marked the climax of such theological investigation which seeks to rediscover the true person of the Galilean peasant who radically changed the world.

Even though the search for the historical Jesus has ended in dismal failure, the modern search for the historical Jesus has within contemporary time revealed itself in various dimensions.[2] This modern fascination for the person of Jesus has subsequently resulted in the resurgence of the quest for the historical Jesus in some modern forms such as the *DaVinci Code* and *Discovery Channel Saga* which claims to have found the tomb of Jesus Christ. What often amaze me, is the diachronic tendencies in the studies of Christology particularly as it lies in the Western propensity to

2. For a basic theological discussion on Christology see Klaas Runia, *The Present-Day Christological Debate* (Leicester: InterVarsity Press, 1984); Alister E. McGrath, *Understanding Jesus: Who He is and Why He Matters* (Grand Rapids: Zondervan, 1987); Murray J. Harris, *Jesus As God* (Grand Rapids: Baker, 1992); Richard Longnecker, *The Christology of Early Jewish Christianity* (London: SCM, 1970); Harold O. J. Brown, *The Image of Christ in the Mirror of Heresy and Orthodoxy From the Apostles to the Present* (Garden City, New Jersey: Doubleday, 1984); David F. Wells, *The Person of Christ: A Biblical and Historical Analysis of the Incarnation* (Westchester, Illinois: Crossway, 1984); Howard I. Marshall, *I believe in the Historical Jesus* (Grand Rapids: Eerdnmans, 1977); Donald Guthrie, *Jesus the Messiah* (Grand Rapids: Zondervan, 1972); C. F. D. Moule, *The Origin of Christology* (Cambridge: Cambridge University Press, 1977); John F. Walvoord, *Jesus Christ Our Lord* (Chicago: Moody, 1969); Millard Erickson, *The Word Became Flesh: A Contemporary Incarnational Christology* (Grand Rapids: Baker, 1991).

divide Christology into two halves, one historical and the other theological. This quest for the historical Jesus has been ongoing without fruitful theological benefit in the long run to the church or the academic community. In arguing that the early church invented the Christ of faith which is often assumed to be a dim reflection of the actual historical Jesus, it is presumed, as modern discussion so far has shown, that the church was theologically correct, but historically wrong.

However, to pursue this present enquiry, we must understand the mechanics of history or historical narration especially in its ancient expression. When we define history as the narration of past events, this modern definition suggests that the work of history is done whenever dates and events are recalled or narrated. However, it should also be observed that the narration of history should include the lenses used in the interpretation of the said historical data. In this regard, narration of "history for history's sake" was a strange phenomenon in the ancient world as rightly attested in the work of Herodotus, Thucydides and Josephus, who even though claim to convey "history for history's sake," fall short of such a lofty goal. Consequently, even within these classical historical works, there were varying interpretative lenses used to interpret and analyze past history. They did not merely relate the events of the past, but they interpreted or filtered these events through the political, sociological and theological hermeneutical lenses, so that everything they related are a partial form of the actual events that took place since another person could have related the same historical data through different hermeneutical lenses and arrive at varying historical conclusions. We have to come to terms with the understanding that the quest to narrate history for history's sake was a development that came with Western civilization and the rationality of modern academia. However, even within these spheres, it is still doubtful whether we have actually attained an impeccable narration of history or past that is devoid of sentimental attachments or whether we could develop one universal historical methodology in order to come to universal historical conclusions on a single particular event. For example, even though the dates and times of the American invasion of Iraq or the September 9/11 are forever ingrained in our memories, there are diverging interpretative lenses employed to understand the source, nature and global implications of these two events. No two historical analysts have agreed on the political, economic and theological or religious source, nature or significance of these events.

If such an objective narration of history is contemporarily a mirage or a delusion of the modern academic enterprise as many honest individuals would readily admit, then our criticisms against New Testament authors that they are historical inaccurate and theologically correct is not right from the onset. These individuals are not interpreting history "for history's sake" as the modern scientific mind would have wished, but they are narrating history, however, as custodians of theological convictions. Thus, theological lenses or motifs guided the selection and the interpretations of the historical materials they are confronted with. For example, the story of the coming of the Holy Spirit in Acts 2 could have been narrated by a historian whose interest was "history for history sake" as a stupor from the drinking of wine that characterized the Jewish celebration of the Pentecost, but on the other hand, the writer of Acts saw in this historical event a Christological significance that has its source in the prophecies of Joel. It is this same predilection that generally motivates the rereading of the life of the historical Jesus in a newer note of faith. In retrospect, the Easter celebration provided the early church with the interpretative fulcrum or lenses to understand the meaning and importance of Jesus Christ.

Thus, dividing Christology into historical and theological or the Jesus of history and the Christ of faith is not only slick solution to the enigmatic character of Jesus, but a misunderstanding of the merger of historical and theological elements in the practice of ancient narration. Seen in this persuasion, ancient Jewish historiography in particular saw history as a collaboration of theological and non-theological elements. They are not related to tell us dates or events, but to tell us the derived theological significance of these events in divine perspective. Thus, history in this understanding becomes a vehicle of theology and the Jesus of history becomes in this regard the Jesus of faith.

In Africa, the thought of weaving theological and historical lines as one and the same is not really a difficult task or an issue at all since often African stories of great men or women began with historical events and persons and thence, the translation of such events and persons turned into some form of prestigious religious tales or supernatural stories. However, underneath these tales are a theological or religious revelation of the significance that Africans attach to such a person or event. Thus, as such the dichotomy between the Jesus of history and the Christ of faith is actually a Western fad, which unfortunately sought to impose a Western twenty-first-century academic agenda on ancient New Testament writings. S. Oyin Abogunrin in his inaugural lecture on *In Search of the Original*

Jesus captured the general feelings of Africa on the subject of the quest for the historical Jesus. He asked, "Of what value to Africa is the current debate on the historicity of the Gospels, as well as the question of the historical Jesus?"[3] Answering this same question, Abogunrin observed, "African Christianity has benefited tremendously from the cumulative labours of Western scholars" however, such quest for historical Jesus is unhealthy for the African people because, according to Abogunrin,

> Majority of Africans still live in the world of the New Testament, where belief in demons and a host of unseen supernatural powers is still potent and real. A Jesus emptied of all such supernaturalism as is contained in the Gospels would therefore be meaningless in the African setting.[4]

Significantly, such theological hypothesis has occasioned the rise of reconstruction of the traditional Christology in the category of the African pre–Christian past rather than historical investigation into the historicity of the Jesus events.[5] The preceding discourse indeed provided a necessary introduction to the understanding of the enigmatic character of Jesus in history, church tradition and scriptures. Traditionally, the doctrine of Christology averred that Jesus Christ was fully God and fully man in one person, and will be thus forever. Hence, the common dictum, *He is hundred percent of the very God and hundred percent of the very Man.* The humanity and deity of Christ is of uppermost significance both within the Bible and church history, it therefore important to understand the main thrust of biblical teaching in this direction especially in the context of contemporary Christological proposals in Africa.

African Christological Quest

Charles Nyamiti has rightly observed that "Christology is the subject which has been most developed in today's African theology."[6] This assertion can readily be seen in the different Christological discussions taking place right now on the African continent. Looking closely at the important works in this direction, there are four dominant Christological methodologies. These four African Christological methodologies are

3. Abogunrin, "In Search of the Original Jesus," 38.

4 Ibid., 39.

5. See S.O. Abogunrin, *et al*, eds., *Christology in African Context*, 1–411.

6. Nyamiti, "African Christologies Today," 3.

namely the comparative Christological methodology, the systematic Christological methodology, the liberationist Christological methodology and the community-oriented Christological methodology.[7] Interestingly, these four Christological methodologies fall broadly within the immanent Christological methodologies and thus as we shall see, these Christological proposals sought to wrestle contextually with the cultural realities in the African context, particularly the traditional religious forms in African pre-Christian past.

The first Christological methodology, the comparative method seeks to reconstruct Christology by the amalgamation of biblical Christological category and the African conception of the universe around him. Often, this model employs the usage of the historical Jesus of the gospel as Christological forms that are compatible with the African general worldview. The starting point of such Christological reconstruction could either begins with the Bible or the African cultural categories, however the Christ that emerges from such a synthesis of the African culture with the biblical material is often distinctively African.[8] The theological presuppositions underlying the quest of African Christology in the comparative definition come from the realization that classical Christologies with the popular appellations such as "messiah," "Christ," "Son of Man," and "Son of David" are understood to have little significance for the African people, While Christological titles such as "servant of God," "Lord," "savior," and "Son of God" are often portrayed in works that undergird this thesis as greatly relevant in the African context. Similarly, Christological works exploring this theological methodology often employs the usage of traditional African cultural categories such as "ancestor,"[9] "elder brother," "firstborn," "chief," "master of initiation" and "healer" as fundamental Christological tools.[10] Kwesi Dickson exploring this model had viewed Christ in the African cultural category of the ancestor.[11] Restating this thesis, Dickson observed,

7. These four theological approaches to African Christology are taken from Okoye, "African Theology," 9–17.*See also* <www.insect–african catholictheology.htm>

8. See McCarthy, "Christology," 29–48.

9. On the correlation between the mediating roles of the ancestors and angels in the inter–testament period see King, "Angels and Ancestors," 10–26.

10. For works exploring this comparative model see the contributions in the work, Schreiter, ed. *Faces of Jesus in Africa* ; Nkwoka, "Jesus as Eldest Brother," 87–103. For the implication of such model particularly the understanding of Christ as proto–ancestor in African ecclesiology see Sankey, "The Church as Clan," 437–49. For the understanding of Jesus as a brother see Kurewa, "Who Do You Say that I Am?" 182–88.

11. For similar construction of Christology using the framework of the ancestors and elder brother in Asia see Phan, "The Christ of Asia," 25–46.

> Christ was the perfect victim; by his death he merits to be looked upon as Ancestor, to use an African image, the greatest of ancestors, who never ceases to be one of the 'living-dead,' who lives because there will always be people alive who knew him, whose lives were irreversibly affected by his life and work... The physical cross, like the staffs and stools looked upon as material representations symbolizing the presence of the ancestor, becomes the symbol of Christ's being the ever-living.[12]

Dickson underscored that the continuous impact of Jesus' life and his eternality are credible basis that warrant his status as the greatest of the African ancestors. Thus, the dual attributes of eternality and the continuous impact of Jesus' life on the living through his death becomes the basis for Jesus' admission into the fold of African ancestorship as the head of the ancestral spirits. However, even within these definitions Christ transcends these said ancestors because he not only shares these attributes in great measure but his supremacy becomes credible since no known single African ancestor had the attributes of eternality and a lasting impact as does Christ from generation to generation.[13]

Similarly arguing for the same Christological reconstruction of Ancestor and the related category of "elder brother," Bediako, using the Akan cosmological background,[14] configured a Christology that primarily takes African spiritual cosmology seriously. For Bediako Christological ancestrology will bridge "the gulf between the intense awareness of the existence of God" and the noxious "'remoteness' in African Traditional Religion and experience"[15] of this same God. Constructing this christological bridge, Bediako noted,

> Our Saviour is our Elder Brother who shared in our African experience in every respect, except in our sin and alienation from God, an alienation with which our myths of origins make us only too familiar. Being our true Elder Brother now in the presence of God, his Father and our Father, he displaced the mediatorial function of our natural 'spirit-fathers' for these themselves need saving, since they originated from among us.[16]

12. Dickson, "The Theology of the Cross," 13.

13. On the perceived misrepresentation of the African ancestors see Dzobo, "African Ancestor Cult," 333–40.

14. For an attempt at developing an Asante Christology see Sarpong, "Asante Christology," 189–206.

15. Bediako, "Jesus in the African Culture," 101.

16. Ibid., 102.

For Bediako, Christ through the agency of his resurrection and ascension becomes the supreme Ancestor who went "to the realm of the ancestor spirits and gods,"[17] and thus became endowed with power and authority that transcends those of the ancestor. Restating this thesis, Bediako observed,

> From the kind of understanding held about the spirit-world, the resurrection and ascension of our Lord also come to assume great importance. He has now returned to the realm of Spirit and therefore of power. From the standpoint of Akan traditional beliefs, Jesus has gone to the realm of the ancestor spirits and the 'god.' We already know that power and the resources for living are believed to come from there, but the terrors and misfortunes which could threaten and destroy life come from there also.[18]

Bediako noted the implication of such understanding of Jesus assuming authority that superseded those of the ancestors. In respect to the implication of such thesis, Bediako revealed that "if Jesus has gone to the realm of the 'spirit' and 'gods,' so to speak, he has gone there as Lord over them in much the same way that he is Lord over us. He is therefore Lord over the living and the dead, and over the 'living-dead,' as the ancestors are also described." Thus, "He is supreme over all 'gods' and authorities in the realm of the spirits. So he sums up in himself all their powers and cancels any terrorizing influence they might be assumed to have upon us."[19] Bediako's thesis is that Christ has become Lord over the ancestral spirits 'in much the same way that he is Lord over us.' Understood in this definition, the Lordship of Christ implies the desacralization of the ancestral spirits whereby the ancestors are reduced to the mere status of humans and devoid of the terror associated with them. For Bediako, Jesus now perceived as Lord of both the living, the dead and the ancestor, successfully "displaces the mediatorial function of our natural 'spirit fathers'" and assumes such roles in very important redefined forms that transcend those of the ancestors.[20] Despite the theological strides recorded in this comparative direction of Christological reconstruction, criticism for such integration and incorpo-

17. Ibid., 103.

18. Ibid.

19. Ibid.

20. For a detailed analysis of Bediako's other christological formulations such as Chief, warrior, saviour, high priest, lord, reformer etc. see Fotland, "The Christology of Kwame Bediako," 36–49. See also, Van den Toren, "Kwame Bediako's Christology," 218–32 and Maluleke Sam, "In Search of 'The True Character,'" 210–19.

ration of forms from African traditional religion with Christian categories has been noted. Bediako himself observed,

> African non-Christian critics have vehemently rejected what they have regarded as African theology's attempt to 'christianise,' and hence to distort, African tradition. For them, the attempt to seek an integration of the pre-Christian religious tradition and African Christian experience is misplaced and unwarranted, being the search for the reconciliation of essentially and intrinsically antithetical entities.[21]

Similar criticisms of such Christological formulations from African traditional religion have also been noted among African Christian writers. Ernest Wendland noted the tendencies toward over-contextualized Christology in contemporary African religious thought, particularly in christological constructions that seek to portray Christ using the anthropological analogies in the triad categories of the Ancestor, Witchcraft and the Liberator.[22] P. N. D. Nwachukwu also observed that the usage of forms such as Ancestor, Healer, Warrior, Liberator and other similar forms from African traditional religion as categories for formulation of Christology poses "some apparent dangers for authentic Christian faith in Africa . . ."[23] because such definition as derived from the African traditional religion for "Christological formulation" are "inadequate and sometime misleading."[24] Others expressed fears that this 'hybrid Christology' that results from the direct mutation of African traditional forms and duly incorporated into biblical Christological categories inevitably has serious syncretic tendencies. Such fears of syncretism have generally necessitated works clamoring for the total uniqueness of Christ because of the assumed tendencies that these christological formulations are the direct antithesis of biblical christological forms.[25] While such fears are real, yet the criticism of these works often fails to translate such Christological criticism into positive Christological formulations that are compatible to the African traditional worldviews. More often than not, the alternative Christologies that are proposed as the "true biblical Christology" are actually Western

21. Bediako, *Jesus in Africa*, 49–50.

22. Wendland, "'Who Do People Say that I Am?'" 13–32.

23. Nwachukwu. *African Authentic Christianity*, 35.

24. Ibid., 35.

25. Abogunrin, "The Total Adequacy of Christ," 9–16. See also Obaje, "Theocentric Christology," 1–7.

Christologies, which are paraded as biblical Christology.[26] Nonetheless, the flaw of the comparative Christological methodology lies in its unhealthy preoccupation with the African pre-Christian forms and the inability to reveal the transcendent and biblical dimension of Christology in the quest to reconstruct an Africanized Christology.

The second approach to Christology in Africa employs the systematic model of constructing Christology. The model seeks to organize African traditional forms and incorporate them into the revealed truth, but also exploring in the process the mysteries connecting Christ and the church.[27] Under this definition, systematic Christology subjects the African themes to a scientific process and from such a procedure seek to recreate a Christology that is significantly colored by African themes. While sharing similarity with the comparative method in choice of themes such as ancestor or elder brother, it significantly differs from this model because of its metaphysical disposition and the understanding of vital participation in the processes of theological systematizing of the highlighted African themes. In this understanding, God and the ancestors are primarily perceived as the custodians of the vital force. The ancestor dispenses the vital energy for the sustenance of the African community particularly in the process of birth of all the African family members. As such, in order to have the life and vital energy necessary for existence proper relationship is thus maintained with God via the intermediaries of the ancestors. Significantly, systematic reconstruction of Christology views Christ's life and death as the true reservoir of the vital energy, which is conceived in traditional African society to be dispensed by the ancestors. In this systematic method, resurrection as part of redemption becomes important only because it initiated the process that empowered and endowed Christ with the vital energy via the death experience in the same way as the African ancestors. Hence, Christ is portrayed in the role of vital mediatorship. Even though this portrayal of Christ is important because it reveals Christological continuity between the African pre-Christian forms and the biblical Christology, such systematic Christological configuration largely reduces Him because it suggests that Christ's power or importance is conferred on Him through the processes of death and resurrection in similar fashion to the African ancestors. Undoubtedly, such a portrayal

26. For the contextual conditioning of western theology see Cook, "Significant Trends," 251–76. See also Sider, "Miracles," 237–50.

27. See Okoye, "African Theology," www.insect–african catholictheology.htm (accessed May 4, 2007).

of Christ is actually an aberration and a demotion of Jesus' Christological significance in traditional Christian thought. Other criticisms of the systematic Christological construction have also been noted particularly in its wrong assumption of the pervading nature of the vital participation of ancestors among African societies. A significant criticism has also been noted by James Okoye who observed,

> Does seeing Christ as ancestor limit his divinity? It would seem also that the African relation to the ancestors is more of a mutual entanglement than a living communion. A celibate, as Christ was, could hardly become an ancestor in the tradition; besides, the manner of Christ's death would not qualify him as an African ancestor. There may be issues of translation. It is not clear whether the people's faith associates Christ with the muzimu, the spirits of the dead toward whom the people entertain some ambivalent feelings.[28]

A study carried out by Timothy Palmer among pastors in theological training who are closely related to the church at the grassroots in northern Nigeria, revealed that the majority of these students vehemently reject the understanding of Christ in terms of the ancestor as suggested by African theological academia. Palmer, in the conclusion of his study, noted that such a sharp disparity between African academia and the voices of the students at the grassroots. Hence he observes that African ancestral Christology might after all be another of the ivory tower inventions of African scholars. At the end of his study, Palmer observed,

> In short, there is an incredible gap between the 'ivory-tower' scholarship of some of the academic professors and the experience of African students who are close to the 'grassroots.' The theology of Christ as an ancestor does not resonate with most of these respondents.[29]

Bluntly, Palmer affirmed, "I would like to suggest that the ancestorship of Christ causes too much confusion and does not meet the pastoral needs of the average Nigerian Christian."[30] The plausibility of Palmer's study may be challenged since the students sampled were not fresh students and thus, might have been already exposed to anti-`ancestral Christological thinking, which is often the hallmark of evangelical conservatism particularly as frequently seen in Western influenced theological institutions, however,

28. Ibid.
29. Palmer, "Jesus Christ: Our Ancestor?" 13.
30. Ibid.

Palmer's observation must be taken seriously since African church members at the grassroots are not largely preoccupied with an ancestral obsession as often insinuated by African academia. Significantly, at the grassroots, African Christian prayers, worship, liturgy and songs hardly reveal any ancestrology as now advocated among African theologians.

The flaw of this Christological construction can also be seen in its continuous tendency to systematize the African religious past,[31] which clearly lacks a legitimate theological ground. An example of such theological systematization can be seen in the works of Charles Nyamiti who sought to systematize the classical Christian Trinitarian concept to fit the African category of the ancestor. In respect to this approach, Nyamiti observed,

> With an understanding of ancestral relationship it is possible to examine the inner life of God (trinity) and discover that there is an ancestral kinship among the divine persons: the Father is ancestor of the Son, the Son is the descendant of the Father. These persons live their ancestral kinship through the Spirit whom they mutually communicate to as their ancestral oblation and Eucharist.[32]

While Nyamiti's systematization of the forms to fit into the Christian doctrinal conception of trinity is well-intentioned yet the configuration of African traditional forms to fit this neatly packaged Christian Trinitarian doctrinal form is at best faulty. The reason is that the tripartite conception of divinity is foreign to African traditional forms and therefore such systematization could never be successful without a distortion of the original components of the two forms that are undergoing theological synthesis. Seen in these antecedents the problems of Nyamiti's postulations become clearer. For example, when he noted that the "Father is ancestor of the Son" what does Nyamiti mean by such statement? Because in the African understanding of ancestorship, attaining to such a status only comes with death, and if this understanding is envisaged the question that follows is the desire to know at what point did the Father die to attain to the status of ancestor? Moreover, within the framework of such categorization, the

31. There are many problems generated by the African past, one such problem is the salvation of the African ancestor. For this discussion see Gehman, "Will the African Ancestors Be Saved?" 85–97.

32. Nyamiti, "The Trinity," 21–22. For Nyamiti's other works about this christological model see Nyamiti, "African Christologies Today," 17–39; *idem, Christ Our Ancestor*, 9–11.

Holy Spirit is merely reduced to the medium of communication of the supposedly "ancestral kinship" between God the Father and God the Son. In this theological scheme, the Holy Spirit loses his personhood, and becomes merely a vital glue to strengthen the ancestral bond. Taking these antecedents into consideration, the next question is whether this radical redefinition of the Christian forms by Nyamiti is not in an actual sense a distortion of the classical Trinitarian doctrinal conception of Christian divinity and hence confirms the fears of some observers as to the syncretic tendencies inherent in the current African reconstruction of Christology? Answering the question in relation to the allegation of syncretism[33] that often results in the adaptation of African traditional religious forms to express Christian truths, Lamin Sanneh observed,

> . . . in a different sense, Christianity itself is one of the most syncretistic of religions, if by that we mean the amalgamation of ideals and realities, of principles and mundane practice, for it is a pre-eminent theological teaching that through the incarnation the transcendent and terrestrial merged in human focus. The Christian poet describes it well: He laid his glory by, He wrapped him in our clay; unmarked by human eye, the Latent Godhead lay.[34]

Even with the tolerance suggested by Sanneh, the synthesis of African traditional forms and Christian categories in Christological formulations inevitably have serious theological consequences. This is because of the inherent modification and adjustment that the two forms in dialogical process undergo, which might not only be injurious to the two variables in question, but also may certainly affect the resulting christological formulation.[35] Thus, the flaw of this Christological methodology is its inherent obsession with African pre–Christian forms and the failure to harness local categories with classical Christological definitions.

The third Christological approach in Africa employs the framework of liberation. It focuses on the life of Christ on earth particularly in His quest to address the injustices and oppressive structures of the first century. Christ, under this definition, is seen primarily as a liberation symbol,

33. On the syncretic tendencies in African theological discourse see Kato, "Theological Issues in Africa," 144–53; *idem, Biblical Christianity in Africa; idem, Theological Pitfalls.*

34. Sanneh, "Reciprocal Influences," 234.

35. On a self–critical relationship to the ancestor see Kiwovele, "An African Perspective," 56–75.

which later became lost in the process of transposing the man Jesus into Christ in the early church.[36] Using the liberation framework of North and South America this Christological construction sought to portray a Christ that will address the injustice and oppression particularly of the South African context and Africa in general. Hence, the classical politically passive Christology is rejected. Similarly, the glowing eschatological Christology in traditional Christology is also rejected and in its place a liberational Christology is developed that is compatible with the yearning and aspirations of the oppressed in the African context. After the South African apartheid struggle, Christology in the South African context also sought to explore the reconciliation processes necessitated by such a context, whereby Christ's inclusive meals and other biblical forms are made to reflect the need of racial reconciliation and forgiveness. Similarly, using the framework of liberation, the African feminist movement made significant Christological formulations exploring the liberative dimension of the Bible and the Christian traditions to destabilize the patriarchal nature of African society and ecclesiastical structures in order to recreate a just society that will be fair to both genders. Exploring the liberative construction, Elizabeth Amoah and Mercy Oduyoye sought to emphasize the necessity of such a theological venture.[37] They understood that African male theologians have dominated christological discussion in Africa and significantly postulated some distinctive ways in which women in Africa see and understand Christ.[38] Terese M. Hinga writing from the Kenyan context captured women's understanding of Christ particularly exploring the liberative connotations of Jesus' titles such as saviour, healer, personal friend and liberator.[39]

However, dominant among these christological configurations in the category of liberation is the work of Jean-Marc Éla and J. N. K Mugambi. Even though their work lacks a systematic presentation of liberational

36. Okoye, "African Theology," www. insect–african catholictheology.htm(accessed May 4, 2007).

37. See Amoah and Oduyoye, "The Christ for African Women," 35–46.

38. For similar African feminist emphases see Ekeya, "The Christ Experience," 178–83; Tappa. "The Christ Event," 173–77. See also, Lagerwerf, "African Women Doing Theology," 1–69; Morny, "Christ Restores Life," 149–54 and Magesa, "Christology," 66–88.

39. See Hinga, "Jesus Christ," 183–94. In the following work, Hinga underscored the necessity whereby inculturation becomes a liberative framework that will lead to the liberation of entire aspects of the African social historical context. See Hinga, "Inculturation," 10–18.

Christologies, nonetheless it reveals a consistent theological emphasis on the christological framework of liberation. In the work of Éla, he explores the christological paradigm of liberation as a basis for political engagement in the African context. He called for the "rereading of the gospel"[40] in order to address the social-political landscape of African society. He noted the problem with missionary Christianity lies in its passivity towards addressing the problem of underdevelopment on the African continent. He observed,

> We Africans have been introduced to the Christian God by means of a theology of suffering, which seems to have been created so black people would learn to accept their historical status as a conquered people. That is the message of the curse on Canaan (9:25)—a myth used in catechisms, preaching, and prayers to record the genesis of an entire people caught up in a tragedy of identity with outcasts.[41]

However, Éla noted that in the midst of the plight of the African people, God has taken sides with the oppressed Africans.[42] Éla revealed, "The center of revelation is that a commitment has been made to the poor, and this commitment is rooted in a history where messianic dynamics are coming to life."[43] Éla appealed to the Exodus as a reflection of divine distaste for injustice and oppression and thus, "Today, through acts, symbols, liturgical gatherings, prayer, and festivals, we must reactivate the experience of that God who brings humanity out of servitude into freedom and service . . ."[44] since *God is not neutral*[45] reasoned Éla as he had already revealed in the Exodus and moreso in the institution of the prophetic office, the incarnation was designed by God to continue the divine desire for justice and freedom from oppression.[46] New Testament Christology is the culmination of such divine intention for the protection of the poor against the oppression of the rich and the powerful, thus for Éla,

> Finally, Jesus of Nazareth comes to reveal the true name of the God of the exodus (John 17:6; 8:28; 13:19; Exod. 3:14). The

40. Éla, *My Faith as an African*, 102.

41. Ibid.

42. Ibid.

43. Ibid.

44. Ibid., 103.

45. Ibid., 102.

46. Ibid., 103.

> incarnation is the supreme event of our faith–God's final word
> to us (John 1:4; Heb. 1:1–2). It is difficult to realize its full sig-
> nificance unless we grasp it through the world of poverty and
> oppression. The real world of the gospel is one of hunger, wealth
> and injustice, sickness, rejection, slavery, and death. It is precise-
> ly through the structures of such a world that God is revealed.
> God is present through Jesus of Nazareth, who, in the incarna-
> tion, reveals God's omnipotence in weakness and establishes a
> form of conspiracy between God and the downtrodden.[47]

The symbol of divine incarnation in Christ, according to Éla, has deep theological implications for us. It places the onus on theology to assert the liberational motif of Christ's incarnation by its refusal to identify with the present structures of power, but to critique it. Éla noted that "God's revelation through the incarnation obliges us to unmask the ultimate scandal of our faith: Jesus Christ made a radical choice in favor of those considered to be the dregs of the world."[48] However, "For a long time, this reality has been covered up by the dominant theology we have inherited down through the centuries. The dominant theology is a theology of the rich. It has always justified and tried to legitimize those ecclesiastical practices in which it is rooted."[49] Consequently, "The church has domesticated the gospel by subordinating its message to the interest of the powerful. We shouldn't be surprised that it has neglected to question the privileges of the rich in the name of the subversive practice of the historical Jesus."[50] "In spite of dog-matic affirmations," Éla noted, "about the realism of the incarnation ("true man")," however, "the dominant theology tends to spiritualize Christ to the point that we forget that he took on human reality with all its ten-sions and conflicts."[51] Éla's Christology is not only committed towards an immanent christological methodology concerning Jesus' incarnation, but extends these considerations to the sphere of Jesus' ministry. Éla revealed,

> From the heart of his radically and uniquely close experience
> of God . . . , Jesus announces the good news, starting with an
> option for the poor. He enters a world divided between rich
> and poor, masters and slaves, educated and uneducated, Gen-
> tiles and Jews. Deliberately, he takes his place among the poor

47. Ibid., 104.
48. Ibid., 105.
49. Ibid.
50. Ibid.
51. Ibid.

and exploited . . . The center of Jesus' preaching and acting is a kingdom of God for the sake of the poor. For it is important to remember that Christianity begins with a criticism of religion, which is, at the same time, a criticism of all of society, of human relationships and of power . . . [52]

Éla's Christology in relation to the ministry of Jesus underscores that Jesus was committed to criticism of the existing religious systems, particularly "the oppressive laws, which assure the prosperity of some at the cost of excluding others."[53] "In the end," Éla observed, "the gospel confronts a strategy of domination leading to hunger, set in a world structure where the administration of the wealth of the earth is monopolized by those who control the economic and political apparatus."[54] Thus, "Jesus reveals God and his option for the poor and the little ones—in the heart of a society built for ideological and religious reasons on the basis of marginalization, misery, and oppression."[55] For Éla, Jesus accomplished these liberational feats by "his refusal to sanctify the system of cleanness and uncleanness that regulated the conduct of life"[56] because "This system gave preference to ritual concerns, and downplayed any struggle to establish justice for the poor and exploitation . . ."[57] Similarly, Jesus accomplished such feat by freeing "people from" oppressive laws "that can reduce people to slavery in order to maintain the *status quo*"[58] in particular, Éla mentioned the Sabbath laws which hinder doing good or eating on the Sabbath day (Mark 3:1ff.; 2:23–38). Lastly, he underscored the symbolic action of Jesus in sharing of bread to the hungry, which for Éla, revealed the divine quest for a "social system" that is based "on accumulation and dispossession."[59] Éla also extended the sphere of divine liberation as revealed in Jesus to encompass the death of Jesus. For Ela,

> Jesus' death cannot be separated either from his life that precedes and illuminates it, or from his resurrection that gives it meaning. It is not a question of magic, but of the basic human reality taken on by Jesus through a life of radical faithfulness

52. Ibid., 106.
53. Ibid., 107.
54. Ibid.
55. Ibid.
56. Ibid.
57. Ibid.
58. Ibid.
59. Ibid.

to his mission. His death is the consummation of that mission. His life of solidarity with the poor and rejected is the key to a credible interpretation of his death in the context of our life today. The death of Jesus is the inevitable dénouement of a drama linked to the whole story of his life—an unending struggle against oppressive socio-religious forces and structures. A victim of repressive violence, Jesus pays for the boldness of his subversive ideas with his life.[60]

In this perspective, "Jesus' death is the result of his option for the poor and oppressed,"[61] thus, its significance lies in the fact that such medium climaxes Jesus' confrontation with "center of political and religious power" in Jerusalem "where the symbolic order of cleanness and uncleanness is institutionalized by the worship in the temple."[62] However, "Even today the death of Jesus must be understood as a situation in which the presence of God is perceived through actions that break away from the dominant religion and society."[63] Consequently, "Jesus transforms the cross from an instrument of humiliation into instrument of struggle against slavery and death."[64] "For Christians and the Church, the liberation of the poor, then, is the basic issue at stake in the death of Jesus."[65] The implication of Jesus' death now according to Éla, is that "Christians must place themselves beside Jesus for the life of the world."[66] Similarly, "The execution of Jesus, with all its gravity of suffering and death, asked us to decide whether we are in fact in solidarity with those who struggle against the forces of death at work in history."[67]

Éla also explored this liberation framework in the understanding of Christ's resurrection. He noted that "In resurrecting the dead once and for all, Jesus proclaims victory over the forces of death and inaugurates a new world. But how can we celebrate the resurrection where millions of men and women live in suffering and oppression? How can the resurrection of Jesus become an historical experience in the struggle for life itself by those who are weak and without power?"[68] In specific connec-

60. Ibid, 108.
61. Ibid.
62. Ibid., 109.
63. Ibid.
64. Ibid.
65. Ibid.
66. Ibid.
67. Ibid.
68. Ibid., 110.

tion of Christ's resurrection to the African continent, Éla asked similar questions. He enquired that "As Africans, how can we live and proclaim the Easter message today when we are already living out the passion of Jesus in history? If the poor and oppressed are the presence of the crucified God, can we read the Bible apart from contemporary situations of poverty and oppression?"[69] Answering this question in the negative, Éla noted that "We must question everything we have learned about the meaning of Jesus' death, about faith in his resurrection—whether from catechisms, theological instructions, devotions, or piety,"[70] because "In the end," as observed by Éla, "does this heritage of catechetics and pietism have any real meaning at all today?" Since "Too often, the church still seems to speak from another world, a world that does not represent the daily life of the poor and oppressed."[71] Contrary to the disposition of the church, Éla noted, "the redemptive cross not only implies an overall critique of a world opposed to God's plan; it also calls for a boundless reservoir of energy for criticism and for change to be used in every basic human situation."[72] For Éla, since "an imperial image of Christ"[73] played a leading role "in the history of colonial conquests, in the massacre of American Indians, . . . in the slave trade"[74] and identification with the status quo, Christology must cease to be mere talk about God or Christ, but to critique the socio-political processes on the African continent.[75] In Éla's opinion, we must find ways of expressing and implementing a christological commitment whereby Christ is not merely "the savior of souls but the hope of the poor and the oppressed."[76] Thus, we must reread the Bible or Christ "couched in this 'word from below.'" As already seen in the preceding discourse, a dominant christological methodology of Éla is in the category of immanence. Éla's christological methodology was determined by his prior commitment to a liberation framework. The rereading of Christ and humanization of him to fit the socio–political milieu is a characteristic shared by all liberation Christologies.

69. Ibid.

70. Ibid., 110.

71. Ibid.

72. Ibid.

73. Ibid., 111.

74. Ibid.

75. Ibid.

76. Jean-Marc Éla, "Christianity and Liberation in Africa," *Paths of African Theology*, ed. Rosino Gibellini, 136–53 (Maryknoll, New York: Orbis Book, 1994), 142.

In the work of Mugambi, a similar framework of liberation was used to interpret and understand Christ. Mugambi employed the understanding of the kingdom in the context of christological reflection.[77] In the dominance of the theme of the kingdom, Mugambi made allowances for a christological rereading of the gospel narrative in the category of liberation. Mugambi observed, "The announcement of the coming of the 'kingdom' by Jesus, is an announcement of the inauguration of an entirely new order, which is absolutely free from all the shortcomings prevalent in ordinary human kingdoms with the dominations, oppressions and exploitations."[78] The implication of this announcement by Jesus according to Mugambi is that "Within present human society, the coming of the kingdom of God means a total rejection of all the trappings and temptations of power, which dehumanize both the rulers and the ruled."[79] In this definition, Mugambi observed that "Such a total rejection would involve a complete and radical transformation of all those who come under the grip of this new awareness."[80] For Mugambi, the concept of the Kingdom does not lie in its material, spatial and temporal sense, but in the "attitudinal dimension."[81] The emphases according to Mugambi on the fourth dimension or the *attitudinal* dimension arose because "In his teaching, Jesus emphasized that the common attitudes which govern human actions tend to destroy the same life and freedom which human beings endeavours to preserve for themselves."[82] Even though, Jesus did not treat the other three dimensions of material, spatial, and the temporal as unimportant, yet "he emphasized that material, spatial and temporal concerns, exclusively, cannot satisfy man's quest for complete fulfillment."[83] This "fourth dimension, the attitudinal dimension is essential" because "This dimension affirms that God helps those who help themselves" and thus, rejects "the other worldly view of salvation."[84] Since, "Even in the public ministry of Jesus the majority of his followers were attracted by the immediate relevance of his teaching, not because of its other-worldliness."[85] Mugambi understood

77. See Mugambi, *African Christian Theology.*

78. Ibid., 77.

79. Ibid.

80. Ibid.

81. Ibid., 80.

82. Ibid.

83. Ibid..

84. Ibid.

85. Ibid.

salvation as synonymous with the fourth dimension and consequently liberation and thus "By standing" for this truth, "he conquered death."[86] In this understanding, "Jesus gave the old Hebrew concept of divine reign an entirely new meaning, a meaning wrapped up in paradox, and emphatic on the attitudinal transformation in the individual person."[87] For Mugambi, the death of Jesus has a great implication for human governments because "In his death Jesus showed that there was an absolute qualitative distinction between the kingdom of God on the one hand, and the kingdom of man on the other. The relationship between the two in his teaching was that the kingdom of God should be the spiritual foundation of human kingdoms."[88] In conclusion, Mugambi noted that "the crucifixion and the resurrection"[89] of Jesus will always remain "the central affirmation of the Christian faith" because they revealed how Jesus illustrated "with his own life what" the kingdom of God "demands here and now on earth,"[90] and the encouragement on the part of Christians "to live up to the demands of the kingdom of God . . ."[91]

Mugambi's Christology in relation to the kingdom of God revealed a preoccupation with immanence in his Christological methodology and the quest to interpret the gospel and the Christian tradition using the parameter of liberation. The exploration of Christology using the paradigm of the kingdom is not in any way new, however the christological implications of this christological development to the African context is what is indeed new. But even at this, Mugambi's analysis of the concept of the kingdom in line with Christology failed to delineate the practical Christological implications for the African people and how such will aid as well as increase an African Christian political participation.

As a whole, the flaw of liberation Christological methodology lies in its narrow Christological agenda in terms of race, gender and political forms. Often, this Christological methodology explores the basic Marxist social interpretation of human society and reduces the human predicament to merely the Marxist hypothesis of class struggle. This secularization of Christology usually rendered such liberational Christology inadequate to deal with the multidimensional realities of the African

86. Ibid., 81.

87. Ibid., 84.

88. Ibid., 87.

89. Ibid., 90.

90. Ibid.

91. Ibid.

context, particularly the spiritual longings of the African people. Similarly, Nyamiti's criticism of liberation methodology must be taken seriously particularly in its originality towards the African socio-cultural and political realities and its slavery to the liberation methodology of Latin America. In this perspective, Nyamiti observed,

> African Christologies of liberation are, methodologically speaking similar to those of Latin America. There is, however, a pressing need for originality in this field. This is true partly because of what I feel to be questionable methodological principles of liberation theology in Latin America, but especially because the African sociocultural situation possesses an almost inexhaustible number of potentialities that can be actualized in original and authentically numbered African liberation Christologies.[92]

The thrust of Nyamiti's criticism is that he rejected the general methodological slavery of most African christological methodologies in their quest to recreate or transplant the theological trends in other regions of the world to African theological discourse. The uncritical transplantation of fully fledged liberation methodologies as done in Latin America to the African socio-political context often makes the liberation models ineffective in the socio-political experiences at the grassroots. In the long run, this development cripples theological originality and renders those Christological proposals a mere duplication of trends elsewhere.

The last christological approach in African theological reformulation is communal-based and often takes place at the grassroots.[93] The content of this Christology is the spiritual and practical realities of the African context, which the presence of the African worldview has clearly fashioned. Interestingly, this Christology has often explored the triumphant victory of Christ over death and dark forces and thus offered African Christians victory over similar evil forces such as witchcraft and demonic powers. In this Christological definition, Christ ceases to become the "philosophical Christ" of the west but a spiritual warrior and victor, who never loses a battle. It is this warring and conquering spiritual Lord that appeals to most Africans rather than the classical Christological formulations as revealed in the Nicean and Chalcedonian Christologies. It is easy to see the attraction that these various forms of local and communal based Christologies holds for many Africans particularly within the African Independent churches, whereby their songs, liturgies, prayers and cultic categories have

---

92. Nyamiti, "Contemporary African Christologies," 73.
93. See Ross, "Current Christological Trends," 160–76.

a strong and lively Christological framework, which has no rival in the mainline denominations. A good example of this grassroots' Christological construction is the work of Philip T. Laryea, who sought to reconstruct the Christology of an influential African Independent churchwoman by the name of Afua Kuma (1900–1987) held from Obo Kwahu in Eastern Region of Ghana.[94] In his study of her poetry, *Jesus of the Deep Forest*, which was written in her mother tongue, Akan, Laryea sought to reconstruct the understanding of Christology in this non-formal and vernacular setting. "Madam Kuma's poems," according to Laryea, "were triggered by certain calamity she faced in her life, and these events were interpreted in the light of her new faith."[95] Laryea also noted that the Christology of Afua Kuma dominantly reflects the Akan traditional religious worldview which is blended with biblical Christology in the context of her existential human experiences. To construct this grassroots Christology, Afua Kuma described Jesus using images from the wealth of her Akan background. These images of Jesus include images of Christ with regards to the Akan constitution and war formation,[96] images of Jesus from the realm of Akan magic and divination,[97] images of Christ from Akan royalty and regal functions,[98] images of Christ drawn from Akan farming and fishing,[99] images of Christ in relation to modern state and institutions[100] and images of Christ in reference to the economy. At the end of his study, Laryea noted,

> A careful consideration of Afua Kuma's prayers and praises reveals what can be termed a 'grassroots theology,' in so far as it focuses on the expression of faith in Jesus in dealing with the concrete realities of life. We can conveniently distil from her poetry two major concerns, namely protection and provision. These are the themes that are most celebrated in her work.[101]

"For most African Christians," Laryea continues, "protection is not merely an academic subject."[102] Thus, "in her poem she demonstrates the reality of an unfriendly world peopled by evil spirits which constantly threaten

---

94. Laryea, "Mother Tongue Theology," 50–60.

95. Ibid., 57.

96. Ibid., 52.

97. Ibid.

98. Ibid., 53.

99. Ibid., 55.

100. Ibid., 56.

101. Ibid., 57.

102. Ibid.

life and well-being. The world of *anosom* (lesser gods), *nsamanfo* (spirits), and evil spirits . . . is engaged by Jesus Christ in a spiritual combat, vividly described in metaphorical language drawn from the traditional as well as the modern setting."[103] Consequently, for many Africans "The battle to survive the relentless onslaught of disembodied powers and forces is fought on all fronts."[104]

Notably, Laryea observed, "The significance of Afua Kuma's work lies in her ability to articulate faith in Jesus by invoking such powerful images to deal with these forces of instability that are destructive of social harmony and peace . . ."[105] Thus, "in Afua Kuma's images of Jesus, we meet one who provides in abundance and beyond imaginable expectations, food, water, clothing and shelter, in a word, security."[106] Furthermore, Laryea noted the political and secular implications of Afua Kuma's Christology in the Ghanaian sphere of governance. He observed,

> If, as spelt out in the Constitution of Ghana the modern insti-
> tutions of state are mandated to create a congenial atmosphere
> in which basic human rights are guaranteed, then Afua Kuma's
> inclusion of the army, the police, the judiciary and the economy
> in her presentations of Jesus, would be reckoned as an impor-
> tant theological contribution. The kingdom of God inaugurated
> by Christ is not complete until it has brought into its fold the
> various [domains of power] that regulate the life and conduct
> of mankind.[107]

"By her proclamation," Laryea observed, "Afua Kuma shows that it is risky to leave the events and institutions that control and shape the life and destinies of peoples everywhere in the hands of principalities and powers of this world."[108] Thus "For Afua Kuma, the process of restoration is to be witnessed in the existential realities of life, where Jesus engages these power structures by correcting and reinvesting them with new images."[109] In other words, "This is a clear witness to the power of the Gospel and an indication that the rule of God in Christ has begun."[110]

103. Ibid.
104. Ibid.
105. Ibid.
106. Ibid.
107. Ibid.
108. Ibid.
109. Ibid.
110. Ibid.

Similarly, Laryea noted the transformation of Akan concepts, metaphors and the language itself from its Akan traditional religious context into the service of Christological reflection.[111] Even though these concepts, metaphors or language are formerly applied to imperfect forms of the Akan cosmology such forms are not transformed and employed to describe the greatness and richness of the spiritual and physical experiences now found in Christ. Concerning the incarnation and deity of Jesus, Laryea also noted, "It is important to observe that the world inhabited by *abosom, nsamanfo,* and evil spirits, is also inhabited by *Onyankopon* (God) except that, as Afua Kuma claims, *nananom* (ancestors) 'did not see' *Onyankopon*."[112] "By this claim," observed Laryea," "Afua Kuma makes a significant theological point regarding the Christian doctrine of revelation, for it is in Jesus that this revelation of God is made manifest. This is an eloquent expression of the belief of Jesus Christ, his pre-existence and incarnation."[113] Laryea revealed that through her engagement with the spirit world and the Supreme Being, Afua Kuma sought to reassert the diversity and the unity of the African spirit worlds which goes against the criticisms of Bediako who observed that in the general obsession of African theology to emphasize "the centrality and uniqueness of God in African traditions, African theology has . . . left the natural forces unaccounted for."[114] Putting Bediako's criticism in perspective, Laryea observed,

> The way to resolve the issue, Bediako contends, is to conceive of the primal world as unified cosmic system, and not a transcendent 'spiritual' world separated from 'the realm of regular human existence. Since human existence itself participates in the constant interplay of the divine–human encounter.'[115]

For Laryea, Afua Kuma incorporated the transcendent and immanent dimensions of the African understanding of the spirit world into her christological reflection. Although credit should be given for such a brilliant merger of transcendent and immanent concerns in Afua Kuma's Christology, her christological computation has an obvious immanent methodological framework since it dominantly explores the redefinition of Christology in terms of the Akan religious worldview and cultural

111. Ibid.

112. Ibid.

113. Ibid., 58.

114. Bediako, *Christianity in Africa: The Renewal of a Non–Western Religion* (Edinburgh: Edinburgh University Press, 1995), 97.

115. Laryea, "Mother Tongue Theology," 59.

categories. Another general problem with this Christological methodology is that it is often based on the oral reflection or mother tongue theology as highlighted in Laryea's study at the grassroots, which often is open to subjective cultural interpretations. Similarly, for purely Christological reflection or reconstruction in oral forms, the quest to make oral Christological forms into an academic treatise often robs these oral Christological constructions of their spontaneity, beauty and meaning.

Generally, despite the obvious differences of these four Christological reformulations that are presently taking place across Africa, there is a binding nexus that is quite discernible. Noting these common concerns of African Christological formulations, Amoah observes that, despite the differences, "throughout Africa unifying elements of emerging Christologies include a strong reliance on the Bible and the use of indigenous African symbolism and imagery; and significant consideration of the socio-cultural context, the real situations in which Africans live."[116] These influential sources for the construction of African Christological theologies can therefore be reduced to two variables, namely the Bible and the African context, and it is interesting that these tools are fundamentally shaping the content, nature and disposition of emerging African Christologies. In particular, the presence and popularity of these emerging christologies already reveal the importance and impact of biblical Christology on the African minds.

Putting these Christological formulations in context, however, one can discern that these four Christological methodologies follow the three major theological trends of African theological discourse in the last two decades. From this perspective, Justin Ukpong discerned three dominant concerns of theological discussion in Africa. According to him, the first theological concern that emerged in African theological discussion is the African inculturation or cultural theological emphases, which is narrowly christened 'African theology.' This theological concern seeks to give African expression to the Christian faith and broadly seeks to give the African pre–Christian past some theological legitimacy. The second concern according to Ukpong surrounds the emergence of South African black theology. This theological current takes after the American black theology and aims at relating the gospel to the social problematic setting of black oppression. Thirdly, the next theological current concerns the use of the liberation framework to understand the realities in Africa, particularly in indigenous socioeconomic settings, the political sphere in terms that are

116. Amoah, "African Christologies," 41–43.

reminiscent of South American Liberation theologies and the dual usage of these approaches to understand the socio-economic and political realities in the African context.[117] These tripartite broad theological concerns are no doubt influential in the already stated Christological formulations in African theological discourse whereby Christ is reflected to feature the theological concerns of the African pre-Christian past, the socio–economic praxis and the political dimensions. In retrospect, the four Christological methodologies analyzed in the pattern of comparative, systematic, liberation and community-based Christological constructions follow the dominant theological discussion in African theological reflection. Consequently, the African Christological quest has expressed itself via these four kinds of Christological methodologies. The various assumptions of these Christological methods are primarily based upon the realization that the Christological emphases of the African continent must reveal the unique cultural, religious and social economical or political dimension of African existence. In this way, Christology must bear the distinct marks of African spiritual and non-spiritual expressions. However, there is the realization that such Christological formulations must also interact or engage the Christian and biblical heritage in determining the cultural elements admissible to such Christological configurations. The validity of this enterprise seems convincing, however, its relevance lies not merely on building credence, but in allowing the African and the international communities to further ascertain the worth of these innovative Christological reflections.

Biblical Teaching on the Person of Christ

Unfortunately, despite its many merits, African Christological discourse has tilted towards an emphasis which underscores the humanity of Christ rather than his deity. Looking at the different Christological proposals on the African continent, it is evident that the quest to make Christ an ancestor, elder brother, liberator, healer or warrior draws largely from an extensive quest to humanize Christ. This humanizing agenda must be complemented with an emphasis on the deity of Jesus Christ. Unfortunately, this Christology draws on the immanent character of biblical Christology without a commitment to the transcendent portrayal of Jesus Christ on the pages of the Bible.[118] The flaw of African Christological proposals

---

117. See "The Emergence of African Theologies," 501–36.

118. Often western Christological discussion merely centered on the person

is its deficient understanding of Christ's divinity and thus exploring the different dimensions of his humanity without an equal emphasis on his divinity. These two poles of Christology have been described as "Christology from below" and "Christology from above" respectively. Concerning the immanent commitment of African Christology as a "Christology from below," Tennent rightly observed,

> . . . the starting point and main concern of African Christology is 'from below,' not 'from above' . . . African thinkers are not as focused on the ontology of Christ and the relationship of his deity and his humanity as Western theologians have been. Africans do not invest a lot of time discussing precisely how the two natures of Christ become united into one theanthropic person. They rarely discuss how the two wills of Christ confirm him as the God-Man without confusion or compromise. Yet, these were all central concerns of the ecumenical councils that tended to focus on the person of Christ.[119]

This consideration suggests that there is vast difference between Western Christological discourse and the African ones.[120] Noting the enigma of the person of Christ, and the difficulty of harmonizing these two aspects of biblical Christology, Millard Erickson also asked, "How do we integrate and understand a Christology 'from above' with a Christology 'from below'?"[121] Unfortunately, Western Christological reflections, especially as preserved in mainline missionary churches, have heavily concentrated on the transcendent or "Christology from above" while African Christological discourse is fundamentally tilted towards a "Christology from below." To bridge this gap, we must pay attention to the biblical teaching on the humanity as well as the deity of Jesus Christ in order to be true to the biblical description of the person of Jesus Christ.

---

of Christ rather than what Christ has done in the life of the Christian believer. To this end, John Pobee has rightly observed that "Christology is not only the person of Christ, but also what he does." [See Pobee, "In Search of Christology in Africa," 10]. In his study of the New Testament Christology, Oscar Cullmann has also observed, "the New Testament hardly ever speaks of the person of Christ without at the same time speaking of his work."[See Cullmann, *The Christology of the New Testament*, 3].

119. Tennent, *Theology in the Context*, 113.

120. See for example Pannenberg, *Jesus*, 189–89; 286–93; 300–303, 324, 360–61, 365, 397.

121. Erickson, *The Word Became Flesh*, 11.

The Humanity of Jesus Christ

The Bible clearly articulated the humanity of Christ. Interestingly, while avowing the deity of Christ, it did not shy away from underscoring his humanity. By virtue of his virgin birth, Jesus became human and was human in every sense of the word, with the exception that he had no sin. The Bible teaches that Jesus was born through the supernatural act of the Holy Spirit without the biological intervention of a father (Matt 1:18; 24–25; Luke 1:34–35; 3:23). Grudem rightly observed that this virgin birth of Christ has three main theological importances in the Bible.[122] Firstly, it shows that salvation must ultimately have its source in the Lord. The virgin birth becomes an everlasting reminder that all human labour or effort to obtain salvation has no biblical base and hence, salvation must be rooted in the divine and not in human effort. Secondly, the virgin birth (or the incarnation) of Christ made it possible to unite full deity and full humanity in one person. The full humanity of Jesus is evident by his birth through a human mother, similarly his divinity or deity is obvious by the active participation of the Holy Spirit during his birth. Thirdly, the virgin birth creates the possibility of Christ being truly human without the potentiality of inherited sin. All humanity inherited a rebellious corrupted nature that had been transferred from one generation to the other. But in the case of Jesus Christ there was a complete absence of this nature in his being, since he did not have a human father (Luke 1:35). Apart from Jesus' virgin birth which engendered His humanity, Jesus' possession of a human body (Luke 2:7, 40, 52; John 4:6, 19:28; Matt 4:2; Luke 23:46), human mind (Luke 2:52; Mark 13:32, cf. Heb 5:8) and human soul and human emotions (John 12:27, 13:21, 11:35; Matt 8:10; Heb 5:7) evinces a human weakness and limitation. But despites the human weakness that Christ subjected himself to by the taking of a human body, the Bible clearly taught that he was without sin (Luke 4:13; John 8:46, 29, 18:38; Rom 8:3; 2 Cor 5:21; Heb 4:15, 7:26; 1 Pet 2:22, 3:18; John 2:1, 3:5; Heb 4:15, 2:18, 4:15–16). But could Jesus have sinned? Or to put it simply, did Jesus have the potential to sin since he possessed a human body? While the Bible did not articulate either a clear yes or no answer, Systematic Theologians have proposed some propositions in this direction. Schaff and Hodge had reasoned that for a temptation to be real, the person concerned must have the tendency of sinning, if not, the temptation is baseless and unreal for a being that does not have the possibility of falling into sin, hence they argued that Jesus was

---

122. Grudem, "The Person of Christ," 230.

peccable in order to make his temptation genuine and in this perspective, he provided for us an example and encouragement to persevere in the face of temptations. But in contrast, Robert L. Dabney proposed an alternative view of the problem of Jesus' impeccability.[123] Firstly, he noted that arguing for the impeccability of Christ is based on the unanimous consensus of the Bible and the creed of the church that the human nature of Christ was not totally separated from the divine. Secondly, this union of the human and the divine made it impossible for Jesus to have sinned since the divine nature provides an 'absolute shield' to the lower human nature, against sin and error (Col 2:9, 19). Thirdly, the human nature of Christ was imbued and empowered with the full influences of the Holy Spirit (Ps 55:7; Isa 6:2, 3, 60:1, 3; Luke 4:21, 4:1; John 1:32, 3:34). Fourthly, Dabney argued that Christ himself seemed to have asserted his own impeccability, for example in the scriptural text, "Satan comes and has nothing in me" and other related passages (John 14:30; 2 Cor 5:21; John 10:36; Heb 10:8). Fifthly, Dabney observed that if Christ did not rise above *posse non peccare* or the inherent ability to be peccable, then there was a possibility of the failure of the divine plans for the redemption of man. Thus, Dabney concluded, "For us all agree, a sinning sacrifice and intercessor could redeem no one. There must have been then at least a descretive necessity, that all his actions should be infallibly holy."[124] Dabney's interpretation of those cited texts is doubtful, but a plausible way to argue for the impeccability of Christ is to base the argument on the unique union between his divine nature and his human nature. Berkhorf, following this supposition noted that, "We ascribe to Christ not only natural, but also moral integrity or moral perfection that is sinlessness. This means not merely that Christ could avoid sinning (*potuit non peccare*) and did avoid it, but also that it was impossible for Him to sin (*non potuit peare*) because of the essential bond between the human and the divine natures."[125] From this great theological premise is the plausibility of Christ's impeccability.

In summation of the humanity of Christ, it is very important to stress the theological importance of Christ's humanity, which warranted the great emphasis of the early Christians (see for example 1 John 4:2–3) against the attacks of unorthodox sects like Docetism and Arianism.[126]

---

123. Dabney, *Systematic Theology*, 470–72.

124. Ibid., 470.

125. Berkhof, *Systematic Theology*, 318.

126. Docetism held the belief that considered Jesus' humanity to be only apparent but not real, while a later Arianism thought of Jesus as neither God nor fully man,

Firstly, Christ's humanity served as the means of fulfilling humanity's need of a representative obedience (John 4:1–13; Gen 2:15—3:7; Rom 5:18–19; 1 Cor 15: 45, 47). And secondly Christ humanity became very important because through it Christ became our substitute sacrifice (Heb 2:16–17, 14). Thirdly, Jesus' humanity made him fully qualified to be a mediator between God and man (1 Tim 2:5) and to sympathize with our weakness (Heb 2:18, cf. 4:15–16), hence creating for us a pattern for life (1 John 2:6, 1 Pet 2:21).

The Deity of Jesus Christ

In the pluralistic religious setting of contemporary times, it is wholly accepted that Jesus is human, but most of the times it is the claim of Jesus to deity that is repudiated. Hence, it is apparently important to investigate Jesus' deity in the light of scriptural teachings for the purpose of evangelical outreach and apologetics in contemporary times. Direct scriptural teachings underscored the deity of Christ. He was called God in many instances (John 1:1, 18; 20:28; Rom 9:5; Titus 2:23; Heb 1:8; 2Peter 1:1, Isa 9:6) and Lord (Luke 2:11, 3:3; Matt 22:44, 1 Cor 8:6; 12:3). Similarly, Jesus specifically claims deity-hood for himself (John 8:58, cf. Exod 3:14, Rev 22:13, Matt 16:13, Luke 9:18 cf. Dan 7:13–14 cf. Matt 26:64). A critical look into Jesus' life reveals divine attributes in his life, for example, the divine attributes of Omnipotence (Matt 8:21–27; 14:19; John 2:1–11), Eternity (John 8:58; Rev 22:13), Omniscience (Mark 2:8; John 6: 64; 2:25, 16:30), Omnipresence (Matt 18:20, 28:20), Sovereignty (Mark 2:5–7; Matt 5:22, 28, 32, 34, 39, 44), and the fact that he often accepts worship (Rev 19:10; Phil 2:9–11; Heb 1:6).

Relating to the subject of Jesus' deity is the theory of Kenosis, which stated that Jesus Christ supposedly emptied himself of divine attributes while he walked on earth in a human body.[127] This assumption is enter-

---

but as a being of intermediate status. It is unfortunate, that it is this brand of heretical Christianity that Muhammad the prophet of Islam derived his primary knowledge of Christianity. Hence, this accounts for those statements in the Koran that deny that Jesus was the Son of God and also that He was really crucified (Bruce, "The Person of Christ," 127.

127. In the nineteenth century, the rise of new scientific theories, including the biological theory of evolution as well as the upsurge of Biblical criticism, contributed to the development of some new perceptions concerning the person of Christ. The purpose was that these non–traditional interpretations were intended to make the miracle of the incarnation more reasonable or more acceptable to the scientific

tained because of the misunderstanding of Philippians 2:5–7. But the text and the context of the text speak of Jesus assuming the status of a servant by his taking on the human form. Hence, the *emptying* is in role and status and not the absence of his essential divine attributes or nature. In African Christianity, there is a strong emphasis on Jesus' victory which is closely connected to his divinity. Significantly, African Christians are not preoccupied with the issues of Kenosis, rather they are highly interested in the exaltation that follows Jesus' Kenosis, thus while Western academic theological reflection has busied itself with Philippians 2:5–8, African popular Christianity is enthralled by the exaltation of Philippians 2:9–11, which reflects the victory of Jesus Christ over the three realms of heavens, earth and the underworld. To this end, Mbiti has rightly observed, Jesus is "first and foremost the Victor over the forces which dominated African life from time immemorial . . ."[128] Hence, "the greatest need among African peoples is to see, to know, and to experience Jesus Christ as the victor over the powers and forces from which Africa knows no means of deliverance."[129]

From this foregoing premise, it is needful to stress the theological importance and implication of Jesus' deity. Firstly, the deity of Jesus Christ presupposes that humanity could in no way bear the penalty of sin and hence the need of a divine remedy. Secondly, the deity of Christ reveals the inadequacy of human race to save themselves and rightly places the onus on the divine. Thirdly, the deity qualified him to act in a mediatorial capacity in reconciling humanity and God (1 Tim 2:5). Insufficient and inadequate perceptions of Christ's divinity have developed from the beginning of the Christian church to the contemporary times, it is therefore needful to stress the three most basic heretical understandings of Christ's deity. The first heretical misconception of Jesus' deity, Apollinarianism,[130] believed that Jesus had a human body but not a human mind or spirit, and that the mind and spirit of Christ were from his divine nature. This Apollinaristic denial of Christ having a human mind and spirit engen-

---

mindset of the century. Hence, "Kenotic theory" of the person of Christ assumed a great point of interest in theological discourse. The term "Kenotic theory" comes from the Greek word keno,w, used by Paul in Philippians 2:7 to describe the action by which Christ "emptied" Himself and taking the form of a servant. See Ward, "The person of Christ," 131–137.

128. Mbiti, "Some African Concepts of Christology," 50.

129. *Ibid.*

130. This heretical school flourished under the tutelage of the bishop of Laodicea in AD 361. Several church councils from the Council of Alexandria in AD 362 to the Council of Constantinople in AD 381 repudiated this heretical teaching.

dered theological debates in church history, but was finally laid to rest because of its faulty implication that it was only our body and not our mind that needed redemption, since our minds or souls are not represented in Christ's redemptive work. This is implied from their assumption that Christ is devoid of a human mind. The second heretical teaching on Jesus Christ's deity, Nestorianism,[131] assumed that two separate persons dwell in Christ, a distinctive human person and a divine person. This heretical teaching goes contrary to the consistent biblical teaching on the single personhood of Christ, who nonetheless has two distinctive, but unified natures. The third heretical teaching, Monophysitism (Eutychianism),[132] presupposes that Jesus is a hybrid of two natures, the resultant nature is neither divine nor human. The human nature of Christ is assumed to be assimilated in the divine evincing a new nature or state that is not human and not quite divine. This hypothetical third kind of nature denies the scriptural teaching on the deity of Christ and his humanity. The Chalcedonian Council refuted the deficiencies of these stated heretical teachings on the person of Jesus Christ and reinstated through creedal affirmation their commitment to the person of Jesus Christ as revealed in the scriptures.[133]

In discussing Christology, some subjects of great importance must be hereby stressed. The three christological subjects under consideration are atonement, resurrection and ascension. Beginning with atonement, we proceed to the other highlighted subjects. 'Atonement' is a term that describes the entire redemptive work that Jesus did in his life and death to secure for us salvation. The cause of atonement is based on two fundamental scriptural propositions that lie in God, which are the love and justice of God (See John 3:16; Rom 3:25–26.). The love of God for humanity made Jesus die to appease or to serve as the propitiation for our sin, in order to meet the great demand of a just God. But is it of a necessity that Jesus had to die? Or to put it simply, was there no other way for God to save humanity apart from the death of his son? To answer this question, one should not overlook the fact that it was not binding on God to save humanity in

131. Nestorius was a famous preacher at Antioch and became bishop of Constantinople in AD 428, it is historically doubtful if he indeed articulated this heretical teaching that later bore his name.

132. The proponent of this heretical teaching in the early church was Eutyches who was a leader of a monastery at Constantinople and lived around AD 378–454.

133. The church leaders met at Chalcedon a city near Constantinople from October to November AD 451 to debunk the heretical teaching of Apollinarianism, Nestorianism, and Monophyisitism, thus forming a critical declaration of faith that challenges the assumptions of these already stated sects.

the first place, but in his love and sovereignty, he decided to redeem, thus not allowing them to perish like the host of rebelling angels (2 Pet 2:4). Many scriptural passages undergird the fact that there was no other possible way that God could save humanity that would show his tender love and the firmness of justice except the death of Jesus on the cross (Matt 26:39; Luke 24:25–26; Rom 3:26; Heb 2:17, 10:4, 9:25–26.). The nature of the atonement comprises broadly of two spheres, namely Christ's Obedience for us (also known as his "active obedience") and Christ's suffering for us (also known as his "passive obedience"). The former is significant because it emphasizes the perfect obedience of Christ to the requirements of divine justice (law) and hence he is representative of us to God the Father. It was not only forgiveness we were given, but also perfect positive merit and acceptance based upon the total obedience of Christ to the will of the Father. Righteousness, which we now receive by faith, is based on a lifetime of unflinching obedience to the requirement of God, which we could not accomplish on our own (Phil 3:9; 1 Cor 1:30; Rom 5:19; Matt 3:15). Complementing his obedience, the latter emphasizes the vicarious suffering of Christ in his life and death to pay the penalty of our sins. Jesus' suffering consists of the suffering of his whole life in becoming and living as a mortal man (Matt 4:1–11; Heb 12:3–4; John 11:35; Isa 53:3; Mark 14:34; Matt 26:56, 27:46; Heb 1:13) and the pains of the cross he endured: the physical pain, death, the pain of bearing sin (Matt 26:38; Mark 15:24; John 19:31–34; Isa 53:6, 12; John 1:29; 2 Cor 5:21; Heb 9:28; 1 Pet 2:24), abandonment (Matt 4:1–11; Heb 12:3–4; John 11:35; Isa 53:3) and bearing the wrath of God (Rom 3:25–26; Heb 2:17; John 2:2, and 4:4). This view of Jesus' death is known as "Penal substitution" or "Vicarious atonement." Penal substitution because he took away the penalty of sin and became our substitute. Vicarious, because like a "vicar" who stands in place of another, Jesus stood in our place.[134] We deserved to die because of the penalty of our sins, to bare God's wrath for our sins, be separated from God and to be in bondage to sin and to the kingdom of Satan. But God in his love and mercy made Jesus the Sacrifice for sin (Heb 9: 25), the Propitiation of the wrath of God (1 John 4:10), the Reconciliator of separated humanity from God (2 Cor 5:18–19) and the Redeemer from the bondage of sin and Satan (Mark 10:45; 1 John 5:19; Heb 2:15; Col 1:13; Rom 6:11, 14), hence, the importance of these other themes in the biblical teaching on salvation.

---

134. For further theological discourse on the penal substitution see Leon Morris, "The Atonement," *Basic Christian Doctrines*, ed. Carl F. H. Henry (New York: Holt, Reinhart & Winston. 1962), 152–57.

There are also diverse views of atonement, these consist of firstly, the Ransom to Satan theory.[135] This view of atonement presupposes that the ransom to redeem humanity was paid to Satan, in whose custody humanity was enslaved and eternally kept. African popular Christianity explores this understanding of atonement because they understood Jesus Christ's victory or atonement to be in terms of liberation from the power of Satan. While such conception of the atonement has certain biblical justification, the problem with this theory is that it gives Satan underserved supremacy, to the extent that God has to pay him ransom. The second theory is the Moral influence theory,[136] this theory asserted that Christ's life and death was not to pay the penalty of sin, but was to show the love of God in the sharing of human suffering, even to the point of death. Hence, Jesus' life and death are very important because they communicate the great teaching of an exemplary life of God's love, which should be appropriated by a grateful attitude and as a result we are forgiven. This theory is in contrast to the teaching of the scripture because it denies the passages that assert Jesus died to pay the penalty of sin. The third theory, the Example theory[137] stated that Jesus' life and death was an[138] example to us to show us how we should live in trust and obedience to God as Jesus did even if this path leads to death. The problem with this view is that it narrows atonement to just a pattern to follow. While it is true that Jesus' life and death provided us with an example, it is incomplete to reduce the whole purpose of atonement to just that. The last theory, the Governmental theory, believed that God did not require actual payment for sin, but that Jesus' death was to show humanity that God as a strict moral law giver demands suffering on the part of Christ to show that when God's laws are broken there must be a penalty. The flaw of this last theory is that it did not emphasize Jesus dying for the penalty of our sin and moreover, it neglects the scriptural teachings on propitiation and narrows atonement just to show that divine laws must be observed.

From the discourse on atonement, we now proceed to resurrection. For the Christian faith, the resurrection of Christ occupies a significant

135. This theory was first held by Origen (AD 186–254) a prominent theologian in Alexandrian and subsequently in Caesarea.

136. The first proponent of this theory was a French theologian, Peter Abelard (1079–1142).

137. The proponent of this theory is Faustus Socinus (1539–1604), an Italian theologian who lived in Poland in 1578.

138. This was developed and propagated by the Dutch theologian and jurist, Hugo Grotius (1583–1545).

place in the early church's narration of Jesus' life. Great attention was given by the Gospel writers in stating how he resurrected by the Gospel writers (Mark 16:1–8; Matt 28:1–20; Luke 24:1–53; John 20:1—21:25). The theology of the book of Acts and the Epistles heavily relies on the assumption that Christ was resurrected. The nature of Christ's resurrection differs from just coming from the grave like Lazarus did-living, aging and then finally dying again (John 11:1–44). But rather, He was the *first fruits* of another kind of human life by which his body was made perfectly different, no longer subjected to the human processes of weakness, aging, and even death. The body is made to live eternally, without an iota of mortal corruption (1 Cor 15:20, 23). But this body, while still having some celestial qualities was no doubt physical as attested by different passages of the scriptures (Matt. 28:9; Luke 24:15–18, 28–29, John 20:20; 21:12–13; 20:15, 27; Luke 24:39; Acts 10:41). There are three doctrinal implications of the resurrection for the individual Christian. Firstly, it insures our regeneration (1 Pet 1:3; Eph 2:5–6; Phil 3:10; Eph 1:19–20; Rom 6:4, 11, 14). Secondly, it insures our justification (Rom 4:25; Eph 2:6). Thirdly, the resurrection insures that we will receive perfect resurrection bodies (1 Cor 6:14; 2 Cor 4:14; 1 Cor 15:12–58). Christ's resurrection evinces three ethical implications; firstly it should make us obedient to God in this life (1 Cor 15:58). Secondly, it should help us to focus on our future heavenly rewards (1 Cor 15:17–19; Col 3:1–4). The last ethical implication of the resurrection is that the onus now is on us not to submit the members of our bodies to sin (Rom 6:12–13). From the discussion on resurrection we now briefly reflect on the subject of Jesus' ascension. The Bible teaches that Christ ascended into heaven and is now seated at the highest seat in the universe, *the right of God* as Lord of the entire creation, and invested with the most prestigious honor and glory imaginable (Luke 24:50–51; Acts 1:3, 9–11; John 17:5; Acts 2:33; Phil 2:9; 1 Tim 3: 16; Rev 5:12; Ps 110:1; Heb 1:3; Eph 1:20–21; 1 Pet 3:22). Christ's ascension had great theological significance for the church and its individual members. Firstly, its importance lies in the light of our union with every stage of Christ's redemption. It foreshadows the future ascension of the church and the certainty of our future home in heaven because we are the bride of Christ (1 Thess 4:17). Secondly, it depicts that the church as well as its individual members have a place of partial authority that they now share in Christ which will be consummated fully in the age to come (Eph 2:6, 6:12, 10–18, 1 Cor 6:3; Heb 2:5–8; Rev 2:26–27, 3:21).

Conclusion

Christology as the foregoing discussion has seeks to prove is the center of New Testament Christianity. Christology is the primary category that distinguished Christianity from Judaism. It is the bedrock of the Christianity of the past, the present and the future. It is the theological matrix or platform on which the edifice of Christianity stands. One could readily say that the absence of a biblical Christology could indeed lead to the disappearance of Christianity. Concerning the lofty place of Christology in Christian theology, Erickson has rightly observed,

> When we come to the study of the person and work of Christ, we are at the very centre of Christian theology. For since Christians are by definition believers in and followers of Christ, their understanding of Christ must be central and determinative of the very character of the Christian faith. All else is secondary to the question of what one thinks of Christ . . .[139]

However, beyond this narrow domain of theology, Christology is indeed the centre of human civilization. Interestingly, the person of Jesus Christ in history has truly captured the fascination of artists, poets, historians, philosophers and statesmen. The basis for this appeal of the person of Jesus Christ to every generation lies in the claims of Jesus Christ and the enigmatic descriptions of him within the sacred pages of the New Testament Gospels and Epistles. The claims of Jesus and the description of his life and death in the scriptures have indeed captured the imagination and thought of every generation. The paradox of the modern period is at this point glaring since the modern period seeks to dislodge religion or redefine the major constitutions of religious beliefs. However, in the person of Jesus Christ, Christianity has towered over all secular systems, idealism, philosophies and cultural institutions and thus more than two thousand years after his death he is still the "man" who has successfully outshone all the great men of the past and the aspiring great men of the present era. His thoughts and convictions have been the backbone of civilization and his philosophies have encouraged neighborliness and regard for the life and welfare of other unhappy species of the entire human race. It is to this end that Oden has noted,

> Whichever path one might take, it seems evident that Christology has a powerful impact for good or ill upon Church praxis,

139. Erickson, *Introducing Christian Doctrine*, 207.

where ancient ecumenical teaching of Jesus Christ is neglected, sermons resort to truisms and moralisms, ethical vitality is vitiated, and religious institutions become quickly demoralized. Where Christ is misplaced, humanitarian acts may remain, medical and relief work may continue, and political action may work for humane interest, yet these often lack the spiritual and moral vitality of that life which is hid in Christ. The deterioration of modern Church life has their main cause in the abandonment of classic Christology. Christology must be attempted amid the collapse of modernity. We live in midst of that collapse. We have no other choice than a post-Modern Christology.[140]

Even though the call for a "Post-modern Christology" by Oden might seem unorthodox to many, the exigencies of contemporary times demand a new re-articulation of classical Christology employing the cultural matrix of the post-modern world. So far, this chapter has highlighted the various issues in the context of Christological discussions particularly as it relates to the African Christological quest and classical Christological discussions.

140. Oden, *After Modernity . . . what?* 130–31.

9

Salvation

Introduction

SALVATION COULD BE CONCEIVED as the central teaching of the Christian faith since almost every teaching in the Bible receives its defining importance in direct relationship to the central theme of salvation. In particular, the Christian gospel has salvation as its defining center and it is no exaggeration to say that a gospel message that has no place for salvation is not the biblical gospel. Despite the unique character of salvation in the biblical revelation, the preoccupation with salvation is not entirely unique to the Christian faith since different religions of the world have also sought and understood salvation in diverse ways. Describing the basic instinct of the human race for salvation, Herman Bavinck rightly observed, "There is not a single religion in which the idea of redemption and of a way to participate in it is entirely lacking."[1] Bavinck also observed the futility of the modern world to seek salvation on its own terms, thus he noted,

> Whereas the arts and sciences may be powerful weapons in the struggle for existence, and culture may serve to make human life more pleasant and to enrich it, they are all powerless to bring human beings lasting happiness and an eternal good. This desire arises in them from much deeper levels of need than those that can be satisfied by the world around them.[2]

1. Bavinck, *Reformed Dogmatics*, 491.
2. Ibid.

The African people have also wrestled with this need for salvation. Even though there is much difference between the biblical understanding of salvation and the African one, there is a converging interest in the theme of salvation because almost every act of religious practice in terms of ritual, festivity, sacrifice, exorcism, divination and other religious experiences of the African people come from the deep desire of the African people to attain some form of salvation or deliverance from the social, spiritual and existential problems of their world. This chapter highlights the materialistic understanding of salvation in the African religious conception in relation to the Christian teaching of salvation as presented in the Bible.

The African Understanding of Salvation

There are scattered myths all over Africa which seek to account for the separation between God and creation. These "fall stories" often describe the divine withdrawal from the world and thus appear as myths, folklores and legends which are primarily told for entertaining purposes and not for serious religious or cultic activities. The failure to use these "fall stories" as a theological baseline in order to interpret, engage or define its religious world, unfortunately, occasioned the embarrassing silence of the African traditional religions on the need for the restoration of the world to its former pristine condition. Embarrassing enough, there are no cult practices, festivities, ritual observances or ethical motivations in Africa that seriously employed or used these "fall stories" as a framework to understand the past, the present or the future of the world. Importantly, the silence or absence of this theological template in the traditional African religions reveals the less forceful status in the claims of these fallen stories especially when compared to the defining emphases of the same within the Judaeo-Christian faith. As a result of the preceding void, there is also the lack of the "theological bridge" which connects these stories of the fall to the subject of salvation in traditional African religions. Noting this absence, Mbiti observed,

> This remains the most serious cul-de-sac in the otherwise rich thought and sensitive and religious feelings of our people. It is perhaps here then, that we find the greatest weakness and poverty of our traditional religions compared to world religions like Christianity, Judaism, Islam, Buddhism or Hinduism.[3]

3. Mbiti, *African Religions and Philosophy*, 99.

The absence of this connection in traditional African religions naturally makes the communication of the biblical teaching of salvation from the fall and its attending problems difficult for the vast majority of African people to comprehend. This is because in Christian thought it is the fall that necessitates salvation, and thus since this concept of the fall is clearly silent in traditional African religion, salvation in terms of redemption of the soul from the fall is also largely missing. Consequently, most African people understand salvation in physical, social, economical and political dimensions without the dominant spiritual emphasis that we find in the Christian faith. In the African religious worldview, salvation basically entails a good harvest, victory over an enemy, abundant food, plenty of children, good health, security or protection from evil spirits. This concept of salvation underscores a fundamentally "this world" orientation of traditional African religion rather than "other worldly" nature of salvation in the world to come or heaven. This understanding of salvation even though wholistic, it is largely driven by the temporal and existential concerns in the world of now rather than later.

It is not surprising that after conversion, many African Christians still understand their new faith within the worldview of their pre-Christian understanding of salvation. This external and materialistic nature of salvation is further pursued because the Bible also emphasizes the physical dimension of salvation especially in the Old Testament. Thus many African Christians understand the Christian gospel as particularly concerned about their physical well-being in this present world rather than the "other world orientation" in salvation of the Christian faith. The temptation to understand or explore the materialistic dimension of salvation by African Christians comes also from the increasing poverty, disease, dysfunctional hospitals, instability, insecurity, famine and other economic and social ills of the African continent, which daily exert pressure on the African people. The presence of these problems often pushes the African people to seek for physical salvation rather than pure spiritual salvation in another world. The problem is also compounded by the presence of Pentecostalism which preaches the materialistic concept of salvation with its captivating message of prosperity, abundance, and good health for anyone who believes in Jesus Christ.[4] For many Africans, coming from a traditional context which understands salvation in these terms, the Pentecostal brand of Christianity becomes more appealing than the "spiritual salvation" of the soul by the mainline denominations.

4. See Ngong, "Salvation and Materialism," 1–21.

Without the imposing nature of the "fall" in its theological conception, the African people blame the deteriorating nature of the world on the forces of evil and their human agents who work to sabotage the well-being of Africans. Even though there are accounts of the pristine condition of the world before its deterioration to this present state, salvation is rarely connected to the events that caused the deterioration of the pristine world. In fact, salvation in traditional African society is primarily defined in the "now" and the "present" without a temporal connection to either the world of the past or the world of the future. In this way, salvation is only confined to the present state of life and not to the time before or after. This concept of salvation comes from the fundamental dominance of the "now" and the "present" in traditional African society which primarily defines human relationships and religious activities around this temporal plane. Consequently, biblical understanding of salvation must engage this African understanding of salvation in the here and now.

The Biblical Understanding of Salvation

In the Old Testament, the Bible also speaks of salvation in the present world without any reference to the next. For example, the exodus is clearly a physical salvation from the oppression of Pharaoh. The Psalmist also prayed for salvation from the wicked and present human afflictions (37:40; 91:3; 34:6, 19). Salvation in the Old Testament understanding also involves freedom from slavery (Deut 24:18), military deliverance (Josh 10:6; Judg 6:15; 1 Sam 10:27; 1 Chr 16:35), and provision of food after famine (Gen 45:7). It also involves deliverance from sin and sickness (See Pss 39:8; 69:29; 41:1–13). The Old Testament also describes salvation in terms of national deliverance (Neh 9:27), protection from pestilence, plague and disaster (2 Chr 20:9). In the New Testament, salvation also entails healing from sickness (Jas 5:15), protection from danger (Matt 8:25; Acts 27:20; Heb 11:7), release from prison (Phil 1:19), deliverance from divine judgment (1 Thess 1:10), and even spiritual and physical death (2 Cor 1:10). Following this biblical description, M. J. Harris observed,

> In biblical usage, salvation is a comprehensive term denoting all the benefits, physical or spiritual, that are graciously bestowed on humans by God. The use of the Hebrew verb hôšîa . . . and the Greek verb sōzō in reference to both physical and spiritual healing reflects the Bible's holistic view of salvation, which can

be summed up in the Hebrew term šālôm ('peace') that refers to personal wholeness and well-being in every sphere.[5]

Chris Wright further observed, "the Bible's description of God acting in salvation includes the whole of human life in every dimension, and is not merely an insurance policy for our souls after death."[6] Consequently, he noted, "We need, in other words, to have a *holistic* understanding of salvation."[7] Distinctively, the New Testament placed the person and works of Jesus Christ at the center of salvation (Rev 7:10; 1 Thess 5:9; 2 Tim 2:10; John 1:29; Matt 1:21; 1 Tim 1:15). For the New Testament revelation, salvation is only found in Jesus Christ, thus the declaration that "Salvation is found in no one else, for there is no other name under heaven given to men by which we must be saved" but the name of Jesus (Acts 4:12). In addition, the New Testament also underscores the active role of the Holy Spirit in the procuring of salvation.

In the Old Testament, the scope of salvation is generally defined around the entire community of Israel even though individuals could also experience the same (Gen 7:7:1–7; Exod 14–15; 1 Sam 1:16–20; Pss 43; 86). In the New Testament, the individual character of salvation is largely acknowledged even though salvation is also defined along the lines of groups such as the Gentile and Jewish divisions (Acts 2:39; 3:25; 28:28; Gal 3:8; Eph 2:13, 17). Similarly, the invitation of salvation is also extended to the entire human race (Rom 10:12–13; Gal 3:28). For the Old Testament, salvation is primarily the initiative of God and the product of his grace and compassion on individuals, communities and particularly the nation of Israel. In this sense, divine saving acts are not necessitated by human works but the outcome of divine love and compassion (Exod 34:6–7; Neh 9:27). In the same way, the New Testament continued this close relationship between salvation and divine grace or love (Eph 2:5; 2 Thess 2:13; Titus 2:11). In addition to these highlighted biblical teachings on salvation, the Bible also connects salvation to the final restoration of everything on earth (Acts 3:21). Thus human salvation also has ecological implications since the fall at the beginning caused the deterioration of the world, in the same way, the salvation of the human race implies the restoration of the vegetation and animal world (Rom 8:19–23 cf. Rev 22:1–3).

From the cosmic nature of salvation, one must acknowledge the holistic nature of salvation in biblical thought which moves from the

5. Harris, "Salvation," 762.

6. Wright, *Salvation Belongs to Our God*, 16.

7. Ibid.

spiritual domain to include physical, social, economic, ecological and cosmic dimensions. As a rule, even though the New Testament gives priority to the spiritual dimension of salvation,[8] the other dimensions are equally stressed, and it is not an accident that the book of Revelation ends with a graphic and physical description of the salvation of the world particularly the salvation of those who have believed in the redemptive sacrifice of Jesus Christ.

The materialistic understanding of salvation within African traditional religion must then be complemented with the other dimensions of salvation as presented in the New Testament revelation. In particular, African Christianity must also underscore the centrality of the spiritual dimension of salvation whereby forgiveness of sins is found in the atoning sacrifice of Jesus Christ, and their faith is equally directed to receive the gift of eternal life found in Christ.

Important Aspects in Biblical Conception of Salvation

We now turn our attention to some related topics in discussing salvation in the Bible. These topics include common grace, election, the gospel call, reprobation, regeneration, conversion, justification, adoption, sanctification, perseverance, death and glorification.

Common Grace

There are many scriptural grounds to suppose that common grace is shared by all humans either saved or unsaved. The Bible teaches that common grace is the innumerable blessings that come to all people everywhere without them necessarily being Christians. This is different from *saving grace*, which comes the way of those who are saved. This biblical teaching does not infer that there are two graces as such, but that the grace of God is one though operating in the world in two different ways. Saving grace

8. Describing the priority in biblical teaching on salvation, Wright observed, "Now, of course we must discern the Bible's own *priorities* within its broad salvation agenda. Some things are certainly more important than others. Certain human needs matter more than others in the end. There are things that we need to be saved from that are more ultimately fatal and destructive than other things. The Bible itself shows that being saved from the wrath of God matters a lot more in the end than being saved from illness or injustice. But the Bible also talks emphatically about *both* as being parts of the saving work of God. We cannot confine the vocabulary of salvation to only one part of what the Bible means by it." See Wright, *Salvation Belongs to Our God*, 16.

differs from common grace in three ways. Firstly, saving grace is different from common grace in those that receive it. Even though both believers and unbelievers are qualified to experience the benefits of common Grace, only believers enjoy the benefits of saving grace. Secondly, common grace differs from saving grace in its purpose. Thus while common grace aims at helping the persons to come to some general knowledge or recognition of God, on the other hand, saving grace brings the beneficiary to the experience of salvation. Thirdly, common grace differs from saving grace in its source. While saving grace is based on the finished work of Jesus Christ, common grace is not directly based on such a foundation. Examples of common grace are evident in the physical sphere of human life in the gracious provision of physical substance, e.g., rain and good harvest (Matt 5:44–45; Acts 14:16–17; Ps 145:9, 15–16). Also, common grace is observable in the intellectual realm, God graciously giving all humanity either Christian or unbelievers the gift of a rational mindset (Acts 17:22–23). Moreover, common grace is seen in the moral domain. Humanity generally, either Christians or unbelievers are not given up to evil, but in many ways prefer virtue over vice and uphold moral consciousness, in a way that we Christians cannot understand. It is through the divine gift of a conscience that keeping this moral boundary becomes possible, even though the unbeliever's conscience sometimes may be dead or weak (Rom 2:14–15; 1 Tim 4:2). Furthermore, God's gracious common grace is also evident in the creative abilities he has given men in the societal dimension. For example, this measure of grace is particularly seen in the quest to uphold the necessity and sanctity of marriage, family and order by human governments and the many religions of the world (Gen 5:4, 17, 19, 26; Rom 13:1; Eccl 3:11). The reason for the divine gift of common grace to humanity is not mysterious, firstly because humanity, though in a fallen state, shares in His image and likeness (Gen 1:26–31). Moreover, God's common grace has salvation as its goal (2 Pet 3:9–10). Also, God's common grace demonstrates God's goodness and mercy (Ps 145:9; Ezek 33:11; 1 Tim 2:4). And lastly, God's common grace demonstrates divine justice and glory respectively (Rom 2:5, 3:9).[9]

9. For further discussion on common Grace see Osterhaven, "Common Grace," 171–77.

Election

In Africa, the term "election" basically has one meaning, that is, the act of voting a person to a political office. In this political meaning, election normally carries the dirty baggage of African political connotations. Since African elections are not always fair and transparent, it is natural that this connotation is similarly transferred to the concept of election in theological discussion. Consequently due to this transference of meaning, the term "election" seems inappropriate to describe the divine choice of Israel or the choice of the Christian believer before the beginning of the world. Such divine choice of Israel or the Christian believer is not conceived in traditional theological discussion as related to the good deeds of Israel or the Christian believer. This divine choice seems partial and arbitrarily done, thus bringing to the mind the unfair political practices of African politicians during the time of election whereby individuals are placed in political offices through fraudulent political practices such as rigging, bribery, tuggery, and other unfair political practices at the time of election. Despite the difficulty of the usage of this theological term within the African context, there is no term at present that can readily capture the biblical idea of divine choice which is clearly articulated in the Bible.

In the Bible, election is a teaching that asserts that God decided and chose us for salvation even before we were born. This choice is not made because of any merit on the part of those chosen, but based upon divine sovereign will and pleasure. The doctrine of election has generated throughout the Christian history and traditions various controversies and debates, especially in relation to the tension between divine sovereign will and human responsibility. D. A. Carson suggests that we can gain more enlightenment on the subject if we explore the tension instead of a smooth answer or theology.[10] The Bible teaches both human responsibility and divine sovereignty. This section will emphasized the latter rather than the former, because it is assumed that the reader is already conversant with the tension and debate surrounding this subject.

For the New Testament writers as well as the Old, Yahweh's predestination of His people was a great theme (Deut 9:1–29; Gen 12:1–4). In the New Testament, beginning with the Gospels, Jesus stressed, "Many are called, but few are chosen." This stance is maintained in the book of Acts (Acts 13:48), and sustained in the Epistles, but with a few amendments. In the Epistles, it was understood in relation to the church (Rom

---

10. Carson. *Divine Sovereignty*, 24.

8:28–30; 9:11–13; Eph 4–6, 12; 1 Thess 1:4–5; 2 Thess 2:13; 2 Tim 1:9; 1 Pet 1:1, 2:9; Rev 13:7–8; 17:8.). For the New Testament writers the teaching of predestination was related in order firstly to give comfort (Rom 8:28–30), secondly, as a reason to praise God (Eph 1:5–6, 12; 1 Thess 1:2, 4; 2 Thess 2:13) and lastly, as a motivation for evangelism (2 Tim 2:10). Many people have misunderstood predestination to mean a fatalistic or mechanistic determinism whereby events are believed to have been predetermined and hence, human beings become like robots or machines in these already planned events, without any way of exercising or asserting their will. In a fatalistic universe everything becomes subject to the impersonal force or forces that determine the course of those events. This is the understanding of the Greek concept of predestination or fate. But in the Bible, God is personally related to things or courses of events or persons He lovingly predestined. Moreover, scripture, whenever it talks about conversion, does not depict the Christian as a robot or machine who does not know the implication of his deeds or choices. Constantly the Bible portrays the Christian as a person who out of his willing choice makes a commitment to Christ (Eph 1:5; Matt 11: 28; Rev 22:17). As observed by Grudem,

> In contrast to the charge of fatalism, we also see a much different picture in the New Testament. Not only do we make willing choices as real persons, but these choices are also real choices because they do affect the course of events in the world. They affect our own lives and they affect the lives and destinies of others.[11]

Hence, the New Testament presupposed equally that men determine their eternal destination through their belief or unbelief in Jesus Christ.[12] Since men's fate is partly determined by them through believing or denying Christ, the onus on every Christian is to preach the gospel so that every soul will have opportunity to either decide for God or against Him.[13]

Reprobation

The doctrine of reprobation is one of the hardest of all biblical doctrines. It states that God decided before creation to bypass others in His election,

---

11. Grudem, *Bible Doctrine*, 285.

12. John 3:16–18.

13. 2 Timothy 4:1–2; Acts 18:9–11. For in-depth study see *Introducing Christian Doctrine*, 287–93.

deciding not to save them and still to punish them for their sins on just grounds. These following scriptural passages teach this doctrine: Romans 9:17–22, 11:7, Jude 4, 1 Peter 2:8. While the source of election evolved always from God in scripture, the source of reprobation is closely related to the hardened will of the sinner. There is obviously a mystery that lies between God bypassing others and their rebellious will against Him.

The Gospel Call

With the increase nature of preaching taking place in African societies an understanding of the gospel call is appropriate. This is because such understanding will encourage the Christian preacher in his quest to preach and evangelize African society. In the Bible, the doctrine of the effective gospel call presupposes that God calls his already predestined children through the medium of the human agents of the gospel that will definitely result in their salvation. Some of the scriptural passages underpinning this teaching are as follows; 1 Cor 1:9; Acts 2:39; 16:14; Rom 1: 6, 7; 8:29–30; 1 Pet 2:9, 5:10, 2 Pet 1:3; 1 Thess 2: 12; 2 Thess 2:14, John 6:44 and similar biblical passages.[14]

Often preachers of the gospel are discouraged because of the little or no fruit in their quest to evangelize. However, they should realize that the gospel call will ultimately lead to the response and even salvation of those who are predestined for the call, and thus there is no need to feel discouraged when men and women are unresponsive to the message of the gospel. There is also the need to recognize that divine timing for salvation might not correspond to our human timing, and thus the necessity of patience as we continue to preach and call men and women to the way of salvation. In the life of Jesus, even though there were secret disciples, it was only the twelve and possibly the seventy-two disciples that made an open commitment to follow him (See Luke 10:1–24). Considering this, it is possible that God is secretly at work in the life of those we are called to preach the gospel to, but because we do not often see these secret activities of the Holy Spirit among people we often believe our preaching of the gospel to be ineffective or even unproductive. We must realize that God is at work to bring those that are his to himself through the preaching of the gospel.

14. For more reflection on the doctrine of effectual calling see Geldenhuys. "Effectual Calling," 178–184.

Regeneration

There are many Christian slogans on the African continent particularly about "giving" and "prosperity." However, the term "regeneration" is definitely not one of these emerging Christian slogans. In the Bible, regeneration is the doctrine that teaches that there is a secret act of divine impartation of spiritual life to the spirit of the believer. Regeneration or the popular term "being born again" is attributed to the work of either the Holy Spirit or God the Father (John 3:3–8; Eph 2:5; Col 2:13; 1 Pet 1:3). The Bible teaches also that the believer is passive in the work of regeneration, which has God the Father and the Holy Spirit as the sole active agents involved in the actualization of the state (John 3:3–8, 1 Pet 1:3; Jas 1:18). The process of regeneration is indeed mysterious mostly because the believer is playing no active role; he is only depicted in the scriptures as having been transformed from the state of spiritual dead to spiritual life. Regeneration also affects the whole personality, and should not be seen narrowly as restricted to the spiritual alone (Rom 8:11; 2 Cor 5:17). The work of regeneration occurs instantaneously and is followed by saving faith. It is the new spiritual awareness or consciousness that dawns on the sinner which truly paves the way for the attainment of saving faith (John 6:44, 65, 3:5; Acts 16:14). These processes occur so closely together that a distinction between them, while possible, yet to the believer it seems to have happened at once. Primarily, the work of regeneration should be followed by a definite either radical or gradual change in the life of the person involved. A change from the lifestyle that characterized one formerly in the light of the imparted new life is inevitable (1 John 3:9, 5:1, 3–4, 2:29, 4:7, 5:18). In traditional African society, initiation rites and ceremonies also had this profound effect in the African community. Young men and women undergo the initiation rite expecting to be changed persons the next day. Even though the change is external, the persons initiated are conceived by African society as truly new members of the society who are expected to carry on the traditions of the past to a new generation that is now represented by young initiates. On the other hand, however, despite the expected external change in the life of the Christian, the work of regeneration primarily takes place internally in the spirit of the believer and this change is expected to be seen in the new life of the Christian.

Conversion

The African continent has witnessed a great conversion in the last century. It has moved from being a mission field to becoming a sending mission station whereby missionaries are sent out from Africa to the rest of the world. This growth of the Christian presence in Africa makes the subject of conversion a very interesting one because there is need to understand the meaning and the implication of one's conversion. In the Bible, conversion is the willing response of a sinner to the gospel message, turning from sin in repentance and turning to God in faith for salvation.[15] Two cardinal processes are discernable in conversion, the process of repentance and the exercising of a saving faith. Saving faith consists of a faith that truly trusts in Jesus Christ to save the person involved. Individually, knowledge of Jesus as a great moral teacher, or approval of his teaching as just very important sermons cannot warrant salvation (Jas 2:19; Rom 1:32; John 3:2; Acts 26:27–28; John 1:12; 3:16; 6:37; 7:37; Matt 11:28–30). Repentance and saving faith are mutually inclusive. Repentance is deep sorrow for sin, renouncing of it and a sincere commitment to forsake it and walk in obedience to Christ. In both processes of repentance and saving faith there is an intellectual understanding of sin or saving faith, emotional approval of the teachings of scriptures concerning a sorrow for sin and the needs for a saving faith, and a personal decision to turn from sin and turn to God. Both processes of faith and repentance continue throughout one's life, while saving faith occurs once in one's life, yet faith or trust in God is a continuous aspect of the Christian life. Moreover, repentance, if narrowed to forgiveness, should continually characterize the life of the Christian.[16]

Justification & Adoption

There is a glaring absence in the African church as to the understanding of the concept of justification. Sermons rarely preach it. There are no songs to celebrate it. Christian discussions hardly mention it. The absence of the doctrine of justification is truly embarrassing since the entire New Testament underscores its importance and it is central to Pauline theology. This is amazing considering the amount of emphases placed on this doctrine

15. See Gilliland, *Pauline Theology*.

16 See Matthew 6:12; Revelation 3:19; 2 Corinthians 7:10; 1 Corinthians 13:13; Hebrews 11:1. For a concise discourse on conversion see Julius Mantey, "Repentance and Conversion," 192–98.

by Western Christian churches. Often African preachers refuse to preach from justification texts in the New Testament because they presume that members would live waywardly, thus most seminary–trained African preachers that I interviewed on the reason for the absence of the doctrine of justification within the African church always told me that the doctrine of justification is only fitting for "theological class," but not appropriate for the larger congregation of the church. They consider the teaching as the one of the "hardest" teachings of the New Testament. They feel that preaching the divine justification of the Christian would lead to spiritual laxity among church members because if God has already declared us as righteous then "whether we commit sin" does not matter in the end since we are now God's Children and hence are going to heaven. The logic of this thinking might appear absurd to most non-African Christians but African Christianity has a works-oriented understanding of salvation rather than an entirely divine undertaking. This is not to suggest that African Christians do not consider salvation as a work of God, but they also understand that human deeds are necessary towards complementing divine efforts in terms of a holy and sanctified life. It is this logic that makes justification the least discussed Christian theme in African churches.

Contrary to this popular conception of justification, the doctrine teaches the instantaneous legal act of God in which He thinks of our sins forgiven and Christ's righteousness as belonging to us hence declaring us to be righteous in His sight. The Greek verb "δικαιόω" translated "to justify" in the New Testament has a wide range of meanings, but basically it has the meaning of "to declare" something or somebody "righteous." It is in the light of this nuance that *justification* is used in reference to believers (Rom 3:20, 26,28; 4:5; 5:1; 8:30; 10:4, 10; Gal 2:16, 3:24; Luke 7:29). Justification as a legal declaration is also in the forensic understanding contrasted to condemnation (Rom 8:33–34). The legal declaration involves the forgiveness of past, present and future sin and the imputation of Christ's righteousness to us, so that we are made righteous in the sight of a holy and a just God (Rom 3:21–22; 4:3, cf. Gen 15:6; Rom 4:6, 5:9, 17). In salvation history, three important occurrences of imputation are worth noting, firstly, the imputation of guilt and sin by the fall of Adam. The fall of Adam, its guilt, sins, and consequences were imputed on his descendants automatically. Hence, God saw every man born after Adam as guilty, sinful and miserable. Secondly, sin was imputed to Christ when Christ suffered and died for our sins. Thirdly, in justification the righteousness was transferred to Christians and making them as righteous as

Christ before God. This aspect of salvation as all other aspects of salvation is entirely based on sheer grace (Rom 3:23–24), though faith in Christ is necessary. Faith itself has no merit on its own; except it is a virtue that stresses our dependence on God instead of ourselves and our works (Gal 2:16; 3:11; 5:4; Rom 4:16; 5:1). The book of James complements Pauline emphasis on faith, by adding that a genuine faith will be evident by good works, therefore there is no conflict between Paul and James. The practical implication of the doctrine of justification is that it offers hope to unbelievers who know they cannot merit divine approval and acceptance on the basis of their works. In addition, the doctrine of Justification serves as basis of confidence for the Christian, since he knows that the penalty of his sins past, present and future has been judged in Christ and his righteousness imputed to him, hence, the removal of guilt and the assurance of a meaningful relationship with God. On the other hand *Adoption* is the act of God, whereby we become members of His family and treated in the loving context of that relationship. The New Testament underscores the fact that we are now members of a family, with God as our Father (Rom 8:14–17; Gal 3:23–26; John 1:12; 1 John 3:2), but formerly we were children of disobedience (Eph 2:2, 3; 5–6) and of the family of the evil one (John 8:41, 42–44). We are now the children of God, yet the fullest realization of that status with all its privileges and blessings awaits a time in the future (Rom 8:23).

Sanctification

Sanctification is often associated with the holiness movement in Africa because in Africa the term itself is a synonym for holiness in the popular mind. The root of this association might come from the close relationship between the verb "to sanctify" and the "noun "holy" in popular understanding and usage. In traditional society, sanctification takes the form of "holy baths" and other ritualistic observances. For example, in the case of ritual baths, the chief priest or herbalist first will diagnose the clients in order to know whether he or she is ritually clean, and when the client is conceived as unclean, the priest advises a certain cleansing ritual. This cleansing exercise is expected to make the client ritually clean. The cleansing ritual is often done at the discretion of the priest who usually carries out ritual cleansing from time to time. Under his supervision and prerogative, the client does everything commanded by the priest in order to achieve the ritualistic cleanness desired by the oracles.

However, the idea of sanctification in the Bible teaches the progressive work of God and man which aims to make us more conformed to the image of Christ and less compatible to the ways of sin. It is not the kind of ritualistic cleanness in traditional African society, but ethical and moral change in the life of the Christian believer. This work of sanctification involves three stages. Firstly, Sanctification begins at regeneration, when a new spiritual nature is imparted to the believer. This impartation of the new spiritual nature at Regeneration brings about a definite radical or gradual moral change because the new nature will not allow us to yield to the power of sin (Rom 6:12–13, 17–18; Titus 3:5). Secondly, the work of sanctification that began at regeneration continues in increasing measure throughout our lives as we give the Holy Spirit place to operate fully in our lives (2 Cor 3:18; Phil 3:9–12, 13–14). Thirdly, Sanctification is completed only at the death of the Christian, not in this life. Completion of the sanctification of the soul is at the point of the death of the Christian, while the completion of sanctification for the physical body awaits the time of the Lord's return (Heb 12:23; Phil 3:21; 2 Cor 7:1; 1 Thess 5:23). Sanctification also involves the corporate act of God and man, making man both active and passive at the same time (Heb 13:20–21; 1 Thess 5:23; 1 Pet 1:2; Gal 5:22–23; Rom 6:13, 19; 8:13; 12:1; Phil 2:12–13; Heb 12:14; 1Thess 4:3; 2 Pet 1:5).

The Perseverance of the Saints

In popular thinking, perseverance is a synonym for patience and endurance. In the African continent, children are even christened "Patience" or even "endurance" because of the frustrating nature of the African political and economic existence which always demands patience and a lot of patient waiting for the transformation of African society to a more humane and better society. Even though perseverance is not entirely a direct synonym to patience in biblical thought, the idea of patience is not foreign to the biblical understanding of the term. There is always some time frame involved in the discussion of the subject of perseverance, hence its correlation to the subject of patience. The African people are doggedly Christian amidst the socio–political crises of their world. The choice to be Christian amidst the problems of their circumstance naturally points to the genuineness of their Christian profession because it is easy to be a Christian in the comfortable luxury of one's environment, but it takes genuine faith to make one's profession in the midst of the troubles of the African continent.

In the Bible, the doctrine of perseverance of the saints states that all believers in Christ will be kept by the power of God and will persevere as Christians until the end of their lives, and that only those who persevere until the end have been truly born again. Fundamentally, the perseverance of the saints hinges on two basic scriptural teachings; the assurance of divine keeping of believers from falling and the part that the believer plays in this process. The scriptures teach that God divinely preserves the believer (John 6:38–40; 10:27–29; 3:36; 5:24; 6:4–7; 1 John 5:13; Rom 8:30; Eph 1:13–14; 1 Pet 1:5). But on the other hand, the scriptures also teach that only the believers that preserve to the end have been truly saved in the first place (John 8:31–32; Matt 10:22; Col 1:22–23; Heb 3:14;1 Pet 1:5). It is also important to note that the scriptures reveal that those that fall away often clearly show external signs of conversion (Matt 7:21–23; 2 Cor 11:26; Heb 6:4–6; 10:26–31). The Believer's assurance of a secure relationship can be seen in three ways. Firstly, the believer's present and continuous faith in Jesus Christ is a harbinger that he or she is already saved (Col 1:12; Heb 3:14; 6:12; 1 John 2:4–6, 23–24; 4:6; John 15:4, 7). Secondly, the assurance of secure relationship of believers in Christ is founded on the evidence of a regenerating work of the Holy Spirit in the heart of the believer (Rom 8:15–16; 1 John 4:13; 8:14; Gal 5:22–23; Matt 7:16–20; 1 John 2:23–24; 4:6). Thirdly, the assurance of a secure relationship in Christ should be seen in a long-term pattern of Christian growth.[17]

Death and the Intermediate State

Death is a condition which every African is exposed to daily whether on the street, at the market, at the office, and even in the comfort of one's home. There is the constant danger of death in the food we eat, the water we drink and the air we breathe. Similarly, there is a high mortality rate in most African countries, and the lifespan of many Africans is currently going down. For example, the average lifespan of an African male living in Zimbabwe is 36years and that of the female African at 40. In fact, each day, the life of an African is confronted with the possibility of death. For people

---

17. See 2 Peter 1:5–8, 10. The doctrine perseverance of the saints is also popularly known as *eternal security*. The usage of term the *eternal security* is misleading because it refuses to take into balanced consideration the two major aspects of the doctrine of the perseverance of the saints; the divine aspect in perseverance of the saint and the continuous profession of the Christian faith by the believer to the end. The former is greatly emphasized always when the theme *eternal security* is used to the detriment of the latter.

living in Africa, there is no need for statistics in order to show the brevity of life because the alarming records of death in Africa are visible for all to see. Every day there are new cases of death from malaria, cholera, cancer, polio, and HIV. The list is endless because there are also cases of death from tribal unrests, regional conflicts, guerrilla warfare, religious violence, school riots, armed robbery and even highway accidents to mention just a few. In this particular world of constant death, ironically, many Africans are yearning to live a happy and fulfilled life.

Even though the presence of death in Africa is the product of socio-political mismanagement and abuse by African leaders, for the Christian believers in Christ, death is not a punishment, but the final outcome of living in a fallen world, which God uses to complete our sanctification (Rom 8:1; 1 Cor. 15:26, 54–55; Heb 2:10; 5:8; 12:6, 10–11; Rom 8:28). This is not to trivialize or justify the death of many Africans languishing in poverty, corruption, and bad government, but to stress the biblical teachings on the subject of death. Concerning death, the scripture teaches that the believer should honour God in life or death (Acts 21:13; 20:24; Phil 1:20; Rev 12:11). Hence, the believer should think of his or her death with joy because of the prospect of going to be with the Lord, rather than an attitude of fear and doubt (2 Cor 5:8; Phil. 1:21–23; Rom 8:38–39; Ps 23:4; Heb 2:15; Rev 14:13). The believer should also see the moment of the death of Christian loved ones as a moment of sober reflection though mixed with sorrow but most important they should be comforting, knowing that those loved ones are with the Lord (John 11:35; Acts 8:2; 1 Thess 4:13; 5:10; Rev 14:13; Ps 116:15). For the death of an unbeliever, the sorrow is great because knowing that they are eternally separated from God, hence the need of evangelism to reach our loved ones near or far with the goodnews of God's salvation in Christ (Rom 9:1–3).

Concerning the intermediate state, the scriptures teach that the soul of the believer goes immediately into God's presence (2 Cor 5:8; Phil 1:23; Luke 23: 43; Heb 12:23). The Bible does not teaches the erroneous Roman Catholic doctrine of purgatory,[18] nor the doctrine of soul hibernation (or sleep)[19] nor saying prayers to the dead (1 Cor 3:12–15; 2 Cor 5:10). The

---

18. The Roman Catholic doctrine of purgatory had its primary source in the Apocrypha writings (2 Maccabees 12:42–45), though some Roman Catholics currently seek to justify this teaching on some misunderstood Biblical text (Matt 12:32; and1 Cor 3:15). The problem with the Roman Catholic doctrine of purgatory is that it seeks to add something to the redemptive work of Jesus Christ because it emphasizes the place of prayers for purification as a means of purifying sinners in the presence of God.

19. The doctrine of soul hibernation stresses scriptural passages that seemingly

scriptures also teach that unbelievers are eternally doomed (Luke 16:24–26; Heb 9:27; Rom 2:5–10; Matt 25:31–46; John 5:28–29; Acts 24:15; Rev 20:12, 15). In Africa, death is received with mixed feelings because it is the termination of life, but also the entrance point to the gathering of the ancestors. Death is treated as negative when it occurs among young people however, among the aged, it is always a welcome blessing. When a young person dies, it is often referred to as a "Premature death" because it is culturally accepted that he or she has not explored the many years allocated to him. It is culturally understood that long life is generally the lot of everybody; however, evil persons such as witches can terminate life and thus render one unable to live his or her life's span. Consequently, as a result of this culturally held belief, whenever a young person dies, he or she is assumed to have been "eaten" by witches or killed by malevolent means. For the elderly, it is assumed that when they die they ultimately join the community of the living dead, that is, the ancestors. Even then, old age is not the warrant or ticket for entering the abode of the living dead, it is the kind of life lived by the old person in question. For the African Christian, there is need to evaluate these culturally held beliefs with the basic teachings of the Bible. Even though the Bible promises long life as a token of one's obedience to God, it is also possible for death to come along the way of young persons. Thus, our understanding of divine sovereignty and divine providence should be able to help us through such periods of great bereavement particularly of young persons.

Glorification

The African religious systems lack a clear concept of glorification of the ancestors. In fact, there is an embarrassing lacuna in African traditional thought on the state of the ancestors especially as pertaining to their glorious state of being. In traditional African society, the ancestors are often described as living in a region of the dead which lacks beauty or glory. Traditional African religiosity lacks the language of paradise or celestial glamour that often colors the ancient and modern thoughts of the afterlife.[20] In particular, even though the African ancestors are described as

---

reflect the inactivity of the soul after death (Matt 9:24; 27:52; John 11:11; Acts 7:60; 13:36; Pss 6:5; 11:115: 17–18; Eccl 9:10; Isa 38:19) , but the dominant picture of the Bible is that people do not live an unconscious existence after death (2 Cor 5:8; Phil 1:23; Luke 23:43; Heb 12:23).

20. Idowu envisages partly the possibility of a prosperous state of being for some

superhuman spirits who could bless or curse, their state of bliss or wellbeing is rarely emphasized. On the other hand, the Bible reveals the blissful state of believers particularly their transformation to the heavenly and celestial state. The scriptural doctrine of the glorification of the saints teaches that the believer's physical body will be transformed at the second coming of Christ into the exact likeness of the resurrected body of Christ. Since man is a tripartite being the redemption of every part of him is important in the plan of God. Salvation in Christ offers present redemption for the soul, but anticipates redemption for the body at the second coming of Christ. Hence, redemption is in part present, but we await a full completion at Christ's coming (Rom 8:23–24, 30; 1 Cor 5:12–58, vv. 22–23, 51–52; 1 Thess 4:14, 16). These resurrected glorified bodies will be in likeness to that of Christ (1 John 3:2; 1 Cor 15:49; Rom 8:29). Some characteristics of these resurrected bodies are given in 1 Corinthians 15:42–44. Firstly, they will be imperishable, by this we can infer that they will not succumb to the process of aging, disease and death. Secondly, they are bodies that will be raised in glory. This presupposes that they will be beautiful, attractive, and eternally youthful mature bodies. Thirdly, they will be bodies that will be raised in power. They will not be weak, frail and mortal human bodies that all humanity has been accustomed to, but superhuman bodies. Fourthly, they will be spiritual-physical bodies. This spiritual body will be a combination of both physical and spiritual elements in the right proportions. Like the body of Christ, it will have flesh and bones and hence can be touched (Luke 24:39). It can also eat food (Luke 24:41–43). While we wait for the redemption of our physical bodies it is needful to do everything possible to improve the condition of our physical, frail, weak and human bodies and to remove possible discomfort by means of proper health care and hygiene. And it is also needful to pursue all possible scientific advancement and technological schemes to improve the status of our physical bodies as we anticipate the glorious, better heavenly ones. On the whole, the subject of the application of salvation has significantly revealed the various dimension of divine spiritual blessing showered on the believer, however, unfortunately such an upward looking emphasis of the application of salvation has often robbed this subject of its contextual interaction with the social and existential dimension of human existence.

---

of the dead in the thought of the Yoruba people about the Afterlife, when he observed, "Death is not the end of life. It is only a means whereby the present earthly existence is changed for another. After death, therefore, man passes into a 'life beyond' which is called Èhìn-Ìwa– 'afterlife.' This Èhìn-Ìwa is of *more* vital importance than the present life, however, prosperous this one may have been." [see Idowu, *Oòdúmare*,189].

In Africa, the spiritualized emphases of these stated categories of regeneration, gospel call, conversion, sanctification, justification, death, intermediate state and glorification have often been developed in alien historical and existential contexts that have little or no relevance to the present existence of the average Christian. It is pertinent to underscore the social-political implications of these highly spiritualized aspects of salvation. Does one's conversion, for example while often perceived as purely individual, extend to the conversion of the system? When for God's sake will the political system or religious structure undergo conversion? Conversion should not really be restricted to individual persons in the society; we must extend the divine quest for a just society based upon divine values to the entire community of human society, so that in the long run, the society and its structures might come under the lordship of Jesus Christ.

Conclusion

Despite the development and advancement of the modern age, the need of salvation as described in the Bible cannot be overemphasized because salvation is not merely a Christian term that is locked in the world of the first century, it has relevance to the contemporary world. Underscoring the importance of salvation to the modern world, Wright rightly observed,

> A glimpse at our modern world underlines the continuing relevance of the biblical message about our need of salvation across very broad front. We can marvel at the amazing progress of the human race in combating disease, improving living conditions for some, raising standards of justice and equality of opportunity in some cultures, and spreading the benefits of education and literacy. Yet any self-congratulation about such patchy progress is outweighed by the crushing poverty of millions, the scourge of HIV-AIDS along with the resurgence of some older diseases, the appalling brutality and violence that blights the lives of millions in wars great and small, the endless misery of long-term refugees. And to all this we must add the reality of two-thirds of the world's population who have little or no access to any understanding of the salvation that Jesus accomplished through his death and resurrection, and who thus live and die in spiritual ignorance of the gospel. For behind all the manifestation and symptoms of our dire human condition lies the fundamental reality of our sin, our deliberate rebellion against God, and all the consequences that it has brought upon us, including what

the Bible clearly and repeatedly calls the wrath or anger of God. We need to be saved, or else there is simply no hope at any level in the present or the future, in this life or for eternity.[21]

As already highlighted, the Christian understanding of salvation is holistic even though priority is given to the spiritual dimension. Consequently, we must emphasize continually these dimensions of biblical salvation by reinstating their importance and place in the modern world. In particular, the African understanding of salvation must be complemented with the spiritual dimension of salvation as described in the Bible. We must also seek to reiterate the centrality of Christ as described in the Bible. In the Bible, there is no salvation without Christ and the Christ of the Bible is primarily a saviour, thus any human quest or noble undertaking to bring salvation to human society in the absence of Christ is basically incomplete from the point of view of biblical revelation. Humanitarian concerns to better the lot of human society physically, socially, morally, economically and even spiritually must derive its importance in direct relationship to the person and work of Christ. Thus for the Christian, salvation has its source, goal and motivation from the person and work of Jesus Christ. In this regard, the African materialistic and temporal quest for salvation in the here and now, must be transformed to embrace the divine plan for salvation now in Christ, which though, having a dominant spiritual emphasis now, will have fuller physical realization at the end of time.

21. Wright, *Salvation Belongs to Our God*, 15.

10

The Holy Spirit

Introduction

The Pentecostal movement has brought to the fore the reality of the person, work and ministry of the Holy Spirit to the modern consciousness in the face of increasing secularization of the modern world and its attending anti-supernatural presuppositions.[1] This reawakening of the significance of the Holy Spirit in the life of the church arose out of certain factors. The key factor is the growing coldness of the mainline churches who often refuse to recognize or allow the free operation of

---

1. Even though Pentecostal fervor has always characterized the life of the church at different times in church history, primarily such Pentecostal emphasis has always being at the fringe of the mainstream church's life. In its modern expression, the origin of Pentecostalism is traced to the Azusa street revival. Describing the origin of Pentecostalism from a small street revival to a worldwide movement, Tennent observed, "In the first one hundred years of Pentecostalism the movement has grown from a few scattered revival meetings to a major global force of a half billion adherents, second in size only to Roman Catholicism. What began as a small flame among an assortment of poor janitors, horse drivers, factory laborers, hotel waiters, washers, and maids has become a whole new branch of Christianity. If one also considers the impact of Pentecostal theology as reflected in the charismatic and neo-Charismatic movements that have deeply influenced both Protestant and Roman churches, then the number swells to nearly 600 million Christians around the world who are Pentecostal in belief, in practice, or by denominational affiliations." In fact, as rightly observed by Tennent, "We ignore to our own detriment the vital role Pentecostalism is playing in shaping theological discourse and practice throughout the world." See Tennent, *Theology in the Context*, 164.

the Holy Spirit in the church's life.[2] This neglect of the active presence of the Holy Spirit often leads to the inability of the church's membership to make sense of the Christian faith, which lacks the vitality to address their various human and spiritual problems. This neglect of the Holy Spirit is not merely a phenomenon of the contemporary times, but has characterized the general life of the church, hence William Menzies observed,

> The ancient church from the second century through the ninth century was almost totally preoccupied with questions pertaining to the identity of Jesus Christ, so that what was said of the Holy Spirit was largely an appendage to theology, and was limited largely to ontology, the Being of God within his inter-trinitarian relationships.[3]

In Africa, the emergence of the Pentecostal movement and their attending emphases on the presence of the Holy Spirit for today's church comes from the diminishing presence and ineffectiveness of the missionary founded churches which often are African versions of the dying European churches. These westernized churches have little emphasis on the active role of the Holy Spirit in the church's life, thus the new converts troop to the Pentecostal congregations which speak to the worldview of the African people by their emphasis on the active presence of the Holy Spirit in the life of the church. This active presence of the Holy Spirit is readily seen in Pentecostal congregations by the emphasis on miracles, healing, prophecy, words of knowledge, visions, dreams, deliverance and other supernatural categories that readily show the power of the Christian God. These Pentecostal emphases often draw largely from the traditional African worldview as well as the biblical revelation where these categories are duly assumed and also practiced. The emphasis on these concerns often make the Pentecostal churches the most populated gatherings in Africa, and thus the "favorite church" of most African Christians. In particular, the Pentecostal emphasis on the victory of Christ over the forces of evil is celebrated as well as the related emphasis on freedom from demons, sicknesses, diseases, and even death. Even though the claims of some Pentecostals can be faulted at various points, on the whole, the Pentecostal congregations have better positioned themselves to address the African worldview than the missionary founded congregations who often pay little or no attention to categories such as miracles, deliverance and power encounter in their

2. For an introduction to issues in contemporary Pentecostalism see Anderson, *An Introduction to Pentecostalism.*

3. Menzies, "The Holy Spirit in Christian Theology," 67.

pastoral ministry. As a result of this neglect, Christian believers in many mainline congregations have deserted these places of worship to attend the so-called new generation churches, and even the members who remain in the old mainline churches, have divided loyalties because some of these members go to the mainline churches on Sunday morning and rush to the Pentecostal churches immediately afterwards. Thus they keep their membership of the old mainline churches in order to fulfill "all righteousness" however, their spiritual edification comes directly from these thriving Pentecostal churches. Looking closely at the two churches, the difference often is not only based on their liturgy and worship, but on the significance which they attach to the place of the Holy Spirit in the life of the church. The old mainline congregations mainly talk of the Holy Spirit as a confessional or doctrinal information which is taught in the baptismal and catechetical classes, however, the Pentecostals have generally made the Holy Spirit an essential component of the Christian's daily life whose presence is emphasized and experienced. Thus, while the Holy Spirit is merely a tenet of the creed of the mainline churches, for the Pentecostals, the Holy Spirit is the sole administrator of the Christian life, and hence an essential personality for the success of the Christian life. From the foregoing, the chapter seeks to provide biblical teaching on the person, work and ministry of the Holy Spirit especially in the context of the African understanding of the good works of the benevolent spirits.

The 'Benevolent' Spirits in Traditional African society

In the traditional African worldview, spirit beings are basically divided into two categories namely the good and bad spirits. The good spirits as well as the evil spirits are impersonal beings who go about roaming the world. The good spirits and the evil spirits are believed to be created by God. However, it is not always clear the reason or origin for their evil or goodness. In particular, the good spirits are believed to offer assistance, guidance, blessing, prosperity, riches, children and other good things of life to those who court their favour. The assistance of these good spirits could be invoked or sought through consultation with traditional diviners or seers who know how to court the favour of these good spirits. In most African societies, there are so many stories which underscore human encounters with these good spirits and the subsequent radical change in their fortune. Often it is believed that these good spirits can manifest themselves physically to take human forms and thus children are cautioned to show courtesy to strangers and the elderly are advised to be hospitable to the same. Often strangers are welcomed and entertained because of this understanding that they may be an incarnation of "good spirits," thus by such "good deeds" they may receive their blessing. In some cases, these "good spirits" are also believed to possess individuals for the purpose of speaking through them. The mouthpiece of these "good spirits" are deemed as "prophets," "prophetesses," or "seers" in traditional African society. Through their human mediums they can act as clairvoyants thus providing "words of knowledge," "prophecy," "guidance," "healings" and even "miracles." Under the influence of these "good spirits" the persons possessed by them often undergo heightened spiritual sensitivity and ecstatic behavior is not uncommon in such states of possession. At such moments, the personality of the possessed person is lost, and he or she assumes another personality. Often the person forgets or loses the memory of his or her behavior during spirit possession.

In Africa, covenants with these "good spirits" are very common because often a particular family brings themselves under the protective power and care of the "good spirits." These "good spirits" are expected to protect, provide, bless and prosper the members of the family. In recognition of the protective presence of these good spirits the family in return also sacrifices at designated periods to further court their favor. The sacrifices are carried out by the family in order to show their gratitude for the activities of these spirits on their behalf. These covenants exist from generation to generation, and the gratitude to these spirits is expected to also continue throughout the lifespan of the family. The presence and activities of these good spirits are underscored in virtually every part of Africa even among Africans who are educated in Western culture and education. African Christians too also assume the presence and activities of these good spirits. The recognition of the activities of these "good spirits" often influences the understanding of the Holy Spirit in the minds of many Africans. While the traditional recognition of the works of these "good spirits" provides a common ground in discussing the person and activities of the Holy Spirit among African Christians, often the understanding of the impersonal nature of these "good spirits" is transferred to the Holy Spirit, thus distorting the biblical understanding of the Holy Spirit. Admittedly, like the "good spirits," the Holy Spirit in the Bible speaks, guides, works miracles, heals, and even resides, fills or possesses the Christian believer, however, the "good spirits" are impersonal beings while the Holy Spirit is a person. Similarly, the "good spirits" operate within the matrix of the African polytheistic context while the Holy Spirit operates in the monotheistic definition of the biblical faith. Significantly, the Holy Spirit is a member of the Godhead, that is, the Holy Spirit is God, while these "good spirits" are merely lower spirits and created beings, thus the Holy Spirit is totally different from the African beliefs in the "good spirits."

The Holy Spirit in Biblical Revelation

In the opening of the Bible, we meet the Holy Spirit hovering like a "bird" over God's creation (Genesis 1:2). In this place, the Holy Spirit works to watch over and uphold God's creation. Throughout the Bible, the work of the Holy Spirit in this and other dimensions are duly noted. In particular, the Holy Spirit's work as rightly stated by Grudem, is *"to manifest the active presence of God in the World, and especially in the church"* (emphasis his).[4] He further observed, "after Jesus ascended into heaven, and continuing through the entire church age, the Holy Spirit is now the *primary* manifestation of the presence of the Trinity among us. He is the one who is most prominently *present* with us now."[5] Even though the Holy Spirit is the active presence of God in the church age, often we miss and ignore his presence and significance. In most cases, He is treated in an offhand way as the "silent member" of the Godhead, whose work is often represented in subservient fashion to the person and work of the first and second members of the Godhead namely God the father and God the Son. In the Bible, the Holy Spirit is not an impersonal force, but a person (Acts 5:3). He is also described as God himself (Isa 63:10; Ps 139:7). In particular, the Old Testament emphasized that the presence or activities of the Holy Spirit is expected to trigger divine blessings (Isa 32:14–18; 44:3). In the future, the Old Testament prophets envisaged a great period of the Holy Spirit's presence and activities (Joel 2:28–29; Ezek 36:26–27; 37:14; 39:29). Concerning the activities of the Holy Spirit, Grudem categorized them into four namely the activities of the Holy Spirit to empower, to purify, to reveal and to unify.[6] In relation to the first work of the Holy Spirit, the scriptures teach that the Holy Spirit gives life (Ps 104:30; Job 34:14–15; John 3:5–8; 6:63; 2 Cor. 3:6; Acts 10:44–47; Titus 3:5; Matt 1:18, 20; Luke 1:35; Rom 8:11). In this life–giving role, the Holy Spirit is also described in the Bible as giving power for service (Num 27:18; Deut 34:9; Judg 3:10; 6:34; 11:29; 13:25;

4. Grudem, *Systematic Theology*, 634.

5. Ibid.

6. Grudem, *Systematic Theology*, 635–47.

14:6, 19; 15:14; 1 Sam. 11:6; 16:13; Exod 31:3; 35:31; 35:34; 63:11–12; Isa 11:2–3; 42:1; 61:1; Luke 4:18). Often the Holy Spirit is described as residing or dwelling in the heart of these individuals (Num 27:18; Deut 34:9; Ezek 2:2; 3:24; Dan 4:8–9, 18; 5:11; Mic 3:8; John 14:17). The greater work of the Holy Spirit in the empowerment of God's people is expected to take place in New Testament times (Acts 1:8; 6:5, 8; Rom 15:19; 1 Cor 2:4; Acts 4:8, 31; 6:10; 1 Thess 1:5; 1 Pet 1:12; 1 Cor 12:11). Secondly, the Bible also teaches that the Holy Spirit participates in the work of purification (1Cor 6:11; Titus 3:5; Matt 3:11; Gal 5:22–23; 2 Thess 2:13; 1 Pet 1:2; Rom 8:4, 13, 15–16; Phil 1:19). Thirdly, the Holy Spirit works in the mediation of revelation. He inspired the prophets and the apostles (2 Pet 1:21; Matt 22:43; Acts 1:16; 4:25; 28:25; 1 Pet 1:21; John 16:3; Eph 3:5). In this work of revelation, the Holy Spirit reveals the divine presence (Num 11:25–26; John 1:32; Acts 2:2–3; 10:44–46; 19:6; Rom 8:16; Gal 4:6; 1 Cor 2:4; 12:7–11; Heb 2:4; Rom 15:19). He also guides and directs God's people (Luke 4:1; Acts 8:29; 10:19–20; 11:12; 13:2; 15:28; 16:6–7; 20:22–23, 28; Rom 8:14; Gal 5:18; 1 Cor 14:29–33). Similarly, the Holy Spirit provides assurance and illumination (Rom 8:16; 1 John 3:24; 4:13; John 14:26; 16:13; Luke 12:12; Acts 11:28; 21:11; 20:23; 21:4; 1 Tim. 4:1; 1 Cor 2:12). Lastly, the Holy Spirit unites God's people (Acts 2:16–18, 44–47; 1Cor 12: 7, 11, 13, 21; 2 Cor 13:14; Phil 2:1–2; Eph 2:2; 4:3). The African church must relate these biblical teachings to the African context in order to correct the various cultural perceptions of the "good spirits" among the African Christians. The Holy Spirit is not merely a "good Spirit" but the "Holy Spirit" who according to the Bible is the third person of the Godhead. Without such distinction, the Holy Spirit becomes merely another "good spirit" in the African traditional worldview thus ultimately reducing the lofty status accorded to the Holy Spirit within biblical revelation.

The Spiritual Gifts

The last area in our discussion on the Holy Spirit is the contentious subject of the spiritual gifts. Beginning with the definition, a spiritual gift is any ability empowered by the Holy Spirit for ministry in the church. The definition embraces the gifts that seem to relate to natural abilities (e.g., teaching, administration, showing mercy) and to "miraculous" abilities (e.g., healing, prophecy, and discernment). The ministry of Spiritual gifts have their background in the Old Testament, where the Spirit of Yahweh descends on individuals to accomplish some divine assignment (Deut

34:9; Judg 6:34; 11:29; 13:25). Spiritual gifts are given for the purpose of equipping the church to carry out its ministry until the return of Christ (1 Cor 1:7; 13:10; 14:12). Furthermore, spiritual gifts are given as a fore-taste of the age to come (1 Cor 1:5, 7; 2 Cor 1:22; 5:5; Eph 1:14). A combination of various texts that talk about spiritual gifts gives a list of 22 gifts (1 Cor 12:28; 8–10; Eph 4:11; Rom 12:6–8; 1 Cor 7: 7; 1 Pet 4:11). It seems that the apostle in these different texts was not obsessed with giving an exhaustive list, but was giving a few of them in relation to the spiritual gifts which the local church he was writing to was abusing, neglecting or misusing. Debates today in contemporary evangelical churches are not about the number of gifts, but whether some of these gifts have ceased. The cessationist view of spiritual gifts appeals to 1 Corinthians 13:8–13 as validating the cessation of some spiritual gifts. On the contrary, a careful analysis of the text does not support the presuppositions of the cessation-ist, but appear to favour the understanding that some gifts are going to continue until the coming of Christ, *when the perfect will have come and the imperfect will pass away* (V. 10) and *when we will no longer see in glass, but will see him face to face* (V. 12 cf. Rev 22:4).[7] The scripture seems to align with the understanding that spiritual gifts were given to equip the church to carry out its ministry through the church age. Hence, the scrip-tures do not hint, as often speculated, that some spiritual gifts will cease because the contemporary church would no longer need them. In respect to this view, four of the most controversial gifts are briefly analyzed. The first of the spiritual gifts under consideration is the gift of prophecy. In the New Testament, the gift of prophecy is not having the perceived powers to "predict the future" nor as "proclaiming a word from the Lord," nor as "powerful preaching" as often speculated but the "telling of the spontane-ous prompting of God" or the "relating of something intuitively that God has brought suddenly to the mind." In the Old Testament prophets wrote and spoke directly from Yahweh communicating expressly the very words of God (Num 22:38; Deut 18:18–20; Jer 1:9; 2:7). Therefore, their words were the very word of God, doubting them was tantamount to doubting God. In the New Testament, the apostles assumed this office. They spoke the direct word of God that later formed the New Testament canon. But whenever the apostle sought to validate their authority to write scriptures they appealed to their office of apostleship, rather than the office of proph-et (Rom 1:1; 1 Cor 1:1; 9:1–2; 2 Cor 1:1; 11:12–13; 12:11–12; Gal 1:1; Eph

---

7. For a detailed refutation of cessionist's understanding of 1 Corinthians 13:8–13 see Grudem, *Bible Doctrine*, 403–406.

1:1; 1 Pet 1:1; 2 Pet 1:1; 3:2). Jesus distinctively called his twelve disciples apostles, not prophets. This is significant because the meaning of the office of prophet acquired a new meaning during the Inter–testamental and New Testament times that is foreign to the Old Testament understanding of the term. Hence, the term 'prophet' comes to assume ordinary usage. The term 'a prophet' or 'prophesying' becomes synonymous to *common human speech* without the Old Testament connotation of *divine authority* or just a spokesman *who predicts the future* or has *supernatural knowledge* (Luke 22:64). The New Testament is the new age of the Holy Spirit as predicted by the Old Testament prophets (Joel 2:28–32 cf. Acts 2:16–18), hence the prophetic office became a ministry for many Christians in the early church and it seemed all local congregation in the early church had ministers who ministered as prophets (Acts 11:27; 13:1; 21:4, 8–9; Rom 12:6; 1 Cor 14:29; 1 Thess 5:20–21). But the New Testament scriptures indicate that this office of prophet assumed a lesser authority compared to the Old Testament understanding. The words of these prophets were not equal to the words of scripture. They were spontaneous words brought to the hearts of these men and women and not authoritative as the very word of God and hence they were subject to the scrutiny of mature Christians (Acts 21:1, 10–11; 1 Thess 5:19–21; 1 Cor 14:29–38). Significantly, in the entire New Testament scripture no acclaimed prophet wrote because their words were not viewed as authoritative to be inscribed in the scriptures. In the same way, the contemporary church should treat prophecy as spontaneous human words, not equal to God's word and should subject the same to the judgment of the canonical scriptures.[8]

In the African Church, the phenomenon of prophecy is closely associated with the African Independent Churches or the so-called prophetic churches. Prophecy within these churches occupies a lofty place since it reveals or signifies the daily presence of God within his people. Thus prophetic utterances in ecstasies, frenzies and drunken–like demonstrations characterize African Independent gatherings. Similarly, the overseer or founder of these churches often clad themselves in prophetic regalia in imitation of the Old Testament prophets. They also frequently speak of their otherworldly, celestial or spiritual experiences such as visions, dreams and trances which they often presume have some theological importance in defining the doctrines of the sect or in the daily leadership of the church depending on the nature of the circumstance or the sect in question. Despite their allegiance to the Bible, particularly the Old

---

8. Grudem, "Gifts of the Holy Spirit," 408–15

Testament, the African Independent Churches in relation to the phenomenon of prophecy draws extensively from their African traditional roots especially in the traditional institution of the diviners, healers and mediums. In traditional African society, guidance is required in critical moments of life such as during sickness, misfortune, embarking on a journey, undertaking a business venture, at birth, marriage and even death. Thus, the traditional institution of the diviner holds a very important place in the life of the African people in providing divine blessing on known courses of action, or in discovering the mind of the ancestor and gods in a course of action that is intended to merit their blessings. From this understanding, the African Independent churches are seeking to fill a cultural, religious, spiritual and psychological void in the psyche of the African people particularly as defined within these culturally accepted backgrounds. In this way, the African Independent Churches are a quest to meet the obvious needs of the African people in providing answers, guidance and blessing of the spiritual world, which is culturally believed to have a dominant influence on events in daily life. Unfortunately, such prophetic institutions are lacking within the walls of the missionary founded denominations, which solely rely on the Bible for guidance during the critical moments in the life of the African people. Such allegiance to the Bible is often shaken at the moment of crisis and most often, African Christians frequent these traditional places of guidance when they are greatly pressed by issues of daily existence. To overcome these syncretic tendencies, however, the task of African Christianity is to provide guidance in traditional forms from the Bible without a relapse into the traditional methods of consulting the spirit of the ancestors or African gods.

The second gift under consideration is the spiritual gift of teaching. The spiritual gift of teaching is the ability to explain the scriptures and to apply it to people's lives. The apostles devote a lot of their time exercising this spiritual gift (Acts 15:35; 18: 11; 2 Tim 2:2; 3:16). The early church teaching manual consists of the Old Testament and the apostolic instructions (2 Thess 2:10). Unlike prophesy, the spiritual gift of teaching is not spontaneous, but was the continuous repetition and explanation of authentic and authoritative apostolic teachings.

The third gift under consideration is the spiritual gift of healing. The redemption secured by Jesus Christ on the cross warrants our healing from bodily as well as spiritual sickness, hence Matthew's usage of Isaiah 53:4–5 in the context of the physical healing ministry of Jesus (Matt 8:16–17) and Peter's usage of the same text for spiritual healing (1 Pet 2:24). The truth is that healing is part of the redemption of humanity from the fall, which while partly in the atonement will be fully realized in the eschaton. We possess some of the blessings of the "already" inaugurated kingdom and its glory, but the fullest actualization of the glorification of the saints awaits the time of the second coming of Christ. The Bible teaches that God heals through means (2 Kgs 20:7; Mark 6:13; 1 Tim 5:23), faith (Luke 8:48; 17:19), and without means or faith (John 5:1–15). But ultimately even with faith or with means people might not always be healed, as we would like them to, because of the fall and the "yet" to be actualized kingdom of God. Nonetheless, the Bible commanded us to pray for the sick (Luke 10:8–9; Matt 10:7–8; Mark 16:15–17). The healing ministry of Jesus certainly demonstrates the willingness of God to grant us a foretaste of the perfect health that we will possess at the second coming. Hence, the book of James gave healing a prominent place in the pastoral ministry of the church (5:14–15). Paul mentioned it as one of the gifts given by the Holy Spirit for the edification of the church.[9]

The last gift under consideration is the spiritual gift of tongues and interpretation. Speaking in tongues is the spirit empowered act of praising or praying in syllables or languages unknown to the speaker. Speaking in tongues, unlike prophecy is directed towards God (1 Cor 14:2). For speaking in tongues to be genuine, it must be a language not understood or known to the speaker (1 Cor 14:2, 11; Acts 2:6). Moreover, the scriptures commanded silence in the absence of an interpreter (1 Cor 14:28). The biblical gift of tongues is devoid of frenzy and ecstatic displays that characterize heathen and pagan religious ceremonies. It is a self-controlled activity because the Spirit of tongues is a spirit of order (1 Cor 14:27–28). The Bible clearly teaches that not all Christians will speak in tongues (1 Cor 12:30). While abuses fault the contemporary ministry of tongues, there is no doubt that speaking in tongues is a gift from the Holy Spirit, unfortunately as the other preceded gifts of prophecy and healing, it is a gift lacking in most Evangelical churches. African traditional beliefs hold a constant appeal to the Christian convert because the traditional African society expresses its spirituality through the agency of these spiritual media.

---

9. 1 Cor 12:9. See the following authors on an in-depth discussion on healing; Blue, *Authority to Heal* and, Springer and Wimber, *Power Healing.*

Conclusion

The concept of the benevolent and good spirits is common among the African people. These good spirits are considered to bring good fortune to those who court their favour. This traditional concept of the 'good spirit" can be readily associated with the "Christian Holy Spirit" who is also thought to give gifts, spiritual power and blessings. Most of the African Independent Churches often have a problematic concept of pneumatology because of this common association. Consequently, the African Christian church should seek ways to help church members to overcome the temptation of associating or classifying the Holy Spirit with the many "good spirits" of the African spiritual world. There is need to emphasize the person of the Holy Spirit in contrast to the impersonal forms of these "good spirits." Significantly, the church should also seek to underscore the Godhood of the Holy Spirit as the third person of the Trinity. In this way, the African Christian will overcome the temptation to classify the Holy Spirit as a Christianized spirit from African spiritual cosmology. Such treatment will stress the distinction between the Holy Spirit and the 'good spirits" of the African spirit world, and thus rightly stress the lofty place accorded to the Holy Spirit in the Christian scriptures. In this emphasis, the Holy Spirit is not "another spirit" of the African spiritual cosmology, but God himself.

However, such distinction and stress on the discontinuity between the Holy Spirit and the "good spirits" of the African cosmology must also seek to also underscore the continuity between them. This consideration will help African Christian to form the mental bridge necessary in crossing from his traditional African worldview to the worldview of the Christian Bible. For many African Christians, such a "crossover" has not yet taken place because Christian life and thought are primarily understood from the vantage point of the traditional African worldview, thus rendering their Christian lifestyle incompatible to the expected lifestyle of the Christian believer. To overcome this problem, the African church must seek appropriate ways to form or forge a "mental bridge" of continuity which seeks to help these Christians make the transition from their past to the present. By such transition, the African Christian will live in the restrains of the biblical worldview rather than on the liberality of his traditional understanding of the spirit world.

11

The Church

Introduction

THE CHURCH IN AFRICA is currently witnessing a tremendous record of daily conversions.[1] Such growth is now primarily defining the meaning and significance of the church. At every street and in almost every corner throughout Africa are buildings and constructions bearing the labels of 'church.' Particularly common are the emerging African Independent Churches and the Pentecostals.[2] The phenomenal growth of the African church has made Christianity a popular religion within the African continent, thus increasing the social prestige which is now attached to one's identification with the Christian church. This social prestige of Christianity often makes the Christian Church another social gathering or some kind of religious assembly devoid of biblical understanding of the church.[3] This chapter presents a biblical understanding of the church and relevant issues in ecclesiology.[4]

1. France, "Critical Needs," 141–49.

2. Akinade, "New Religious Movements," 316–32; Appiah-Kubi, "Indigenous African Christian Churches," 241–49.

3. Concerning the relationship of church and society see Osei-Mensah, "The Theology of Church and Society," 1–7.

4. See Orobator, "Perspectives and Trends," 267–82.

African Clan and Tribal Arrangements

The clan and tribe are formidable structures in traditional African society. This emphasis on "clan and tribe" could be easily seen in modern Africa especially in the constant allegations of tribalism against public officers. In traditional society, the tribe is the authority that defines what is right or wrong. It is the custodian of the traditions, values and beliefs. It helps the education, assimilation and incorporation of the newly born African child. It provides the African child with its religion, trade, and cosmic vision. In particular, it provides each individual with the worldview needed for the interpretation of reality. It also provides the individual with ethnic pride or ethnocentrism that is necessary for the continuous survival of its African beliefs and values. They determine his taste, fashion, aesthetics, language, and other cultural predilections. Significantly, it provides the individual with personhood, that is, identity and its attending characteristics or qualities. In this understanding, the tribe has formidable power over the individual and thus helps to chart the path of an individual before he or she is even born. The controlling power of the tribe works to engender goodwill and kinship among people of the same tribe, and help them in their quest for existential survival against opponents or conceived enemies. In this traditional society, the individual places himself at the dictates of the tribe or clan. Speaking of this sense of tribal kinship among African people, Mbiti rightly observed,

> The deep sense of kinship with all it implies, has been one of the strongest forces in traditional African life. Kinship is reckoned through blood and betrothal (engagement and marriage). It is kinship which controls social relationship between people in a given community. It governs marital customs and regulations, it determines the behaviour of one individual towards another. Indeed, this sense of kinship binds together the entire life of the tribe . . .[5]

In the modern time, this group or tribal spirit can be seen almost everywhere in Africa because it cuts across the religious, political, economic and social divides. Due to the pervasive nature of such tribal sentiments, the first point of identification is often the question, 'which tribe did he or she come from?' Unfortunately, people in leadership positions get to such offices because of tribal considerations rather than merits or morality. In office, government often manipulates tribal sentiments in order to

5. Mbiti, *African Religions and Philosophy*, 104.

keep themselves in office. Almost everything in Africa is done out of some calculated tribal considerations or influence. Noting the functions of these African kinship ties especially as expressed in African clans, Mbiti further added,

> Apart from localizing the sense of kinship, clan systems provide closer human co–operation, especially in times of need. In case of internal conflicts, clan members joined one another to fight their aggressive neighbours, in former years. If a person finds himself in difficulties, it is not unusual for him to call for help from his clan members and other relatives e.g., in paying fines caused by an accident (such as accidental wounding or killing of another person or damage to property); in finding enough goods to exchange for a wife; or today in giving financial support to students studying in institutes of higher education both at home and abroad.[6]

These strong tribal ties often enter the church with terrible consequences. For example, the genocide in Rwanda demonstrated the terrible nature of tribal sentiment. In the tribal crisis there, the Christian Hutu and Tutsi killed one another because of strong tribal differences.[7] Unfortunately, the commitment towards tribal interests dominated their commitment towards the Christian faith. Consequently, the church was divided on tribal and ethnic lines rather than on Christian and non-Christian divisions. There is a miniature Rwanda in almost every church across Africa with people committed to tribal sentiments in the church rather than to the binding vision of a new community in Christ. The understanding of the church is often blurred in the context of such tribal conflicts because

6. *Ibid.*, 106.

7. In relation to the tension between African nationalism and tribalism, Mbiti said, "Nationhood scratches on the surface, it is the conscious mind of modern Africa. But the subconscious of tribal life is only dormant, not dead. The two levels do not always harmonize, and may even clash in an open conflict to the detriment of both sides. 'Tribalism' is a new phenomenon within and endangering nationhood . . . on the material or economic level, the trend is clearly the cultivation of individual and national prosperity. But in the emotional and psychological level, it is towards tribal solidarity and foundations. Modern African nations have no solidarity with a long tradition and firm foundations similar to tribal solidarity which evolved over a long period." In addition, Mbiti also noted, "on the material or economic level, the trend is clearly the cultivation of individual and national prosperity. But on the emotional and psychological level, it is towards tribal solidarity and foundations. Modern African nations have no solidarity with a long tradition and firm foundations similar to tribal solidarity which evolved over a long period." See Mbiti, *African Religions and Philosophy*, 222.

often it is tribal considerations that dominate and control the decisions of the church. The church has becomes a tribal organization with many tribal churches springing up whose commitment to Christ is often questionable because they often use the church as a venue to perpetuate their ethnic agendas. Often people say "blood is thicker than water" in order to justify their tribal propensity and bias, however, it is often forgotten that the "blood" of Jesus should be able to bind Christian together irrespective of their tribal, racial, social and political affiliations. The African church must rediscover the true meaning of the "church" and thus highlight its relevance in dispelling the tribal sentiments that have now entered the African Church.

Biblical Teachings on the Church

In the Bible, the church is the community of all true believers for all time. This community of faith consists of men and women in both the Testaments.[8] The church is invisible and visible, local as well as universal (2 Tim 2:17–19; Heb 12:23; Acts 20:29–30; Matt 7:15–16; Rom 16:5; 1 Cor 16:9; 1:2; 2 Cor 1:1; Acts 9:31; Eph 5:25). Many metaphors are used in the scriptures to describe the relationship that exists between the church and Christ. A few of these metaphors are namely; the bride of Christ (Eph 5:32; 2 Cor 11:2), a family (1 Tim 5:1–2), branches on a vine (John 15:5), an olive tree (Rom 11:17–24), a field of crops (1 Cor 3:6–9), a building (1 Cor 3:9), and a harvest (Matt 13:1–30; John 4:35), a new temple (1 Pet 2:5), a new group of priests (1 Pet 2:5), God's House (Heb 3:6) and the body of Christ (1 Cor 12:12–27; Eph 1:22–23; 4:15–16; Col 2:19). The scriptures also reveal the purposes of the church on earth. Four key purposes of the church are quite obvious in the scriptures. Firstly, the scriptures teach that the church was built for the worship of God (Col 3:16; Eph 1:12; 5:16–19). Secondly, the church was founded for the edification of

---

8. Linguistically, the Septuagint translated the Hebrew word lhq as ekklhsiaj in Deuteronomy 4:10, describing the congregation of Israel with the favourite New Testament word for the church. The writer of the book of Hebrew in his translation of Psalm 22:22 described the psalmist as saying, "In the midst of the church I will praise you" (ἐν μέσῳ ἐκκλησίας ὑμνήσω σε) Theologically, the community of the Israelites in the wilderness was described by Stephen as τῇ ἐκκλησίᾳ ἐν τῇ ἐρήμῳ (the church in the wilderness). Moreover, the writer of the book of Hebrews described the Old Testament saints as part of the cloud of witnesses that currently surrounds the believer (11:4–32). It is based on these premises to say that the church consists of believers in both Testaments. See Grudem, Bible Doctrine, 363–4.

believers (Col 1:28; Eph 4:12–13). Thirdly, the church was established to reach out in evangelism and social concern to the world (Matt 28:19; Acts 11:29; 2 Cor 8:4; 1 John 3:17). It is needless to say that the contemporary church has lost the purpose of its existence. It seems many Christians do not understand the purpose of the church. They have mistaken the church to be a human organization, a vast empire that needs newer policies and administrative geniuses to keep it running.[9] These human political structures divert the focus of the church from its main purpose. Hence, great attention is given to great projects, and the building of gigantic church structures instead of the primary purpose of the church as stated above.[10] Lastly, the biblical church is a vision of a new community where "there is no longer Jew or Greek, slave nor free, male nor female, for you are all one in Christ Jesus" (Gal 3:28). Similarly, Paul also said in Colossians 3:11 that "Here there is no Greek or Jew, circumcised or uncircumcised, barbarian, Scythian, slave or free, but Christ is all, and is in all." However, this vision of a new community of God's people has not yet been realized in Africa because of the tribal and ethnic considerations which often destroy the equality, brotherhood and love that are expected in the divine vision of a new community, namely the church.

Two areas of biblical teachings on the church will occupy our present discussion. The first area of ecclesiology is the rite of baptism. Baptism is the ordinance of Christ, at times called a sacrament.[11] The nature of baptism varies from one denomination to the other, some advocate infant baptism (paedobaptism),[12] others emphasize adult baptism at an age when

9. On the problem of the African church see Adeyemo, "An African Leader," 151–60.

10. On the hermeneutical functions of the church see Arrastia, "The Church," 18–25.

11. Baptism should be understood as an ordinance, rather than a sacrament. It is an ordinance because it was commanded by Christ (Matt 28:19–20), but not a sacrament which by Roman Catholic and Lutheran's understanding produce spiritual regeneration or spiritual change in the person being baptized. See Erickson, *Introducing Christian Doctrine*, 349.

12. The argument for infant baptism is firstly based on the premise of the perceived likeness of circumcision with baptism. Baptism is conceived to be the same as circumcision; hence as children are baptized in the Old Testament so also children should be baptized in the New Testament. Secondly, in the New Testament there are cases of household baptism (Acts 16:15; 16:33; 1 Cor. 1:16), thus, proponents of infant baptism argue for the validity of infant baptism. Arguments for refuting infant baptism is based on the fact that while baptism and circumcision share some similarity for entrance into the covenant community in both the Old and New Testament, it would be a great mistake to stretch this similarity too far because circumcision is carried out

believing in Christ is possible. Some denominations stress baptism by sprinkling[13] while others advocate baptism by immersion. The scriptures teach that baptism firstly has a strong connection to being united with Christ in his death and resurrection (Rom 6:1–11). Secondly, the scriptures also teach that baptism is closely linked to the act of believing, while one's salvation has nothing to do with baptism, yet baptism is the open declaration of one's faith in Christ (Acts 2:37–38; Mark 16:16). Hence, baptism becomes a sign or symbol of what has taken place inwardly in the heart of the believer.[14]

The last area of consideration within our discourse of ecclesiology is the rite of the Lord's Supper. The Lord's Supper has its background in the Old Testament in the special blessing of eating in the presence of Yahweh (Exod 24:9–11; Deut 14:23, 26; Gen 2:16–17). It is the second ordinance of Jesus Christ, baptism being the first. The Lord's Supper is significant because it celebrates Christ' death, our participation in his death, our spiritual nourishment, the unity of believers, and the anticipation of his second coming (1Cor 11:26; Matt 26:26; John 6:53–57; 1 Cor 10:17). The presence of Christ in the rite of the Lord's Supper has caused serious theological debates in the history of the church. The Roman Catholic believes in *transubstantiation*. The term describes the Roman Catholic belief that the two elements (the bread and wine) in the Lord's Supper become actually

---

on every Israelite either having inward faith in YHWH or not, but baptism is a symbol of one's spiritual regeneration and hence not appropriate to equate with circumcision. Secondly, the ground for refuting infant baptism is based on the fact that in those cases of household baptism, there is indication that the individuals involved have individually comes to faith in Jesus Christ. For more theological refutation of infant baptism within Roman Catholic Church and Protestant churches see Grudem, *Bible Doctrine*, 380–384 and for more theological support for infant baptism see Berkhof, *Systematic Theology*, 632–643.

13. Theological refutation of the Roman Catholic practice of baptism by sprinkling is firstly based on the understanding of the Greek word bapti,zw which connotes, "to dip, to plunge, "and hence immersion. More so, on the narrative passages on baptism, which clearly shows a baptism by immersion (Mark 1:5, 10; John 3:23; Acts 8:36, 38–39). Most importantly, a theological refutation of baptism by sprinkling is based on the fact baptism symbolizes a union with Christ in his death, burial, and resurrection and hence requires a baptism by immersion (Rom 6:3–4; Col 2:12).

14. The Roman Catholics and Lutherans understand baptism as a means of saving grace. According to them, baptism is a means by which God imparts saving grace and results in the remission of sin. On the other hand, the traditional reformed and Presbyterian theologians believe that baptism is a sign and the seal of the covenant as circumcision in the Old Testament. See for further discussion of the different views on baptism, Erickson, *Introducing Christian Doctrine*, 346–349.

transformed into the body and blood of Christ. Martin Luther rejected the Roman Catholic's transubstantiation but insisted that the phrase, "This is my body" had to be taken in some sense literal. His supposition is that the physical body of Christ is *present in, with and under* the bread of the Lord's Supper. Luther's position, like that of the Roman Catholic Church, failed to see the symbolic nature of the phrase, "This is my body."[15] The most biblical understanding of the phrase is that the elements of the Lord's Table are symbolic representations of the presence of Christ. They gave a visible sign of the fact that Christ himself is truly present during the Lord's Supper. Hence, the presence of Christ is spiritually present in the fellowship and communion that the Lord's Supper affords us.

The prerequisites for fellowshipping at the Lord's Table are nowhere stated in the Bible. But it could be inferred from certain texts that the participants should be persons having a spiritual relationship with the Lord Jesus Christ at whose table they are having communion. Moreover, they should be mature enough to discern the body of the Lord (1Cor 11:29). In addition, they should not be living in flagrant sin (1 Cor 5:1–5). Should this flagrant sin in the African context include polygamy? The problem of polygamy is intricately related with issues of African values, Western cultures and the Bible. To this end, Yusufu Turaki revealed that "Polygamy is the most difficult theological issue to deal with in Africa because of the apparent uncompromising and irreconcilable views of African culture and religion and Western Christianity."[16] The presence of increasing polygamous relationships in Africa is attested by Mbiti when he observed, "Getting married to two or more wives is a custom found all over Africa, though in some societies it is less common than in others."[17] Aidan Southall also observed, "Africa remains a continent of polygamy. Polygamy is the undoubted goal of men in rural society, though comparatively few reach it until their later years . . ."[18] Significantly, Southall noted, "We are therefore justified in assuming that most Africans still consider that sexual access to a plurality of women is a male right. Islam supports this and

---

15. Other views include Zwinglian and the Reformed position. The Reformed or Calvinistic view believes that Christ is not present physically or bodily, but spiritually, while the Zwinglian position advocated that the Lord's Supper is essentially a commemoration of Christ's death. See for a detail discussion on these different views: Erickson, *Introducing Christian Doctrine*, 352–57.

16. Turaki, *Christianity and African Gods*, 35.

17. Mbiti, *African Religions and Philosophy*, 142.

18. Southall, "The Position of Women," 53.

Christian teaching has made little headway against it." In his definition of Polygamy, Mbiti noted,

> Technically the term 'polygamy' should mean what its Greek components imply, and that is, marrying 'many' (wives, husbands. . . .). But in popular usage it is applied to mean the state of marriage in which there is one husband and two or more wives. This should be referred to as 'polygyny'; and where one wife has two or more husbands this is 'polyandry.'[19]

Mbiti revealed the benefit of polygamy in the traditional African setting particularly its benefit in terms of children, immortality of the man, social status, corporate existence, reduction of unfaithfulness and prostitution.[20] Mbiti also noted, some of the problem associated with African polygamy such as internal conflict between the wives and children, favouritism, financially related problems, family care and disciplining of children.[21] After illustrating the benefits and problems of African polygamy, Mbiti observed, "It needs to be pointed out that the problems of polygamous families are human problems and are not necessarily created by polygamy as such; nor have they been solved or avoided in monogamous families either in Africa or Europe and America."[22]

Similarly, Samuel Waje Kunyihop following similar recognition of the theological difficulty polygamy poses to the African society, however, he further observed, "There are still people from both the old and young, the educated and uneducated, the religious and pagan, Christians and non-Christians who still practice polygamy."[23] Idowu revealed that among the Yoruba people "polygamous relationship is common," however, "It is realized that the basis of conjugal happiness is in the faithfulness of both parties; that is so, even in a polygamous community."[24]

From this dominance of polygamous relationships in Africa, an ethical concern is the denominational barricade stopping polygamous couples from partaken of the Lord's Table. If the primary concern of the Lord's Table is for the remembrance of Jesus Christ, is not proper for such polygamous couples to also partake in order to remember him? Thus the central concerns of the contemporary African church is not whether Jesus

19. Mbiti, *African Religions and Philosophy*, 142.

20. Ibid.

21. Ibid., 143.

22. Ibid., 144.

23. Kunhiyop, *African Christian Ethics*, 314.

24. Idowu, *Oòdúmare*, 157.

is literally or symbolically present in the elements of the Holy Communion as debated by the Western church in the past, but whether polygamous couples could partake in the Communion? The early missionary barred many genuine Christians having polygamous relationships from joining the Church. In many places, they were anathemazed because of their polygamous relationships. Due to such developments, significant numbers of intending converts or Christians were lost to Islam. From such historical lessons, is it proper to re-evaluate such denominational stipulations or to re-evaluate scriptural understanding of such unions? Superficially, these African polygamists read the Bible and see polygamous relationships characterizing some of the holy patriarchs of Old Testament faith such as Abraham, Jacob, Moses and David and they are at a roadblock, and they often ask "how could such unions be lawful for these holy men and be unlawful for us?" While the issue of polygamy and Holy Communion is controversial, it is important that denominational constitutions and bye laws should find ways of discouraging polygamous relationships without jeopardizing the right of the polygamous Christian in participating from the Communion table.

Conclusion

The African church is confronted with various ecclesiological problems that center on Baptism and the Lord's Supper. Concerning the first, the African church is struggling to maintain the membership of those who indeed have had a spiritual conversion experience and other ones who do not. Often it is hard to know who have had a direct spiritual experience of conversion in the midst of multitudes trooping into the church. Thus, as it should be expected, nominalism becomes common and insincere spiritual commitment is often popular. On the other hand, baptism has become a prestigious religious experience in the African church because it is the entry point towards the recognition of one as a committed member of the church. Often, people undergo the experience of baptism without the corresponding spiritual understanding of the significance of this religious ritual, thus unfortunately many get baptized in order to participate or attain the social prestige accorded by the church to its baptized members. In this regard, some Africans joined the church and subsequently seek baptism because they want the church to give them a befitting burial at the time of their death or for the church to identify with them during their moment of crisis or problems. In this capacity, the church acts or replaces the traditional social institutions or specifically the clan kinship which is traditionally designed to carry out the said burial functions. In this way, the church is actually dispensing the cultural defined role of the clan gatherings. Seen from this perspective, it is not surprising the church in many places in Africa has become a glorified tribal or clan gathering.[25] Similarly, many African people get baptized because they want the flamboyant church's wedding especially the wearing of the white gown for the bride and the suit-dress code for the bridegroom. The prestige accorded to this westernized church's wedding has forced the African church to use this event as a bait for baptism, and hence they insist on only conducting the wedding ceremony for members who are baptized. Consequently, baptism in Africa is an outward indicator of one's good standing with the church and also indicates the promise of social or material benefits to the one who is being baptized. In almost the same understanding, partaking of the Lord's Supper, in Africa, is one of the socially or spiritually prestigious indicators of one's spirituality, thus strict denominational legislation is common which is intended to guard against the unscrupulous taking of Holy Communion. Such denominational concern often reveals itself in the barring of polygamists, disallowing them to partake in the remembrance of the Lord at the Table of Holy Communion. To this end, the chapter presents various biblical teachings in these and other ecclesiastical concerns of the African church.

---

25. See Sankey, "The Church as Clan," 437–49.

12

The Future Hope

Introduction

MBITI RIGHTLY OBSERVED THAT "[t]he Christian faith is intensely eschatological . . ."[1] or in other words, the Christian faith is largely preoccupied with issues of the future world. This assertion is readily seen in the close relationships between the various doctrines of the Bible and the theme of the other world. In particular, the biblical teachings on God, Christ, salvation, ethics and even ecology have inherently eschatological dimensions that one cannot successfully do justice to these subjects without adequately considering their eschatological implications in relation to the future. In fact, one can readily say that the Christian message becomes meaningless without a right emphasis on its eschatological vision or description of the persons and events of the next world. The message of the Christian faith ends in the book of Revelation with a graphic description of the world of the future whereby all the wrongs of the present world are made right and the dawning of a new world order without death, sickness, poverty, and other ills that have continually battered the pride of human attainments and advancement. Consequently, the message of the Christian Bible closes with a message of hope.

On the other hand, despite the dominance of the theme of eschatology in biblical thought, Mbiti also noted the docile nature of the Christian eschatology and its tendency to encourage passivity among Christian

---

1. Mbiti, "New Testament Eschatology," 17.

believers in the world of "the here and now." In this criticism of Christian eschatology, Mbiti significantly critiqued the futuristic and forward–looking nature of Christian theology, hence he observed,

> This presentation of eschatology directs the attention of Christians only to the next world, thus evading them responsibilities and involvement in the Christian life here and now. They hope for a reward in heaven, comprising all the good things which they believe to be denied them here on earth.[2]

However, the specific claims of Mbiti that the African worldview lacks a forward–looking or futuristic dimension of time has been hotly debated because it presumes the impossibility of the African people to adopt the temporal frame of a Christian eschatology, which is basically forward or futuristic driven. Unfortunately, this conception of the African understanding of time as hypothesized by Mbiti often ignores the domineering power of the present in the merger of the two temporal planes in traditional African thought. In fact, the description of the past in traditional African society is largely enmeshed in the present at basic points. Histories, stories and cultic practices of the past are narrated or told by African people because of their close relationship to the issues or events of the present. In the thought frame of the African people, there is a close proximity between the past and the present. Indeed, a corresponding and entwined relationship exists between these two horizons that the separation of the two frames or horizons is technically impossible since the interest of the present often forms the basis for a reference to the past. Consequently, events are presented from the horizon of the past, but in their relationship or interest to the present. Often, it is the present that overwhelmingly shapes our description of the past. In fact, the present is the time frame by which the past is reinterpreted or understood. Everything in the past is narrated or told because of its direct significance to the present. Thus the present plays an important role in the traditional worldviews of the African people. For most African people, an interest in the past for the sake of the past is strange because the past is only useful in terms of its service to the present.

Similarly, Carl G. Jung in his discourse on the "Modern Man in Search of a Soul," noted,

> The Modern man or, let us say again, the man of the immediate present—is rarely met with. There are few who live up to the

2. Ibid., 20.

name, for they must be conscious to a superlative degree. Since to be wholly of the present means to be fully conscious of one's existence as a man . . .[3]

Thus Jung concluded "He alone is modern who is fully conscious of the present."[4] In this regard, according to Jung, many people are not modern because being modern is closely associated with an intensive consciousness of the present. There is also a relationship between Jungian logic and the African traditional description of time at this point since both of them have a high regard for the present even though they differ in the terms of this relationship. In particular, Christianity falls within the "un–modern classification" if a Jungian definition is used since Christianity has dominant eschatological motifs that place theological emphases from the domain of the present to those of the future. After World War II, Jung recognized the skepticism towards eschatology when he noted,

> Think of nearly two thousand years of Christian ideals followed, instead of by the return of the Messiah and the heavenly millennium, by the World War among Christian nations and its barbed-wire and poison-gas. What a catastrophe in heaven and on earth! . . . I realize only too well that I am losing my faith in the possibility of a rational organization of the world, that old dream of the millennium, in which peace and harmony should rule, has grown pale. The modern's skepticism regarding all such matters has chilled his enthusiasm for politics and world-reform . . .[5]

While Jungian thesis could be right that contextual problems have a way of dimming eschatological longings, however, often it is the problems of a human setting that fanned its eschatological vision. Consequently, on the African continent often it is the despicable standard of living, unstable politics and other harsh facts of the African existential context which has brought to the fore significantly its emphasis on eschatology. Thus, many African Christians from the discomfort of the continent seek a psychological refuge or consolation in the eschatological message of the Christian faith. As is always the case, such unbalanced eschatological emphases often degenerate into passive engagement with the social and political ills of the society and thus sabotaging ultimately the needed contribution of the Christian person in the public sphere. Within the Christian faith, the

3. Jung, *Modern Man*, 196.

4. Ibid. 167.

5. Ibid., 199.

theology of the future consists of three major events namely the second coming of Christ, the millennium reign of Christ and the final judgment, which are presented in the New Testament as cardinal elements of the Christian hope. These major events are briefly analyzed below.

Traditional African Eschatologcal Expectations

There are few or even no eschatological expectations in traditional African society because most African traditional beliefs have no room for a clearly defined eschatological vision apart from scattered ideas of afterlife which often lace its religious imagination. The end of eschatological vision is narrowly defined around the "abode of the dead" in traditional African society. The living Africans look forward to this place as the final destination of their journey on earth. The idea of a "millennium" or "cosmic" judgment" is absent in traditional African thought because its entire eschatological imagination ends with the "land of the dead." Ironically, despite its communal inclination, there is the absence of a collective resurrection or eschatological vision which speaks of a collective millennium that is characterized by an eternal time of peace and prosperity for the entire human community. To this end, Tokunboh Adeyemo observed, African people "do not have any doctrine of the resurrection of the body in such a dramatic, eschatological sense as the graves giving up their dead at the consummation of all things as stated in the Bible."[6] In this same way, Mbiti has also noted, "As far as our evidence goes, African people do not expect any form of individual or collective resurrection to rise again: he lost that gift in the primeval period, and he knows of no means to regain it."[7] A similar point has been made by Idowu in his study of the concept of the afterlife among the Yoruba people.[8] He notes that the Yoruba people are one of the few African peoples that have a concept of reward and punishment as part of their belief in the afterlife. In relation to this view, Mbiti said,

> Apart from these few ideas [among Yoruba and Lodagaa people], we have no concrete evidence of the hereafter being pictured in terms of punishment or reward. For the majority of African peoples, the hereafter is only a continuation of life more or less as it is in its human form. This means that personalities are retained, social and political statuses are maintained,

6. Adeyemo, *Salvation in African Tradition*, 66.

7. Mbiti, *Concepts of God in Africa*, 14.

8. Idowu, *Oòdúmare*, 200.

sex distinction is continued, human activities are reproduced in the hereafter, the wealth or poverty of the individual remains unchanged, and in many ways, the hereafter is a carbon copy of the present life. Although the soul is separated from the body it is believed to retain most, if not all, of the physical-social characteristics of its human life.[9]

To this end, Mbiti further noted, ". . . there is no 'world to come,' such as is found in Judaism and Christianity."[10] In particular, the African eschatological vision is primarily narrowed around the families rather than a cosmic vision for the entire human race. The dead soul is expected to join the deceased ancestors, thus ending his entire journey on earth. The condition of the dead in this "abode of the dead" is often shrouded in mystery because the new dead arrivals gradually lose their personhood and identity, and they become faceless spirits of the region of the dead.[11] The dead are welcomed and reunited to their dead family members, thus the eschatological vision is primarily defined around the family or clan. This family kind of eschatological vision comes from the emphasis of the African people on a binding familial kinship which transcends the boundaries of the grave. However, such dominance of a family orientation to eschatology does not provide the needed place for a cosmic one. Similarly, even though the creation or the beginning of the world is clearly envisaged in African cosmology as readily seen in different myths and legends, there are no eschatological visions about the end of the world. Even places where such an eschatological vision is entertained, the presence of such eschatological longing may have come partly from the influence of the Judeo–Christian heritage. The factor responsible for this absence could be traced to a philosophical assumption which could not imagine an end to a "good thing" such as the world because despite its many problems the world is generally good since it provides the African people with food, cattle, land, children and other blessings. Hence for the African people, it becomes largely impossible to visualize the end or termination of this world.[12] Similarly, ontologically speaking, the fate of the human race is

9. Mbiti, *African Religions and Philosophy*, 161.

10. Ibid, 23.

11. On theological issues of resurrection, reincarnation and transmigration see Adeyemo, *Salvation in African Tradition*, 66–68.

12. Mbiti further observed that the desire for the continuation of this life is so well entrenched that "For peoples who think that the hereafter is in another world or a distant place, food and weapons may be buried with the dead body to sustain and protect the person in the journey between the two worlds or places." See ibid, 159.

as a necessity tied to the continuation of the world because the continuous existence of the world provides the place for giving birth to children, which is an ontological necessity in traditional thought for the continuance of the human race. In traditional African thought, even the dead live again in their children, hence the traditional belief in the reincarnation of a deceased father or mother. In fact, the African person is truly dead only when he or she has no children who will succeed him. Thus the barren persons are ontologically dead, that is, they do not exist or live. Through this traditional reasoning the continuance of the world is seen as a true necessity for the continuous importance and survival of the human race. In this traditional African understanding, human beings cannot exist or survive without some relationship with the world. The African people could not imagine a "celestial world" that has no connection whatsoever with this physical world. It cannot imagine another world that will logically continue after the termination of the present one. Consequently, the African eschatological imagination does not emphasize the termination of this world because this present world is necessary for the continuation of the next, that is, even the ancestors need this present world to continue since without this continuance they, ontologically speaking, become truly dead.

The Second Coming

The first subject under this categorization is the second coming of Christ. According to Bruce Milne, "The centre of the Christian hope is Christ himself and his glorious appearing."[13] The early church described the second coming of Jesus Christ as the "blessed hope" (Titus 2:13). The scriptures teach that Jesus Christ will come back again physically (Acts 1:11). The consciousness of Jesus' return was so imminent in the early church that Christians in Thessalonica refused to work and daily waited looking forward for his return (2 Thess 3:10). The New Testament teaches that Jesus' second coming will be sudden, personal, visible and bodily (Matt 24:4; John 14:3; Acts 1:11; 1 Thess 4:16; Jas 5:8; Rev 1:7; 22:20). The scriptures also teach that we should eagerly long for his return (Rev 22:20; Titus 2:12–13; Phil 3:20; 1 Cor 16:22). However, the scriptures also teach that we do not know when Christ will return (Matt 24:44; 25:13; Mark 13:32–33; Luke 12:40). Many verses in the scriptures teach the suddenness and the unexpected nature of his return (Matt 24:36–39, 42–44; Mark 13:32–33;

13. Milne, *Know the Truth*, 326.

Luke 12:40; 1 Cor 16:22; 1 Thess 5:2), while other verses seem to advocate that there will be signs that precede his return. The signs that will precede his return include; the preaching of the gospel to all nations (Mark 13:10; 24:14), the great tribulation (Mark 13:19–20), coming of the false prophets working signs and wonders (Mark 13:19–20. cf. Matt 24:23–24), signs in the heavens (Mark 13:24–26; cf. Matt 24:29–30; Luke 21:25–27), the coming of the man of sin and the rebellion (1 John 2:18; 2 Thess 2:1–10; Rev 13) and the salvation of Israel (Rom 11:25–26). The obvious tension could be resolve with the understanding that it is unlikely but possible that these signs have already been fulfilled, and hence we simply cannot tell precisely at any point in history whether all these signs have been fulfilled. This theological stance presupposes a possibility that some of these signs have been fulfilled in the past, but also anticipates the fulfillment of greater part of them in the future. This attitude is very good for the Christian life because Christians living in each generation will seriously watch for the coming of their Lord and Master as each world event blues and fades. In particular, four important purposes of the second coming can be highlighted. First, the second coming of Jesus Christ is a very important element of the Christian's future hope because his coming ultimately brings to an end the life of persecution and pain as brought about by the fall and the hostility of the present world to the church (Matt. 24:12, 21ff). Through his coming, Christ will begin the process which leads to the completion of the "redemptive purposes of God across the ages" when "All God's enemies, sin, death and the devil will be removed from God's world."[14] This ultimate victory of God over evil (See 1 Cor 15:22–28, 42–57; Rev 12:7–11; 20:10; 22:1–15; 2Pet 3:1–13) makes the second coming of Christ a very important ingredient of Christian hope. In addition, the coming of Jesus Christ is a moment of great joy because we will be rewarded for every service done in his name (2 Cor 5:8–10; 1 Thess 2:19–20). Lastly, the second coming of Christ will bring about reunion with Christians who are dead in the Lord. It will be a joyous occasion when we will be reunited with the loved ones who have died in the Lord. The resurrection of these loved ones at his coming has provided Christians throughout the history of the church with element of hope (1Thess. 4:13–18).

14. Milne, *Know the Truth*, 315.

The Millennium Reign

The second theme under the definition of eschatology or Christian future hope is the subject of the millennium. The thousand years' reign of Christ commonly known as the Millennium is a period when Christ will reign on earth. However, theologians are divided on the time as well as the nature of the one thousand years reign. Three views concerning the millennium are generally held. The first of these views is the amillennial view of the millennium. The amillennial position is that the millennium is taking place currently in the church age. For the proponent of amillennism, Revelation 20:1–10 is fulfilled in the ministry of the church age, because through the redemptive work of Christ and the gospel, Satan is bound and his deception unveiled. Hence for the advocate of the amillennial position, the reign of Jesus is not a physical–bodily reign, but a spiritual–heavenly reign.[15]

The second view on the millennium reign is the postmillennial. The postmillennial position believes that Christ will return after the thousand years. According to them, the church age will transform society, hence ushering in the millennium. It is then that Christ will return after the one thousand years to execute judgment and then comes the eternal state. The third view of the millennial, the premillennial, believes that the church age will end by a period of tribulation. Thence, Christ will come to establish a physical millennial kingdom on earth, with dead Christians whose bodies will reunite with their spirits to rule the earth with him. The primary premises for a premillennial understanding of the millennium are based on three fundamental theological thrusts. Firstly, this position did justice to many Old Testament scriptural passage that describe some future stage in the history of redemption that is far greater than the present church but that still does not see the removal of all sin and rebellion and death from the earth (Isa 65:10; 11:2–9; Ps 72:8–14; Zech 14:6–21; 1 Cor 15:24; Rev 2:27; 12:5; 19:15). Secondly, there are New Testament passages other than Revelation 20 that suggest a future millennium (Rev 2:26–27; 12:5–6; 19:15; 1 Cor 15:23–25). Thirdly, Revelation 20 indeed teaches a future millennium by the greater restriction of Satan, which seems future in verse 2–3 and a bodily resurrection in verse 4.[16]

Equally, there are diverse views on tribulation. The proponents of pretribulation presuppose that there will be the rapture of the church

15. For a theological defense of Amillennism and a critique of Premillennism see Berkhof, *Systematic Theology*, 708–16.

16. See for more discussion on plausibility of the Premillennial's position, Grudem, *Bible Doctrine*, 438–51.

before the events of the great tribulation, a period in the Bible that is regarded as a moment of intense difficulty and hardship for the inhabitants of the earth. On the other hand, the advocates of posttribulation believe that the Church will go through tribulation. Other positions like the midtribulation believe that the church will be raptured in the middle of the tribulation. It seems that the dominant biblical understanding about tribulation is tilted towards the posttribulation. Many passages indicate that the church will go through the tribulation (Matt 24:29–31), though there might be the possibility of protection from its severity (Rev 3:10; 1 Thess 4:17). Moreover, the biblical worldview stresses the trials and harsh conditions that believers will pass through rather than removal from these adversities.[17] Throughout the history of the African church, it has continually wrestled with the problem of pain and suffering that comes from persecution. Even though its churches, due to the influence of Western Christianity, have professed allegiance to the pretribulation or midtribulation schools of thought, in her daily experience she has always gone through tribulation, and often with the added severity of dysfunctional political, economical and social sectors. Thus it appears the African church has remained in a perennial state of tribulation.

The Resurrection

Bodily resurrection is a cardinal teaching of the Christian faith, which lies at the heart of New Testament teaching.[18] In fact, the New Testament describes the centrality of Christ's bodily resurrection and the expected resurrection of the bodies of the believers in likeness to his resurrected body. Thus Paul said, "But our citizenship is in heaven. And we eagerly await a Savior from there, the Lord Jesus Christ, who, by the power that enables him to bring everything under his control, will transform our lowly bodies so that they will be like his glorious body" (Phil 3:20–21). Paul based the resurrection of the believers on the fact that Jesus Christ had resurrected, thus providing the believer with the hope of resurrection.

17. For more theological arguments in support of the Pretribulation position see Erickson, *Introducing Christian*, 382–94.

18. The Old Testament speaks of a bodily resurrection, thus for example Isaiah 26:19 said, "but your dead will live; their bodies will rise. You who dwell in the dust, wake up and shout for joy. Your dew is like the dew of the morning; the earth will give birth to her dead." See also Ezekiel 37:12–14. The understanding of bodily resurrection in the Old Testament is closely connected to the dawning of a new world order at the eschaton.

In his discourse on resurrection in 1 Corinthians 15, Paul established the basis of the believer's hope for resurrection on Christ's resurrection, and unequivocally asserted that "our preaching and faith is useless if Christ has not resurrected" (1 Cor 15:14). In this understanding, Jesus is the "first-born from the dead" (Col 1:18) and the "first to rise from the dead" (Acts 26:23). The resurrected life of Jesus Christ is expected to characterize the life of the believer now, which by the power of God's Spirit gives him a foretaste of the victorious resurrected life now, and the future hope also for a bodily resurrection after death. Underscoring the unique character of biblical teaching on bodily resurrection in comparison to the Asian or African conception of the afterlife, Roland Chia rightly observed,

> The centrality of the resurrection of the dead is unique to Christianity and cannot be found in the religions and philosophies of Asia [or even Africa]. Most Asian religions gravitate towards the idea of the reincarnation or rebirth of individuals according to what they have done in their previous lives.[19]

However, he further noted, "The resurrection of the dead is the essence of biblical individual eschatology."[20] In a sense, the resurrection of the believers in Christ is a culmination of the divine program for the world, and the satisfaction of the hopes and yearnings of humanity for immortality. Significantly, it appears the New Testament is largely preoccupied with the subject of resurrection for believers in Christ, and often makes only a passing reference to the resurrection of unbelievers (Dan 12:2; John 5:28–29; Rev 20:11–15). The possible reason for such distinction may come primarily from the understanding that resurrection for the believer is a joyous event, while for the unbeliever it is the beginning of the process of eternal damnation. Thus the resurrection of the believer in Christ provides eternal hope and presents the future in glorious way.

The Final Judgment

The last subject under consideration is the reality of final judgment and eternal punishment. The scriptures teach that there will be final judgment, when the world will be judged (Acts 17:30–31; Rom 2:5; Matt 10:15; 11:22,24; 12:36; 25:31–46; 1 Cor 4:5; Heb 6:2; 9:27; 2 Pet 2:4; Jude 6; Rev 20:11–15). The time for this judgment will be after the millennium and the

19. Chia, *Hope for the World*, 76.
20. Ibid.

rebellion that follows it (Rev 20:1–6, 7–8, 9–10, 11). Jesus will be the judge on that great day (2 Tim 4:1; Acts 10:42cf. 17:31; Matt 25:31–33; John 5:26–27). The unbelievers as well as believers will be judged. The distinction is that the believer is already judged in Christ, hence for the believer the judgment will be a time of rewards for faithful services to God (2 Cor 5:10; Rom 2:6–11; Rev 11:18; 20:12,15; John 5:24; 1 Cor 4:5; Col 3:25; Mic 7:19; Ps 103:12; Isa 43:25; Heb 8:12), while for the unbeliever it will be a time of punishment and torment. The unbelievers will be judged according to "what they have done," (Rev 20:12, 13) hinting that the punishment will be grade by grade (Luke 12:47–48; Matt 11:22; Luke 20:47). But even the rewarding of the believers will also be according to the measure of their service and faithfulness (1 Cor 3:12–15; 2 Cor 5:10; Luke 19:17, 19). Similarly, angels will be judged (2 Pet 2:4; Jude 6; 1 Cor 6:3). God in the final judgment will show Himself just and righteous for all eternity, because at last sin and unrighteousness is judged (Rev 19:1–2; Rom 2:11; 3:19; 1 Pet 1:17). Four moral implications are inevitable in dealing with the doctrine of final judgment and eternal punishment. Firstly, the doctrine of final judgment satisfies our inward quest for justice in the world (Col 3:25; Rev 20:12; Mal 3:16). Secondly, the doctrine of final judgment enables us to forgive others freely (Rom 12:19; 1 Pet 2:22–23; Luke 23:34; Acts 7:60). Thirdly, the doctrine of final judgment provides a motivation for righteous living (Matt. 6:20; Rom. 3:18; 2 Pet 3:3–4). Lastly, the doctrine of final judgment provides a great motivation for evangelism.[21]

Equally related to the doctrine of final judgment is the doctrine of hell. In traditional African religion, the concept of hell is absent. Describing this absence, Steve Biko observed, "There was no hell in our religion. We believe in the inherent goodness of man—hence we took it for granted that all people at death joined the community of the saints and therefore merited our respect."[22] However within the Christian thought, hell is a place of eternal conscious punishment for the wicked. In fact, the scripture teaches the reality of hell.[23] But on the other hand, the scripture also

21. Grudem, *Bible Doctrine*, 458–459.

22. Biko, *I Write What I Like*, 93.

23. Matthew 25:30, 41, 46; Mark 9:43, 48; Luke 16:22–24; Revelation 14:9–11. Many object to the eternal nature of the punishment of the wicked, instead they propose annihilation of the wicked, in the place of a conscious eternal torment of the wicked. They argue for annihilation based on the premises that some scriptural passages advocate the destruction of the wicked (Phil 3:19; 1 Thess 5:3; 2 Thess 1:9; 2 Pet 3:7). Moreover, they reasoned there is an apparent inconsistency of eternal conscious punishment with the love of God. In addition, they argue that there is an apparent

teaches that believers are going to live eternally with God in the New Heaven and New Earth (Matt 25:34; Rev 22:3; Isa 65:17; 66:22; 2 Pet 3:13). The scripture also teaches that heaven is not a state of mind, but a place (Acts 1:9, 11; cf. Luke 24:51). The scripture also reveals that the physical creation will be renewed, and we will continue to exist and act in it (2 Pet 3:13; Rev 21:1; Rom 8:19–21). Moreover, this new creation will be a place of great beauty and abundance and joy in the presence of God (Rev 21:2–3, 4, 6, 11, 23, 27; 22:5).

Conclusion

The human race has become increasingly disillusioned with the thought of the earth becoming a peaceful, edenic and heaven–like habitation because of the increase of wars, diseases, and other existential problems. From the religious point of view, many have abandoned the thought of a millennium on earth where all the problems or ills of the world will cease. After the two world wars and the continued conflicts among nations of the world, the hopes of realizing the humanistic dreams of science and the idealism of the Christian religion for a paradise at the end of human history appears unattainable. In the same way, skepticism has generally continued unabated, particularly with the declining standard of living in human societies and the growing religious and political conflicts around the regions of Africa, Asia and Latin America.

However, despite contemporary skepticism, the modern world reveals a consistent quest to change the world into a better place. Thus humanistic quest has manifested itself in the continued ecological and political campaigns to transform human society into a habitable place for the continuous survival of the human race. This kind of humanistic eschatology has fundamentally influenced some theological schools of thought which argue that the millennium will be realized through human programs, reforms and administrations. Contrary to such theological understanding, the Bible presents the realization of the millennium as

---

injustice involved in the punishment of sin that occurs in time and punishment that is eternal. Against these presuppositions, Grudem proposes that the passages that seemingly advocate annihilation do not actually support this because they speak of the harmful and destructive effects of the final judgment on the wicked. Moreover, Grudem has argued that the reason we perceive the unfairness involved is because we wrongly assume that we know the extent of the evil done when sinners rebel against God. For more theological discourse on these issues see Grudem, "The Final Judgment and Eternal Punishment," *Bible Doctrine*, 460–62.

fundamentally based on God's initiative and not on human planning and programs. While the Bible indeed encourages us to engage in the transformation of human society, the transformation of the world in eschatological terms is not a gradual process or the outcome of human activity but the product of a sudden divine activity. In Africa, eschatological hopes are always high because of the frustration of the economy, the chaotic politics, rising crime, falling standard of living, unemployment, insecurity and epidemics. In this worrisome context, it is not surprising that many prophetic or eschatological churches have come to give the African populace the hope of a better life in the millennium. Unfortunately, such eschatological hopes do not often impose on the African people a quest to change the society in the present. As the economy of Africa improves and the dividends of democracy are realized, there is no doubt such eschatological hopes will dwindle or translate into some kind of social, economic and political programs for the African continent. Consequently, African Christianity must explore the two temporal dimensions of biblical eschatology in providing hope for the now, but looking beyond the now to the culmination of God's program in eternity.

13

Conclusion

A FRICAN TRADITIONS HAVE OBVIOUSLY survived despite the consistent attacks by the forces of modernity and Western civilization. In fact, African traditions have accommodated modernity and Western civilization as readily seen in its contemporary cultural sway over the African continent especially in Sub-Saharan Africa. Even though such sway is not in its pristine traditional form, African traditions have continually held the constant admiration and adherence of millions of the human race. In Sub-Saharan Africa in particular, there is a growing resurgence of African traditions among the elite and the educated classes despite the increasing westernization of the African political, economical, social and religious systems. For example, African traditional healing has become increasingly patronized by even the educated class as good and effective remedies to cure sickness which orthodox or Western medicine could not cure. Thus one constantly now hears Africans saying "This sickness is not for hospital" or in pidgin English, "This sickness no be hospital own na traditional method fit solvam." Patients with such sickness are referred by even African scientifically-trained medical doctors to seek the help and expertise of the traditional African witchdoctor or herbalist in order to cure the sickness. This understanding has become so commonplace that one hears on radio and television advertisement of the efficacy of one traditional African herbal practitioner or the other. Even though one could readily say that the patronizing of alternative African traditional medicine by the African people comes from the failure of the African health sector especially in providing modern medical care and cure to the patients in hospitals and clinics. However, it is also possible that this growing contemporary phenomenon is the product of African traditions seeking to usurp the monopoly of orthodox medicine with its profoundly scientific and Western assumptions.

Apart from the health sector, African traditions have also sought to usurp or influence contemporary religious elements in place within African society. In particular, the tenacity of the African traditions is readily seen in the various expressions of African Christianity. For example, African Christianity has birthed a unique brand of Christianity, which is fundamentally shaped by African traditions and worldview. This brand of Christianity is known as "African Independent Churches" or "African Prophetic Churches" and shows the continuous power of African traditions which continue to wrestle with the claims of Christianity, and the overarching quest to Christianize African traditions or to Africanize Christianity. Either way, African tradition becomes a formidable partner or opponent which African Christianity must adequately seek to understand, interpret and confront.

Historically, African traditions received a major political boost during the time of independence from Western countries and the recognition by the then African fledging states that African traditions are basic ingredients which are necessary for building of an African identity. Since then African traditions have become accepted, encouraged and promoted by African elites such as the politicians, professors at the universities, celebrities and influential African personalities. It is not surprising that in the post-colonial world, African traditions have remained strong on the African continent despite Western influences.

Due to the defining nature of African tradition on the continent of Africa, the present study sought to describe various Christian teachings in the context of some particular or common African denominators and practices in order to encourage a deeper interaction between Christianity and the African people at the level of traditions. Thus since Christian theology has also understood itself as a kind of tradition which is handed down from the biblical apostles to the church, the interaction between Christianity and the African people is enriched because African people have also assumed that their traditions have been handed down to them through generations of ancestral mediations of communal wisdom. This makes the encounter between Christianity and the African people a confrontation to be understood at the level of traditions. It is important that Christian theology must resolve the conflict arising from this encounter between the apostolic tradition and the age-old traditions of the African people in order for Christianity to become meaningful to the African people. Without such clear understanding of this encounter, Christianity, even though now given some forms of recognition, will at the end become merely one of the many religious cults on the African continent, thus losing its exclusive biblical character. This nominal status of Christianity is already practiced especially in the growing jettisoning of Christian values and beliefs at the most critical moments of life. It is not surprising to note that many African Christians at critical moments of birth, marriage, death, burial and other problems of real life strongly identify with their African traditions rather than biblical or Christian traditions. Thus for example, African people give strong emphasis on the traditional marriage ceremony rather than the Christian wedding, and often the former is given precedence over the latter. In the same way, African Christians are comfortable in seeking traditional modes of supernatural guidance rather than Christian forms such as reading the Bible. These incidences show the powerful and persistent influence of African traditions, and thus necessitate the need of interaction between Christian theology and various expressions of these traditions. The present work uses "traditions" rather than the usual nomenclature of "culture" because tradition is an all-embracing term that encompasses many cultures, but most importantly, this use of "tradition" shows not merely the longevity but the durability of these African cultural practices. Consequently, tradition goes deeper than culture and also shows the challenging nature of the entire encounter between Christianity and the African continent since it is an encounter between two inherited traditions. The African traditions make claims that its traditions are necessary towards the construction of its identity. Thus we could ask the pertinent question whether one can jettison African traditions and still remain an African, or to put this another way, by taking on the Christian traditions are Africans not taking on a foreign identity since it is assumed that traditions of a particular people are key to the formation of the identity of such people? The contention of this work is that Christian theology should encourage taking on the positive elements of the African traditions and positioning these elements in dialogue with the teaching of the scriptures. Through such dialogue between the traditions of the Bible and the African traditions it will result in a new identity for the African Christian that is biblically founded, but distinctively African. This transformed Christian identity will understand the African world from the vantage point of the Judeo-Christian traditions while duly acknowledging the positive elements of the African traditions. Consequently, such engagement will help to provide an African Christian with an identity that is not particularly based on African traditions alone, but on the biblical traditions as expressed in the Judeo-Christian form. Thus an African Christian becomes heir of the Judeo-Christian faith while he or she also allows this heritage to transform the various traditions of his African world. At the end, the encounter between Christianity and the African continent is an encounter between the Judeo-Christian traditions and the age-old African traditions. For the African Christian, his loyalty is to the noun rather than the adjective that describes him, thus "African Christian" becomes first and foremost committed to the "Christian" in this label, and it is such "Christian" commitment that determines his general attitude to the "African" and the adjectival nomenclature that further describes him.

Bibliography

Abogunrin, S. O. *University of Ibadan Inaugural Lecture, 1997/98: In Search of the Original Jesus.* Ibadan: M. Alofe Enterprise, 2003.

―――. J. O. Akao, D. O. Akintude, G. M. Toryyough, eds. *Christology in African Context: Biblical Studies Series* no. 2 (2003): 1–411.

―――. "The Total Adequacy of Christ in the African Context." *Ogbomoso Journal of Theology* (1986): 9–16.

Abrams, Daniel. "The Boundaries of Divine Ontology: The Inclusion and Exclusion of the Metatron in the Godhead." *Harvard Theological Review* 87.3 (1994): 291–321.

Ada, Juliana Mary and Elizabeth Isichei, "Perceptions of God in the Churches in Obudu." *Journal of Religion in Africa* 7.3 (1975): 165–73.

Adamo, David Tuesday. "The Use of Psalms in African Indigenous Churches in Nigeria." In *The Bible in Africa: transactions, trajectories and trends,* eds. Gerald O. West and Musa Dube Shomanah, 336–49. Leiden: Koninklijke Brill, 2000.

Adeyemo, Tokunboh. *Salvation in African Tradition.* Nairobi, Kenya: Evangel, 1997.

Aerthayil, James. "Interiority: A Universal Search for Contemplative Experience." In *Light from the East: Essays in Commemoration of the Golden Jubilee of Carmel Vidya Bhavan (19430'93),* ed. James Aerthayil, 279–88. Bangalore, India: Dharmaram Publications, 1993.

Akinade, Akintunde E. "New Religious Movements in Contemporary Nigeria: Aladura Churches as a Case Study." *Asia Journal of Theology* 10.2 (1996): 316–32.

Allen, D. C. "Milton and the Love of Angels." *Modern Language Notes* 76.6 (1961): 489–90.

Amoah, Elizabeth. "African Christologies." *Dictionary of Third World Theologies,* eds. Virginia Fabella & R. S. Surgirtharajah, 41–43. New York: Orbis Books, 2000.

―――. and Mercy Amba Oduyoye, "The Christ for African Women." *With Passion and Compassion: Third World Women Doing Theology: Reflections from the Women's Commission of the Ecumenical Association of Third World Theologians,* eds. Virginia Fabella and Mercy Amba Oduyoye, 35–46. Maryknoll, New York: Orbis Books, 1988.

Anderson, Allan. *An Introduction to Pentecostalism.* Cambridge: Cambridge University, 2004.

Anselm of Canterbury, vol. III, eds., trans. J. Hopkins and Both. Richardson, Toronto & New York, Mellen, 1976.

Appiah-Kubi, Kofi. "Indigenous African Christian Churches: Signs of Authenticity." *Bulletin of African Theology* 1.2 (1979): 241–49.

Aquinas, Thomas. *Selections form Writings of St. Thomas.* Translated by Vernon J. Bourke. New York: Washington Square, 1960.

Augustine, *St. Augustine City of God and the Christian Doctrine*. A Select Library of the Nicene and Post-Nicene Fathers of the Christian Church. Vol. 2. ed., Philip Schaff. Translated by Marcus Dods. Grand Rapids, Michigan: Eerdmanns, 1890.

Austin, Lisa M. "Person, Place or Things? Property and the Struggling of Social Relations." *University of Toronto Law Journal* 60 (2010): 445–65.

Arrastia, Cecilio. "The Church: A Hermeneutical Community." *Occasional Essays* 9.2 (1982): 18–25.

Barth, Karl. *Church Dogmatics*, vol. 2, G. W. Bromiley and T. F. Torrance, eds. Edinburgh: T. & T. Clark, 1961.

———. *Protestant Theology in the Nineteenth Century: its Background and History*. Valley Forge: Judson, 1973.

Barr, James. *The Semantics of Biblical Language*. London: Oxford University Press, 1961.

Basinger, David. *The Case for Freewill Theism*. Downers Grove, IL: InterVarsity, 1996.

Bavinck, Herman. *Doctrine of God*. Grand Rapids: Eerdmans, 1951.

Bediako, Kwame. *Christianity in Africa: The Renewal of a Non-Western Religion*. Edinburgh: Edinburgh University Press, 1995.

———. *Jesus in Africa: The Christian Gospel in African History and Experience*. Yaounde: Editions Clé, 2000.

———. "Jesus in the African Culture: A Ghanaian Perspective." In *Emerging Voices in Global Christian Theology*, ed. William A. Dyrness, 93–121 Grand Rapids, Michigan: Zondervan, 1994.

———. "Understanding African Theology in the 20th Century." *Themelios* 20.1 (1994): 14–20.

Berkhof, Louis. *Systematic Theology*. Carlisle, PA: The Banner of Truth Trust, 1988.

Berkouwer, G. C. *General Revelation*. Grand Rapids: Eerdmans, 1955.

Bettenson, Henry. *Documents of the Christian Church*, 2nd ed. London: Oxford University, 1963.

Bews, Mike. "The Concept of the 'High God' in Traditional Igbo Religion." *International Journal of Frontier Missions* 2.4 (1985): 315–21.

Biko, Steve. *I Write What I Like*, ed. Aelred A. Stubbs. London: Bowerdean, 1978.

Blue, Ken. *Authority to Heal*. Downer Grove, IL: InterVarsity, 1987.

Bockmuehl, Klaus. *The Unreal God of Modern Theology*, trans. Geoffrey W. Bromiley. Colorado Springs, Colorado: Helmers & Howard, 1988.

Bosch, David J. "God in Africa: Implications for the Kerygma." *Missionalia* 1.1 (1973): 3–20.

Boyd, Gregory. *God of the Possible*. Grand Rapids: Baker, 2000.

Bray, Gerald L. *Creeds, Councils and Christ: Did the Early Christians Misrepresent Jesus?* Fearn, Ross-shire: Mentor, 1997.

———. *The Doctrine of God*. Downers Grove, IL: InterVarsity, 1993.

———. "Rescuing Theology from the Theologians." *Themelios* 24.2 (1999): 48–57.

Bromiley, G.W. "Angel." *Evangelical Dictionary of Theology*, ed. Walter Elwell, 46–47. Grand Rapids: Baker, 1984.

Brown, Harold O.J. *The Image of Christ in the Mirror of Heresy and Orthodoxy From the Apostles to the Present*. Garden City, New Jersey: Doubleday, 1984.

Brown, Robert McAfee. *Theology in a New Key: Responding to Liberation Themes*. Philadelphia: Westminster, 1978.

Bruce, F. F. "The Person of Christ: Incarnation and Virgin Birth." *Basic Christian Doctrines*, ed. Carl F. H. Henry, 124–30. New York: Holt, Reinhart & Winston, 1962.

Brunner, Emil. *Man in Revolt: A Christian Anthropology.* Philadelphia: Westminster, 1947.

Bultmann, Rudolf. *Theology of The New Testament*, Vol. 1., trans. Kendrick Grobel. New York: Scribner's, 1951.

———. *Essays Philosophical and Theological*, trans. James C. G. Greig. New York: Macmillan, 1955.

Buswell, Oliver J. *A Systematic Theology of the Christian Religion.* Grand Rapids: Zondervan, 1962.

———. *A Systematic Theology of the Christian Religion.* Grand Rapids: Zondervan, 1971.

Caldwell, William. "The Doctrine of Satan : I in the Old Testament." *Biblical World* 41.1 (1913): 29–33.

———. "The Doctrine of Satan: II Satan in Extra-Biblical Apocalyptical Literature." *Biblical World* 41.2 (1913): 98–102.

Carroll, Noel. "Nightmare and the Horror Film: The Symbolic Biology of Fantastic Beings." *Film Quarterly* 41.4 (1981): 16–25.

Carson, D.A. and John Woodbridge, eds. *Hermeneutics, Authority, and Canon.* Grand Rapids: Zondervan, 1986.

———. *Divine Sovereignty & Human Responsibility: A Biblical Perspectives in Tension* Eugene, OR: Wipf & Stock, 1994.

———. *Exegetical Fallacies.* Grand Rapids: Baker, 1984.

———. *How Long, O Lord? Reflections on Suffering and Evil.* Grand Rapids: Baker, 1990.

Chafer, Lewis Sperry. "Biblical Theism: Divine Attributes of God (Concluded) part 3." *Bibliotheca Sacra* 96.381 (1939): 5–37.

———. "Trinitarinism part 2." *Bibliotheca Sacra* 97.386 (1940): 137–65.

———. "Unabridged Systematic Theology." *Bibliotheca sacra* 91.361 (1934): 8–23.

———. *Systematic Theology*, 8 vols. Dallas, TX: Dallas Seminary Press, 1947.

Calvin, John. *Institutes of the Christian Religion*, trans. Henry Beveridge. Grand Rapids: Eerdmans, 1994.

Charnock, Stephan. *Discourses upon the Existence and Attributes of God*, 2 vols. Grand Rapids: Baker, 1979.

———. *The Existence and Attributes of God*, repr. ed. Evansville, Indiana: Sovereign Grace Book Club, nd.

Chia, Roland. *Hope for the World: The Christian Vision.* Leicester: InterVarsity, 2006.

Clark, Stephen B. *Man and Woman in Christ: An Examination of the Roles of Men and Women in Light of Scripture and the Social Sciences.* Ann Arbor: Servant, 1980.

Clouser, Roy. *Knowing with the Heart: Religious Experience and Belief in God.* Downers Grove, IL: InterVarsity, 1999.

Cook, David. "Significant Trends in Christology in Western Scholarly Debate." In *Sharing Jesus in the Two Thirds World: Evangelical Christologies from the Contexts of Poverty, Powerlessness, and Religious Pluralism*, eds. Vinay Samuel and Chris Sugden, 251–76. Grand Rapids: Eerdmans, 1984.

Coppedge, Allan. *Portraits of God: A Biblical Theology of Holiness.* Downers Grove, IL: InterVarsity, 2001.

Cottrell, Jack. *What the Bible says about God the Creator*. Joplin: College Press, 1983.

————. *Feminism and the Bible: An Introduction to Feminism for Christians*. Joplin, Missouri: College Press, 1992.

Cosby, John F. "The Twofold Source of the Dignity of Persons." *Faith and Philosophy* 18.3 (2001): 292–306.

Craig, William Lane. *The Only Wise God*. Grand Rapids: Baker, 1987.

Cranford, Ronald E., and David Randolph Smith, "Consciousness: The Most Critical and Moral (Constitutional) Standard for Human Personhood." *American Journal of Law & Medicine* 13.2–3 (1987): 233–48.

Cullmann, Oscar. *The Christology of the New Testament*. Philadelphia: Westminster, 1963.

Dabney, R. L. *Systematic Theology*. Edinburgh: The Banner of Truth Trust. 1871.

Daneel, Marthinus L. "African Independent Church Pneumatology and the Salvation of All Creation." *Theologia Evangelica* 25.1 (1992): 35–55.

————. "The Encounter between Christianity and Traditional Culture: Accommodation or Transformation?" *Theologia Evangelica* 22.3 (1989): 36–51.

Davies, B. *Thinking About God*. London: Churchman, 1985.

D'Costa, Gavin. "The End of Systematic Theology." *Theology* 95 (1992): 324–34.

Demarest, Bruce A. "Creeds." In *New Dictionary of Theology*, eds. Sinclair B. Ferguson et al, 179–81. Leicester: InterVarsity, 1988.

————. *General Revelation: Historical Views and Contemporary Issues*. Grand Rapids: Zondervan, 1982.

————. "The Quest for God in African Ways." *Evangelical Missions Quarterly* 18.2 (1982): 99–101.

Dickason, C. F. *Angels, Elect and Evil*. Chicago: Moody Press, 1975.

Dickson, Kwesi A. "The Theology of the Cross in Context." In *Biblical Exegesis in African Perspective. Journal of African Christian Thought* (Journal of the Akrofi-Christaller Memorial Centre for Mission Research and Applied Theology, Akropong-Akuapem, Ghana), 6.1 (2003): 9–14 .

Dockery, David S. *Biblical Interpretation Then and Now: Contemporary Hermeneutics in the Light of the Early Church*. Grand Rapids: Baker, 1992.

Dzobo, Noah K. "African Ancestor Cult: a Theological Appraisal." *Reformed World* 38.6 (1985): 333–40.

Ekeya, Bette. "The Christ Experience of African Women Doing Theology." In *Third World Women Doing Theology: Papers from the Intercontinental Women's Conference, Oaxtepec, Mexico, December 1–6, 1986.*, ed. Virginia Fabella and Dolorita Martinez, 178–83. Port Harcourt, Nigeria: Ecumenical Association of Third World Theologians, 1987.

Éla, Jean-Marc. "Christianity and Liberation in Africa." In *Paths of African Theology*, ed. Rosino Gibellini, 136–53. Maryknoll: Orbis, 1994.

————. *My Faith as an African*. Maryknoll, New York: Orbis, 1988.

Eliade, Mircea. *The Sacred and the Profane*, trans. W. R. Trask. New York: Harcourt, Brace and World, 1959.

Elwell, Walter. *Evangelical Dictionary of Theology*. Grand Rapids: Baker, 1984.

Erickson, Millard J. *A Basic Guide to Eschatology*. Grand Rapids: Baker, 1998.

————. *Christian Theology*, 2nd ed. 1998. Reprint, Grand Rapid: Baker Academic, 2009.

————. *God the Father Almighty: A Contemporary Exploration of the Divine Attributes.* Grand Rapids: Baker, 1998.

————. *The Word Became Flesh: A Contemporary Incarnational Christology.* Grand Rapids: Baker, 1991.

Evans, C. Stephen. *Philosophy of Religion.* Leicester: InterVarsity, 1982.

Farah, Martha J. and Andreas S. Heberlein, "Personhood and Neuroscience: Naturalizing and Nihilating," *The American Journal of Bioethics* 7.1 (2007): 37–48.

Fatula, Mary Ann. *The Triune God of Christian Faith.* Collegeville, MN: Liturgical, 1990.

Fisher, Christopher. "Animals, Humans and X-Men: Human Uniqueness and the Meaning of Personhood." *Theology and Science* 3.3 (2005): 291–314.

France, Dick. "Critical Needs of the Fast-Growing African Churches." *Evangelical Missions Quarterly* 14.3 (1978): 141–49.

Fee, Gordon D. and Douglas Stuart, *How to Read the Bible for all its Worth.* Grand Rapids: Zondervan, 1982.

Feinberg, J. S. *The Many Faces of Evil: Theological Systems and the Problem of Evil.* Grand Rapids: Zondervan, 1994.

————. *No One Like Him.* Wheaton: Crossway, 2001.

————. *Theologies and Evil.* Washington D.C.: University Press of America, 1979.

Feinberg, Paul. "Inerrancy and Infallibility of Bible," *Evangelical Dictionary of Theology,* ed. Walter Elwell, 141–45. Grand Rapids: Baker, 1984.

Foh, Susan. *Women and the Word of God: A Response to Biblical Feminism.* Phillipsburg, New Jersey: Presbyterian and Reformed, 1980.

Fotland, Roar. "The Christology of Kwame Bediako." In *Christ in African Experience-Reflections from Homeland and Diaspora. Journal of African Christian Thought* (Journal of the Akrofi-Christaller Memorial Centre for Mission Research and Applied Theology, Akropong-Akuapem, Ghana) 8.1 (June 2005): 36–49.

Frame, John M. *The Doctrine of God: A Theology of Lordship.* Phillipsburg: P. & R., 2002.

Freddoso, Alfred J. *Review of God, Time, and Knowledge* by William Hasker, *Faith and Philosophy* 10.1 (1993): 105–6.

————. "The 'Openness of God': A Reply to Hasker." *Christian Scholars Review* 28.1 (1998): 124–33.

Freeland, Cynthia. *The Naked and the Undead: Evil and the Appeal of Horror.* Boulder: Westview, 1999.

Gbadegesin, Segun. *African Philosophy: Traditional Yoruba Philosophy and Contemporary African Realities.* New York: Peter Lang, 1991.

Gehman, Richard J. "Will the African Ancestors Be Saved?" *Africa Journal of Evangelical Theology* 14.2 (1995): 85–97.

Geisler, Norman L .and J. S. Feinberg, *Introduction to Philosophy: A Christian Perspective.* Grand Rapids: Baker, 1980.

————. *Christian Apologetics.* Downers Grove, IL: InterVarsity, 1970.

————., ed. *Biblical Inerrancy: An Analysis of Its Philosophical Roots.* Grand Rapids: Zondervan, 1981.

————. *Philosophy of Religion.* Grand Rapids: Zondervan, 1974.

————. *The Roots of Evil.* Grand Rapids: Zondervan, 1978.

Geivett, R. Douglas and Brendon Sweetman, *Contemporary Perspectives on Religious Epistemology.* Oxford: Oxford University Press, 1993.

Geldenhuys, J. Norval. "Effectual Calling." *Basic Christian Doctrines,* ed. Carl F. H. Henry. New York: Holt, Reinhart & Winston, 1962.

Gerstner, John H. "An Outline of the Apologetics of Jonathan Edward: The Proof of God's Special Revelation, the Bible." *Bibliotheca Sacra* 133.531 (1976): 195–201.

Gilliland, Dean S. *Pauline Theology and Mission Practice*. Jos: Albishir Bookshops Nigeria Ltd, 1983.

Gragg, A. *Charles Hartshorne: Makers of the Modern Theological Mind*, ed. B. E. Patterson. Waco: Word, 1973.

Graham, Billy. *Angels: God's Secret Agents*. Waco: Word, 1986.

Grenz, Stanley J. and Roger E. Olson. *20th Century Theology: God and the World in a Transitional Age*. Downers Grove, IL: InterVarsity, 1992.

———. *Theology for the Community of God*. Grand Rapids: Eerdmans, 2000.

Grudem, Wayne. *Bible Doctrine: Essential Teachings of the Christian Faith*, ed. Jeff Purswell. Leicester: InterVarsity, 1999.

———. *Systematic Theology: An Introduction to Biblical Doctrine*. Leicester: InterVarsity, 1994.

Guthrie, Donald. *Jesus the Messiah*. Grand Rapids: Zondervan, 1972.

Gutiérrez, Gustavo. *A Theology of Liberation*. Maryknoll: Orbis, 1973.

———. *The Power of the Poor in History*. Translated by Robert R. Barr. Maryknoll: Orbis, 1983.

Hagan, George P. "Divinity and Experience: The Trance and Christianity in Southern Ghana." In *Vernacular Christianity: Essays in the Social Anthropology of Religion Presented to Godfrey Lienhardt*, ed. Wendy James and Douglas Hamilton Johnson, 146–56. New York: Barber, 1988.

Haley, John W. *Alleged Discrepancies of the Bible*. Grand Rapids: Baker, 1977.

Hall, Douglas John. *God and Human Suffering: An Exercise in the Theology of the Cross*. Minneapolis: Augsburg, 1986.

Harnack, Adolph. *History of Dogma*, vol. 1. New York: Dover, 1961.

Harrington, Curtis. "Ghoulies and Ghosties." *The Quarterly of Film Radio and Television* 7.2 (1952): 191–202.

Harris, Murray J. *Jesus As God*. Grand Rapids: Baker, 1992.

———. "Salvation." In *New Dictionary of Biblical Theology*, T. Desmond Alexander *et al*, 762–67. Leicester: InterVarsity, 2000.

Hartouni, Valerie. "Reflections on Abortion Politics and the Practices Called Person." *Fetal Subjects, Feminist Positions*, eds. L. M. Morgan and M. W. Michaels. Philadelphia: University of Pennsylvania Press, 1999.

Hartshorne, C. *The Divine Relativity: A Social Conception of God*. New Haven: Yale University Press, 1948.

Hasker, William. "The Openness of God." *Christian Scholars Review* 28.1 (1998): 111–39.

Helm, Paul. *The Divine Revelation*. Westchester, IL: Crossway, 1982.

Hemer, Susan R. "*Piot*, Personhood, Place, and Mobility in Lihir, Papua New Guinea." *Oceania* 78 (2008): 109–25.

Herring, Stephen L. "'A Transubstantiated Humanity:' The Relationship Between the Divine Image and the Presence of God in Genesis i 26f." *Vetus Testamentum* 58 (2008): 480–94.

Heschel, Abraham J. *The Prophets*, vol. 2. New York: Harper, 1962.

Hilary of Poitiers, *St. Hilary of Poitiers Select Works*. A Select Library of Nicene and Post-Nicene Fathers of the Christian Church. Translated by E. W. Watson, L. Pullan, *et al*. Edited by W. Sanday. Grand Rapids: Eerdmans, 1983.

Hinga, Terese M. "Inculturation and the Otherness of African: Some Reflections." *Inculturation: Abide by the Otherness of Africa and the Africans: Papers from a Congress (October 21-22, 1993, Heerlen, the Netherlands) at the Occasion of* 100 *Years SMA Presence in the Netherlands*, eds. Peter Turkson and Frans Jozef Servaas WijsenKampden, 10-18. The Netherlands: J. H. Kok, 1994.

———."Jesus Christ and the Liberation of Women in Africa." *The Will to Arise: Women, Tradition, and the Church in Africa.* Edited by Mercy Amba Oduyoye and Musimbi R. A. Kanyoro, 183-94. Maryknoll: Orbis, 1992.

Hirsch, E. D. Jr., *The Aims of Interpretation.* Chicago: University of Chicago Press, 1976.

Hodge, Charles *Systematic Theology*, vol. 2. Grand Rapids: Eedmans, 1993.

Hodgson, Leonard. *The Doctrine of the Trinity.* New York: Scribners, 1944.

Hollenweger, Walter J. "The Theological Challenge of Indigenous Churches." *SEDOS Bulletin* (1990): 244-46.

Hood, Robert E. "Must God Remain Greek." *African Philosophy: Anthology*, ed. Emmanuel Chukwudi Eze, 462-67. Malden: Blackwell, 1998.

Horgan, John. *Rational Mysticism: Dispatches from the Borders between Science and Spirituality.* Boston, Massachusetts: Houghton Mifflin, 2003.

Horrell, J. Scott. "Towards a Biblical Model of Social Trinity: Avoiding the Equivocation of Nature and Order." *Journal of Evangelical Theological Society* 47.3 (2004): 399-421.

Howell, Nancy R. "The importance of Being Chimpanzee." *Theology and Science* 1 (2003): 179-91.

Hubbeling, H. G. "Some Remarks on the Concept of Person in Western Philosophy." In *Concepts of Person in Religion and Thought*, eds. Hans G. Kippenberg *et al*, 9-24. Berlin: Mouton de Gruyter, 1990.

Idowu, Bolaji. *Olòdúmare: God in Yoruba Belief.* London: Longman, 1962.

———. *Towards an Indigenous Church.* London: Oxford University Press, 1965.

Jenkins, Philip. *The Next Christendom: The Coming of Global Christianity.* London: Oxford University Press, 2002.

John of Damascus, "Exposition of the Orthodox Faith." A Select Library of Nicene and Post-Nicene Fathers of the Christian Church. Translated by S. D. F. Salmond. Grand Rapids: Eerdmans, 1983.

Jung, Carl G. *Modern Man in Search of a Soul.* New York: Harvest, 1933.

Jung, Leo. "Fallen Angels in Jewish, Christian and Mohammedan Literature: A Study in Comparative Folklore." *Jewish Quarterly Review* 16.3 (1926): 287-336.

———. "Fallen Angels in Jewish, Christian and Mohammedan Literature: A Study in Comparative Folklore." *Jewish Quarterly Review* 16.3 (1925): 171-205.

Jurji, Edward J. *The Phenomenology of Religion.* Philadelphia: Westminster, 1963.

Kagame, Alexis. "The Problem of 'Man' in Bantu Philosophy." *The African Mind: A Journal of Religion and Philosophy in Africa* 1.1 (1989): 35-40.

Kapolyo, J. M. *The Human Condition: Christian Perspectives Through African Eyes.* Leicester: InterVarsity, 2005.

Kato, Byang. "Theological Issues in Africa." *Bibliothesacra* 133.530 (1976): 144-53.

———."Contextualization and Religious Syncretism." *Biblical Christianity in Africa.* Achimota, Ghana: Africa Christian Press, 1985.

———. *Theological Pitfalls in Africa.* Kisumu, Kenya: Evangel, 1975.

Kayode, J. O. *Understanding African Traditional Religion.* Ile-Ife: University of Ife Press, 1984.

Kelly, J. N. D. *Early Christian Doctrines.* Peabody, Massachusetts: Prince, 2004.

Kevin, Springer, and Wimber John, *Power Healing.* Cambridge: Harper & Row, 1987.

King, Fergus J. "Angels and Ancestors: A Basis for Christology?" *Mission Studies* 9.1 (1994): 10–26.

Kiwovele, Judah. "An African Perspective on the Priesthood of All Believers," *Theology and the Black Experience: The Lutheran Heritage Interpreted by African and African-American Theologians,* eds. Albert Pero and Ambrose Moyo, 56–75. Minneapolis: Augsburg, 1988.

Klem, Herbert V. "The Bible as Oral Literature in Oral Societies." *International Review of Mission* 67.268 (1978): 479–86.

Kuhn, Harold B. "Angelology of Non-Canonical Jewish Apocalypses. "*Journal of Biblical Literature* 67.3 (1948): 217–32.

Küng, Hans. *On Being a Christian.* Translated by Edward Quinn. New York: Doubleday & Garden City, 1968.

Kunhiyop, Samuel Waje. *African Christian Ethics.* Kaduna: Baraka, 2004.

Kurewa, J. W. Zvomunondita. "Who Do You Say that I Am?" *International Review of Mission* 69.274 (1980): 182–88.

Kushner, Harold S. *When Bad Things Happen to Good People.* New York: Avon, 1983.

Lagerwerf, Leny. "African Women Doing Theology--A Survey." *Exchange* 19.1 (1990): 1–69.

Langton, Edward. *The Ministries of Angelic Powers According to the Old Testament and Later Jewish Literature.* London: Clarke Ltd, 1936.

Laryea, Philip T. "Mother Tongue Theology: Reflections on Images of Jesus in the Poetry of Afua Kuma." *Theology in Africa in the 21st Century: Essential Foundations. Journal of African Christian Thought* (*Journal* of the Akrofi-Christaller Memorial Centre for Mission Research and Applied Theology, Akropong-Akuapem, Ghana) 3.1 (2000): 50–60.

Lewis, C. S. *The Problem of Pain.* New York: Macmillan, 1962.

Linville, Mark D. "A Defense of Human Dignity." *Faith and Philosophy* 17.3 (2000): 320–32.

Loewen, Jacob A. "Which God Do the Missionaries Preach?" *Missiology* 14.1 (January 1986): 3–19.

Longnecker, Richard. *The Christology of Early Jewish Christianity.* London: SCM, 1970.

Louis Berkhof, *Principles of Biblical Interpretation.* Grand Rapids: Baker, 1950.

Ludwig Feuerbach, *The Essence of Christianity,* trans. George Eliot. New York: Harper, 1957.

Lucano, Thomas. *Them or Us: Archetyphal Interpretations of Fifties Alien Invasion Films.* Indianapolis: Indiana University Press, 1988.

MacDonald, David B. "Pushing the Limits of Humanity? Reinterpreting Animal Rights and 'personhood' Through the Prism of the Holocaust." *Journal of Human Rights* 5 (2006): 417–37.

Macleod, Donald. *Shared Life: The Trinity and the Fellowship of God's People.* Inverness, Scotland: Christian Focus, 1994.

Magesa, L. "Africa's Struggle for Self-definition during a Time of Globalization." *Sedos* 31 (1999): 235–39.

———. "Christology, African Women and Ministry." *The African Ecclesial Review (AFER)* 38.1 (1996): 66–88.

Mantey, Julius. "Repentance and Conversion." *Basic Christian Doctrines*, ed. Carl F.H. Henry. New York: Holt, Reinhart & Winston. 1962.

Marshall, Howard I. *I believe in the Historical Jesus*. Grand Rapids: Eerdnmans, 1977.

Mazrui, Ali. *Political Values and the Educated Class in Africa*. London: Heinemann, 1978.

Mbiti, John. *African Religions and Philosophy*. London: Heinemann, 1969.

———. *The Akamba and Christianity: New Testament Eschatology in African Background*. London: Oxford University Press, 1971.

———. *Bible and Theology in African Christianity*. Nairobi: Oxford University Press, 1986.

———. "'Cattle are Born With Ears, Their Horns Grow Later' Towards an Appreciation of African Oral Theology." *Africa Theological Journal* 8.1 (1979): 15–25.

———. *Concepts of God in Africa*. London: SPCK, 1970.

———. "Dreams as a Point of Theological Dialogue between Christianity and African Religion." *Missionalia* 25.4 (1997): 511–22.

———. "Some African Concepts of Christology." In *Christ and the Younger Churches*, ed. Georg F. Vicedom, 61–62. London: SPCK, 1972.

McCarthy, Caritas. "Christology from a Contemporary African Perspective." In *Pluralism and Oppression: Theology in World Perspective*, ed. Paul F. Knitter, 29–48. Lanham, MD: University Press of America, 1991.

McComiskey, T. E. "Angel of the Lord." In *Evangelical Dictionary of Theology*, *Evangelical Dictionary of Theology*, ed. Walter Elwell, 47–48. Grand Rapids: Baker, 1984.

McDonald, H.D. *Theories of Revelation: An Historical Study*. Grand Rapids: Baker, 1979.

McDowell, Josh. *Evidence That Demands a Verdict*. San Bernardino: Here's Life, 1972.

McFadyen, Alistair I. *The Call to Personhood: A Christian Theory of the Individual in Social Relationships*. Cambridge: Cambridge University Press, 1990.

McGrath, Alister E. *Understanding Jesus: Who He is and Why He Matters*. Grand Rapids: Zondervan, 1987.

Menkiti, Ifeanyi A. "Person and Community in African Traditional Thought." In *African Philosophy: An Introduction*, ed. Richard Wright, 171–82. Lanham, MD: University Press of America, 1984.

Menzies, William W. "The Holy Spirit in Christian Theology." In *Perspectives on Evangelical Theology*, ed. Kenneth Kantzer and Stanley Gundry, 67–79. Grand Rapids: Baker, 1979.

Michael, Matthew. "African Christological Discourse: A Prolegomena to the Emerging Christological Methodologies." In Unpublished Lectures at Jos ECWA Theological Seminary on June 5th 2007.

Mickelsen, Alvera, ed. *Women, Authority, and the Bible*. Downers Grove, IL: InterVarsity, 1986.

Mnyandu, M. "Ubuntu as the Basis of Authentic Humanity: An African Perspective." *Journal of Constructive Theology* 3.1 (1997): 77–86.

Moltmann, Jürgen. "Hope and History." *Theology Today* 25 (1972): 369–99.

———. "Is the World Coming to an End or Has Its Future already Begun? Christian Eschatology, Modern Utopianism and Exterminism." In *The Future As God's Gift: Explorations in Christian Eschatology*, eds. David Fergusson and Marcel Sarot, 129–38. Edinburgh: T. & T. Clark, 2000.

———. "Politics and the Practice of Hope." *Christian Century* 11 (1970): 288–91.

————. *The Theology of Hope: On the Ground and the Implications of a Christian Eschatology*. New York: Harper & Row, 1965.

————. *The Experiment of Hope*. Philadelphia: Fortress, 1975.

————. "Theology as Eschatology." In *The Future of Hope: Theology as Eschatology*, ed. Frederick Herzog, 1–50. New York: Herder & Herder, 1970.

Moody, Janis. "Dementia and Personhood: Implications for Advance Directives." *Nursing Older People* 15.4 (2003): 18–21.

Morgan, Lynn M. "Life Begins When They Steal your Bicycle: Cross–Cultural Practices of Personhood at the Beginnings and Ends of Life." *Journal of Law, Medicine and Ethics* (2006): 8–15.

Morny, Mabel S. "Christ Restores Life." In *Talitha, Qumi!: Proceedings of the Convocation of African Women Theologians, Trinity College, Legon–Accra, September 24– October 2, 1989*. Edited by Mercy Amba Oduyoye and Rachel Angogo Kanyoro, 149–54. Ibadan: Daystar, 1990.

Morris, Thomas V. *Our Idea of God*. Downers Grove, IL: InterVarsity, 1991.

Moule, C. F. D. *The Origin of Christology*. Cambridge: Cambridge University Press, 1977.

Mugambi, J. N. K. *African Christian Theology: An Introduction*. Nairobi, Kenya: Heinemann, 1989.

Nash, Ronald H. *The Concept of God*. Grand Rapids: Zondervan, 1983.

Ngong, David Tonghou. "Salvation and Materialism in African Theology." *Studies in World Christianity* 15 (2009): 1–21.

Nkwoka, A. O. "Jesus as Eldest Brother, (Okpara): An Igbo Paradigm for Christology in African Context." *Asia Journal of Theology* 5.1 (1991): 87–103.

Nwachukwu, P. N. D. *African Authentic Christianity: An Inculturation Model for the Igbo*. New York: Peter Lang, 2003.

Nyamiti, Charles. "African Christologies Today." In *Faces of Jesus in Africa*. Edited by Robert J. Schreiter, 17–39. Maryknoll: Orbis, 2005.

————. "Contemporary African Christologies: Assessment and Practical Suggestions." In *Paths of African Theology*. Edited by Rosino Gibellini, 62–77. Maryknoll: Orbis, 1994.

————. *Christ Our Ancestor: Christology from an African Perspective*. Gweru, Zimbabwe: Mambo, 1984.

————. "The Trinity: An African ancestral perspective." *Theology Digest* 45.1 (1998): 21–22.

Obaje, Yusufu Ameh. "Theocentric Christology as a Basis for a More Relevant Doctrine of Christ for the African Christian." *Ogbomoso Journal of Theology* 5 (1990): 1–7.

————. "Theocentric Christology as a Basis for a More Relevant Doctrine of Christ for the African Christian." *Ogbomoso Journal of Theology* 5 (1990): 1–7.

Oden, Thomas C. *How Africa Shaped the Christian Mind: Rediscovering the African Seedbed of Western Christianity*. Downer Grove, IL: InterVarsity, 2007.

————. *The Living God: Systematic Theology*, vol. 1. San Francisco: Harper & Row, 1987.

Oduyoye, A. *Hearing and Knowing. Theological Reflection on Christianity in Africa*. New York: Orbis, 1986.

Okoye, James. "African Theology." *Dictionary of Mission: Theology, History, Perspectives*, eds. Karl Müller, Theo Sundermeier, Stephen B. Bevans, Richard H. Bliese, 9–17. Maryknoll: Orbis, 1997.

———."African Theology." No Pages. Online: http://Error! Hyperlink reference not valid.

Oosthuizen, George C. "Interpretation of Demonic Powers in Southern African Independent Churches." *Missiology* 16.1 (1988): 3–22.

Orobator, Emmanuel. "Perspectives and Trends in Contemporary African Ecclesiology." *Studia Missionalia* 45 (1996): 267–82.

Osei-Mensah, Gottfried. "The Theology of Church and Society." *Perception* 10 (1977): 1–7.

Osterhaven, M. Eugene. "Common Grace." In *Basic Christian Doctrines*. Edited by Carl F. H. Henry, 171–77. New York: Holt, Reinhart & Winston. 1962.

Otto, Rudolf. *The Idea of the Holy*, trans. J. W. Harvey. New York: Oxford University Press, 1967.

Packer, J. I. "Infallibility and Inerrancy of the Bible." In *New Dictionary of Theology*. Edited by S. B. Ferguson, D. F. Wright and J. I. Packer, 337–39. Leicester: InterVarsity, 1988.

———."Scripture." In *New Dictionary of Theology*. Edited by S. B. Ferguson, D. F. Wright and J. I. Packer, 627–31. Leicester: InterVarsity, 1988.

———. *"Fundamentalism" and the Word of God*. London: InterVarsity, 1958.

Palmer, Timothy. "Jesus Christ: Our Ancestor?" *TCNN Research Bulletin* 42 (2004): 4–17.

Pannenberg, Wolfhart. *Jesus: God and Man*, 2nd ed. Translated by Lewis Wilkins and Duane Priebe. Philadelphia: Westminster, 1977.

Pato, Luke Lungile. "Being Fully Human Being from the Perspective of African Culture and Spirituality." *Journal of Theology for Southern Africa* (1998):53–61.

Paul Tillich, *Systematic Theology*, vol. I. Chicago: The University of Chicago Press. 1951.

Pelikan, Jaroslav. *The Christian Tradition: A History of the Development of Doctrine*, vol. 4. Chicago: The University of Chicago Press, 1984.

Peters, E. H. *Hartshorne and Neoclassical Metaphysics*. Lincoln: Univ. of Nebraska Press, 1970.

Peterson, Michael L. *Evil and the Creation*. Grand Rapids: Baker, 1982.

Phan, Peter C. "The Christ of Asia: An Essay on Jesus as the Eldest Son and Ancestor." *Studia Missionalia* 45, (1996): 25–46.

Pinnock, Clark H. "Theology and Myth: An Evangelical Response to Demythologizing." *Bibliotheca sacra* 128, no. 511 (1971): 215–26.

———. et al., *The Openness of God*. Downers Grove, IL: InterVarsity, 1994.

———. *Biblical Revelation*. Chicago: Moody Press, 1971.

———. "God Limits His Knowledge." In *Predestination and Free Will*, eds. David and Randall Basinger, 142–62. Downers Grove, IL: InterVarsity, 1986.

———. *Flame of Love*. Downers Grove: InterVarsity, 1996.

Piper, John. *What's the Difference? Manhood and Womanhood Defined According to the Bible*. Westchester, IL: Crossway, 1990.

Plantinga, Alvin. *God, Freedom and Evil*. New York: Harper & Row, 1974.

Plato, *Dialogues of Plato*. Translated by J. D. Kaplan. New York: Pocket Books, 1950.

Plutarch, *Fall of the Roman Republic*. London: Penguin, 1980.

Pobee, John. "In Search of Christology in Africa: Some Considerations for Today." In *Exploring Afro-Christology*, ed. John S. Pobee, 9–20. New York: Peter Lang, 1992.

Radin, Margaret J. *Reinterpreting Property*. Chicago: Chicago University Press, 1993.

Retsikas, Konstantinos. "Being and Places: Movement, Ancestors, and Personhood in East Java, Indonesia." *Journal of Royal Anthropological Institutes* 13 (2007): 969–86.

Riesman, Paul. "The Person and the Life Cycle in African Social Life and Thought." *African Studies Review* 29.3 (1986): 71–138.

Rice, Richard. "Divine Knowledge and Free-Will Theism." In *The Grace of God and the Will of Man*. Edited by Clark Pinnock, 121–39. Minneapolis: Bethany, 1985.

―――. *God's Foreknowledge and Man's Free Will*. Minneapolis: Bethany, 1985.

Ross, Kenneth R. "Current Christological Trends in Northern Malawi." *Journal of Religion in Africa* 27.2 (1997): 160–76.

Runia, Klaas. *The Present-Day Christological Debate*. Leicester: InterVarsity, 1984.

Sam, Tinyiko Maluleke. "In Search of 'The True Character of African Christian Identity': A Review Article of the Theology of Kwame Bediako." *Missionalia* 25.2 (1997): 210–19.

Sanders, Clinton R. "Killing with Kindness: Veterinary Euthanasia and the Social Construction of Personhood." *Sociological Forum* 10.2 (1995): 195–214.

Sanders, John. *The God Who Risks*. Downers Grove, IL: InterVarsity, 1998.

Sankey, Paul J. "The Church as Clan: Critical Reflections on African Ecclesiology." *International Review of Mission* 83.330 (1994): 437–49.

Sanneh, Lamin. "Reciprocal Influences: African Traditional Religions and Christianity." In *Third World Liberation Theologies: A Reader*. Edited by Deane William Ferm, 231–39. Maryknoll: Orbis, 1986.

Sarpong,Peter K. "Asante Christology." *Studia Missionalia* 45 (1996): 189–206.

Schaeffer, Francis. "He is There and He is not Silent: Philosophy's Metaphysical Problem As Answered in the Existence of the Infinite-Personal, Triune God." *Bibliotheca Sacra* 128.510 (1971): 99–108.

Schmithals, Walter. *An Introduction to the Theology of Rudolf Bultmann*. Translated by John Bowden. Minneapolis: Augsburg, 1968.

Schreiter, Robert J. ed. *Faces of Jesus in Africa*. Maryknoll: Orbis, 1991.

Sider, Ronald J. "Miracles, Methodology, and Modern Western Christology." *Sharing Jesus in the Two Thirds World: Evangelical Christologies from the Contexts of Poverty, Powerlessness, and Religious Pluralism*. Edited by Vinay Samuel and Chris Sugden, 237–250. Grand Rapids: Eerdmans, 1984.

Singer, Paul. *Animal Liberation: A New Ethics for our Treatment of Animals*. New York Review/Random, 1975.

―――. *Ethics, Human and Other Animals: An Introduction with Readings*. Edited by R. Hursthouse. London: Routledge, 2000.

Sobrino, Jon. "Theology in a Suffering World: Theology as Intellectus Amoris." *Pluralism and Oppression: Theology in World Perspective*. Edited by Paul F. Knitter, 153–78. Lanham, MD: University Press of America, 1991.

Spiegel, Marjorie. *The Dreaded Comparison: Human and Animal Slavery*. Mirror Books, 1997.

Still, William. "Holiness of God and His Redeemed People." *Reformation and Revival* 4.2 (1995): 15–40.

Storrie, Robert. "Equivalence, Personhood, and Relationality: Processes of Relatedness among the Hoti of Venezuelan Guiana." *Journal of Royal Anthropological Institutes* 9 (2003): 407–28.

Strong, Augustus H. *Systematic Theology: A Compendium*. Old Tappan, New Jersey: Revell, 1907.

Surin, K. "The Self-Existence of God: Hartshorne and Classical Theism." *Sophia* 21 (1982): 28–29.

Swinburne, Richard. *The Coherence of Theism*. Oxford: Clarendon, 1977.

Tangwa, Godfrey. "The Traditional African Perception of a Person: Some Implications for Bioethics." *Hasting Center Report* 30.5(2000): 39–43.

Tappa, Louise. "The Christ Event from the Perspective of African Women." *Third World Women Doing Theology: Papers from the Intercontinental Women's Conference, Oaxtepec, Mexico, December 1–6, 1986*. Edited by Virginia Fabella and Dolorita Martinez, 173–77. Port Harcourt, Nigeria: Ecumenical Association of Third World Theologians, 1987.

Tennent, Timothy C. *Theology in the Context of World Christianity*. Grand Rapids: Zondervan, 2007.

Thielicke, Helmut. *A Little Exercise for Young Theologians*. Grand Rapids: Eerdmans, 1962.

Thiessen, Henry. *Lectures in Systematic Theology*. Grand Rapids: Eerdmans, 1977.

Tiénou, Tite. *The Theological Task of the Church in Africa: Theological Perspectives in Africa*. Ghana: African Christian Press, 1990.

Tillich, Paul. *Theology of Culture*. New York: Oxford University Press, 1959.

Turaki, Yusufu. "God's Universal Moral Laws: Ordering Human Life and Creation." Lecture Notes, JETS, 2007.

———. *Christianity and African Gods: A Method in Theology*. Potschestroomse: Potschestroomse Universiteit, 1999.

———. *Tribal Gods of Africa: Ethnicity, Racism, Tribalism and the Gospel of Christ*. Jos: Crossroads Media Services, 1997.

———. *The British Colonial Legacy in Northern Nigeria: A Social Ethical Analysis of the Colonial and Post-Colonial Society and Politics in Nigeria*. Jos: Challenge Bookshop, 1993.

Tutu, Desmond. *An African Prayer Book*. London: Hodder & Stoughton, 1995.

Twitchell, James B. *Dreadful Pleasures: An Anatomy of Modern Horror*. New York: Oxford University Press, 1985.

Ujomu, P. "The Crisis of African Identity," *Scepticos* 1 (1997): 14–17.

Ukpong, Justin S. "The Emergence of African Theologies." *Theological Studies* 45 (1984): 501–36.

Van Til, Cornelius. *An Introduction to Systematic Theology*. Phillipsburg, New Jersey: P. & R., 1978.

Van den Toren, Benno. "Kwame Bediako's Christology in its African Evangelical Context." *Exchange* 26.3 (September 1997): 218–32.

Vincent, David. "Dreams as an Aid to Personal Development." *Catalyst* 22.1 (1992): 31–50.

Walls, Andrew F. "Africa in Christian History: Retrospect and Prospect." *Journal of African Christian Thought* 1.1 (1998):

———. *The Missionary Movement in Christian History. Studies in the Transmission of Faith*. Mary Knoll: Orbis, 1996.

———. "Towards an Understanding of Africa's Place in Christian History." *Religion in a Pluralistic Society*, ed. J. S. Pobee. Leiden: Brill, 1976.

Walton, John H. *Ancient Near Eastern Thought and the Old Testament: Introducing the Conceptual World of the Hebrew*. Grand Rapids: Baker Academic, 2006.

Walvoord, John F. *Jesus Christ Our Lord*. Chicago: Moody, 1969.

————. "The Person of the Holy Spirit: The Holy Spirit Relation to the Unsaved World." *Bibliotheca Sacra* 98.390 (1941): 55–168.

Ward, Wayne E. "The person of Christ: The Kenotic Theory." In *Basic Christian Doctrines*. Edited by Carl F. H. Henry, 131–37. New York: Holt, Reinhart & Winston, 1962.

Ware, Bruce A. "An Exposition and Critique of Process Doctrines of Divine Mutability and Immutability." *Westminster Theological Journal* 47.2 (1985): 175–95.

Warfield, Benjamin B. *Benjamin B. Warfield: Selected Writings*, vol. 2. Edited by John E. Meeter. Phillipsburg, NJ: P. & R., 2001.

————. *Limited Inspiration*. Philadelphia: P. & R., 1962.

Wendland, Ernst. "'Who Do People Say that I Am?' Contextualizing Christology in Africa." *Africa Journal of Evangelical Theology* 10.2 (1991): 13–32.

Wells, David F. *The Person of Christ: A Biblical and Historical Analysis of the Incarnation*. Westchester, IL: Crossway, 1984.

West, Robert H. "Milton's Angelological Heresies." *Journal of the History of Ideas* 14.1 (1953): 116–23.

Wierenga, Edward. *Review of the Openness of God by Clark Pinnock et al.*, in *Faith and Philosophy* 14.2 (1997): 248–52.

William, James. *The Varieties of Religious Experience*, New York: Longmans, Green, & Co., 1902.

Wiredu, Kwasi. "Person and Community in Akan Thought." *African and Community*. Edited by Kwasi Wiredu and Gyekye, 101–22. Washington D.C: Council for Research in Values and Philosophy, 1992.

————, Kwasi Wiredu, "An Oral Philosophy of Personhood: Comments on Philosophy and Orality." *Research in African Literatures* 40.1 (2009): 8–18.

————. "An Oral Philosophy of Personhood: Comments on Philosophy and Orality." *Research in African Literatures* 40.1 (2009): 8–18.

Wong, Sophia Isako. "The Moral Personhood of Individuals Labeled 'Mentally Retarded': A Rawlsian Response to Nussbaum." *Social Theory and Practice* 33.4 (2007): 579–94.

Wright, Chris. *Salvation Belongs to Our God: Celebrating the Bible's Central Story*. Leicester: InterVarsity, 2008.

Subject Index

Made in the USA
Middletown, DE
03 February 2019